Beginning Artificial Intelligence with the Raspberry Pi

WITHDRAWN

■ ■ ■

Donald J. Norris

Apress®

Beginning Artificial Intelligence with the Raspberry Pi

Donald J. Norris
Barrington, New Hampshire, USA

ISBN-13 (pbk): 978-1-4842-2742-8   ISBN-13 (electronic): 978-1-4842-2743-5
DOI 10.1007/978-1-4842-2743-5

Library of Congress Control Number: 2017943462

Cover image designed by Freepik

Managing Director: Welmoed Spahr
Editorial Director: Todd Green
Acquisitions Editor: Aaron Black
Development Editor: Jim Markham
Technical Reviewer: Massimo Nardone
Coordinating Editor: Jessica Vakili

Distributed to the book trade worldwide by Springer Science+Business Media New York, 233 Spring Street, 6th Floor, New York, NY 10013. Phone 1-800-SPRINGER, fax (201) 348-4505, e-mail orders-ny@springer-sbm.com, or visit www.springeronline.com. Apress Media, LLC is a California LLC and the sole member (owner) is Springer Science + Business Media Finance Inc (SSBM Finance Inc). SSBM Finance Inc is a **Delaware** corporation.

For information on translations, please e-mail rights@apress.com, or visit http://www.apress.com/rights-permissions.

Apress titles may be purchased in bulk for academic, corporate, or promotional use. eBook versions and licenses are also available for most titles. For more information, reference our Print and eBook Bulk Sales web page at http://www.apress.com/bulk-sales.

Any source code or other supplementary material referenced by the author in this book is available to readers on GitHub via the book's product page, located at www.apress.com/978-1-4842-2742-8. For more detailed information, please visit http://www.apress.com/source-code.

Printed on acid-free paper

This book is dedicated to my good friend and colleague, Dr. Lundy Lewis. Dr. Lewis and I both teach in the Information Technology and Computer Science Department at Southern New Hampshire University, located in Manchester, NH.

Lundy is a recognized expert in the field of artificial intelligence and robotics, often sought after to present talks on those subjects at international conferences and universities. He has been both a mentor and advisor to me in the exciting field of artificial intelligence.

Contents at a Glance

Contents

About the Author

Donald J. Norris has a degree in electrical engineering and an MBA specializing in production management. He is currently teaching undergrad and grad courses in the computer science subject area at Southern New Hampshire University. He has also created and taught several robotics courses there. He has over 33 years of teaching experience as an adjunct professor at a variety of colleges and universities.

Don retired from civilian government service with the US Navy, where he specialized in acoustics related to nuclear submarines and associated advanced digital signal processing. Since then, he has spent more than 23 years as a professional software developer using C, C#, C++, Python, MicroPython, Node.js, and Java, as well as 6 years as a certified IT security consultant.

He has written and published six books, including two on the Raspberry Pi, how to build and fly your own drone, MicroPython, the Internet of Things, and the Edison microprocessor.

Don started a consultancy, Norris Embedded Software Solutions (dba NESS LLC), which specializes in developing application solutions using microprocessors and microcontrollers. He likes to think of himself as a perpetual hobbyist and geek and is always trying out new approaches and out-of-the-box experiments. He is a licensed private pilot, photography buff, amateur extra-class radio operator, and an avid runner.

About the Technical Reviewer

Massimo Nardone has more than 22 years of experience in security, web/mobile development, and cloud and IT architecture. His true IT passions are security and the Android.

He has been programming and teaching how to program with Android, Perl, PHP, Java, VB, Python, C/C++, and MySQL for more than 20 years. He holds a Master of Science degree in computing science from the University of Salerno, Italy.

Massimo has worked as a project manager, software engineer, research engineer, chief security architect, information security manager, PCI/SCADA auditor, and senior lead IT security/cloud/SCADA architect.

His technical skills include security, Android, cloud, Java, MySQL, Drupal, Cobol, Perl, web and mobile development, MongoDB, D3, Joomla, Couchbase, C/C++, WebGL, Python, Pro Rails, Django CMS, Jekyll, Scratch, and more.

He currently works as chief information security officer (CISO) for Cargotec Oyj.

He also worked as visiting lecturer and supervisor for exercises at the Networking Laboratory of the Helsinki University of Technology (Aalto University). He holds four international patents (PKI, SIP, SAML, and Proxy areas).

Massimo has reviewed more than 40 IT books for different publishing companies. He is the coauthor of *Pro Android Games* (Apress, 2015).

Preface

Artificial intelligence, or AI, is an exciting field and my purpose in writing this book is to convey some of that excitement to you. I will be using the Raspberry Pi single-board computer as the primary tool through which you can explore how AI works and, consequently, gain additional insight on how you might incorporate AI into your projects and/or applications.

I do want to make something perfectly clear at the outset: reading this book and completing all the projects will not make you an expert in AI. This is analogous to the situation where a layperson taking a first aid course could never claim to be a medical doctor or a nurse after taking that course. Becoming an AI expert requires that you take many college courses—both undergraduate and graduate—in a variety of areas, including mathematics, computer science, logic, and even philosophy. There are also AI experts who come from other spheres of interest, including music and the allied arts. Having made the previous statements, I do want you to understand that gaining a reasonable introduction to AI is very achievable by reading this book and other readily available resources. It is just that you should not try to claim that you are an AI expert after reading this book.

I will next discuss why the Raspberry Pi is a good platform with which to examine AI. You should first note that it is a very capable computer on its own merit. Why certainly not as fast nor as memory capable as a modern PC or Mac, it is no slouch, especially when using a Raspberry Pi 3. This model has a clock speed of 1 GHz, uses four cores, and has 1 GB of dynamic ram. This is quite impressive when you realize that this performance comes with a price tag of only $35 (USD). However, the key feature that makes the Raspberry Pi so attractive for AI demonstrations is that it is a microcontroller. This means you can directly control things based upon the outcome of AI events. Microcontrollers also allow sensors to be easily connected to them, thus allowing AI applications a means to interact with the real world.

While PCs can also be set up to both sense and control, it often requires expensive and complex interfaces to achieve these capabilities. The Raspberry Pi was initially designed to be able to sense and control devices with minimal interface requirements, and perhaps more importantly, minimal software requirements. PC software interfaces are often very complex, expensive, and typically proprietary—meaning making user changes or modifications is a difficult-to-impossible task.

The Raspberry Pis that I use in this book use a Raspian Linux distribution named Jessie. This distribution is completely open source and freely available from the Raspberry Pi Foundation's download website. It is a very stable operating system (OS) and supports several extremely large open-source applications repositories. This means that all the software used in this book is freely available and easily downloadable into the Raspberry Pi.

I use a variety of languages and applications in the book's various demonstrations and projects. The languages used are mainly Python, Prolog, and the Wolfram Language. Each of these languages brings some unique features that allow the book demonstrations to be quickly and easily implemented.

The main application that I use is Mathematica, which is a full-featured symbolic processing program that also happens to be part of the Jessie distribution. Mathematica is also a commercial program that ordinarily costs hundreds of dollars, but is provided gratis due to the very generous gift of the Wolfram Corporation and Dr. Stephen Wolfram (CEO) in particular.

I tried to layout the book in a logical manner by first introducing AI in Chapter 1. It is difficult to explain AI to people who have never heard of it, although it is often surprising to inform that them that AI often affects them in their daily lives. I have provided a considerable amount of detail in the first chapter by trying to define AI and how it is commonly applied in everyday life situations. It will soon become apparent to you how invasive AI has become in modern society, whether you like it or not. Please note that I used the term *invasive* in a non-derogatory way, simply to point out that AI is commonly applied in many areas, some of which will surprise you. In addition, I also discuss the topic of business intelligence (BI), as it is very closely allied to AI and is often the vehicle through which AI affects most people. Some AI practitioners often refer to BI as simply *AI applied in a business setting.* You will learn that it is much more than that, however. I adopt it because it is a useful simplification.

I next explore some basic AI concepts in Chapter 2. There is initially some discussion regarding basic logical constructs, as they are important to understand inference, which is an AI core foundation. Expert knowledge systems are next discussed, which constitute a major portion of the more general knowledge management systems (KMS)—an important part of BI. The discussion then turns to machine learning, which is a huge research area in modern AI. Finally, I conclude the chapter with an introduction to fuzzy logic (FL), which is thoroughly demonstrated in a later book project.

Chapter 3 shows you how to implement a practical expert system using the Prolog language. I explore some key Prolog features and explain how this somewhat specialized language is so useful in implementing AI concepts, without requiring extensive programing support as would be necessary if general-purpose languages such as C/C++ or Java were used for the same purposes. A simple console question-and-answer program is used in the practical demonstration.

Chapter 4 focuses on using AI with games. Admittedly, the games are quite simple; however, the chapter's goal is to simply demonstrate how AI is incorporated into gaming logic. These gaming AI concepts may then be easily expanded to handle much more complex games. I used Python to implement the games, which are controlled through a traditional text-console interface. Do not expect to see *World of Warcraft* (*WoW*)-quality graphics in this chapter, but rest assured that *WoW* does use AI in its games.

In Chapter 5, I return to using Prolog to implement some fuzzy logic controls for a practical project demonstration. There is also a simplified expert rules system incorporated into the project. A Raspberry Pi system using both temperature and humidity sensors will control a virtual heating and cooling system.

Chapter 6 introduces the concept of shallow machine learning. A Python program is created, in which the computer "learns" your favorite color and make "decisions" regarding color selection. Finally, I close the chapter with a discussion of adaptive learning, which plays a large role in BI.

Chapter 7 continues the machine learning topic with an examination of machine learning using artificial neural networks (ANN). ANNs are by far the most prevalent AI method used to implement machine learning. I go through a detailed discussion on how an ANN is constructed, and then demonstrate an actual neural network created with Python.

The machine learning continues into Chapter 8, where deep learning is discussed. In this chapter's project I go through a detailed discussion on how a multi-layer ANN functions incuding the gradient search feature.

Chapter 9 contains two demonstrations of deep learning using multi-layer ANNs. The first one recognizes hand-wriiten numbers based on the MNIST training and test dataset. The second one uses a Pi Camera with a Raspberry Pi to image a hand-written number and then uses the previously trained ANN to determine the closest match.

Chapter 10 deals with evolutionary computing (EC), which encompasses, but is not limited to, evolutionary programming, genetic algorithms and genetic programming. I have provided several interesting demonstrations highlighting some of the EC features to provide you with a good introduction to this fascinating field.

Chapter 11 discusses subsumption, which is a behavior-based robotic study area. It is closely allied with AI. I use the robot car first introduced in Chapter 7 to conduct several demonstrations. You will quickly realize that a robot employing subsumption behaviors can remarkably mimic actual human behavior, thus completing the AI loop between human thinking and motor behavior.

I am quite confident that after reading through this book and duplicating most—if not all the projects and demonstrations, you will come away with an excellent appreciation of AI and how to incorporate it into your future projects.

CHAPTER 1

■ ■ ■

Introduction to Artificial Intelligence

This chapter provides a straightforward introduction to artificial intelligence (AI), which in turn helps provide a framework for comprehending what AI is all about and why it is such an exciting and rapidly evolving field of study. Let's start with some historical facts about the origins of AI.

AI Historical Origins

Remarkably, AI, or something akin to it, has been around for a very long time. It has been recorded that ancient Greek philosophers discussed automatons or machines with inherent intelligence. In 1517, the Prague Golem was created; it is shown in Figure 1-1.

© Donald J. Norris 2017

D. J. Norris, *Beginning Artificial Intelligence with the Raspberry Pi*,
DOI 10.1007/978-1-4842-2743-5_1

Figure 1-1. *Prague Golem*

The Golem is made of clay, but according to Jewish folklore, it could be animated to carry out various acts of vengeance and retribution to parties responsible for anti-Semitic acts.

René Descartes, a famous French philosopher, wrote in 1637 about the impossibility of machine intelligence in his *Discourse on Method* treatise. Descartes was not advocating AI, but the treatise does show it was on his mind.

A more fanciful AI experiment example—or more appropriately stated, a hoax—is an automated chess player that made the rounds in Europe in the late 18th to mid-19th centuries. It was known as The Turk. A lithograph of it on a modern stamp is shown in Figure 1-2.

Figure 1-2. Automated chess player

It was purported to be an intelligent machine that could play a game of chess against a human opponent. In reality, there was a human chess player jammed into the machine's supporting box. He operated manipulators to move the machine's chess pieces. I would suppose that there must have been a miniature periscope or peephole available to allow this hidden chess player the opportunity to surveil the chessboard. The odd name *The Turk* is from the German word *Schachtürke*, which means "automaton chess player." The typical human chess master hidden in the box was so skilled that he would often win matches against notable opponents, including Napoleon Bonaparte and Benjamin Franklin. It was not until many years later that a real machine was available to actually play a reasonable chess game.

The advent of a scientific AI approach waited until 1943, upon the publication a paper by McCulloch and Pitts, in which they described "perceptrons," a mathematical model based on real biological brain cells called neurons. In their paper, they accurately described how neuron cells fired in a binary fashion, similar to electronic binary circuits. They also went well beyond that simple comparison to show how such cells could dynamically change their function with time, essentially creating rudimentary behavioral actions. This seminal paper was the first in a long series that established an important AI research area concerned with neural networks. I discuss this topic in greater detail in a later chapter.

In 1947, Alan M. Turing wrote:

> *In my opinion, this problem of making a large memory available at reasonably short notice is much more important than doing operations such as multiplication at high speed. Speed is necessary if the machine is to work fast enough for [it] to be commercially valuable, but a large storage is necessary if it is to be capable of anything more than rather trivial operations. The storage capability is therefore the more fundamental requirement.*

Turing, who many readers may recognize as the genius behind the effort to decode the German Enigma machine that considerably shortened the duration of WWII, also recognized in this short paragraph that any future machine "intelligence" would be predicated upon having sufficient machine memory available and not be solely reliant on computing speed. I have more to say about Turing a bit later in this chapter when the Turing test is discussed.

In 1951, a young mathematics PhD candidate named Marvin Minsky, along with Dean Edmonds, designed and built an analog computer based on the perceptrons described in the McCulloch and Pitts paper. This computer was named the Stochastic Neural Analog Reinforcement Computer (SNARC). It consisted of 40 vacuum tube neuron modules, which in turn controlled many additional valves, motors, gears, clutches, and actuators. This system was a randomly connected network of Hebb synapses that made up a neural network learning machine. The SNARC was possibly the first artificial self-learning machine. It successfully modeled the behavior of a rat traversing a maze in a search of food. This system exhibited some rudimentary "learning" behaviors that allowed the rat sim to eventually negotiate the maze.

A real turning point in AI progress happened in 1956 during an AI conference at Dartmouth College. This meeting was held at the behest of Minsky, John McCarthy, and Claude Shannon to explore the new field of AI. Claude Shannon has often been referred to as the "father of information theory" in recognition of his brilliant work accomplished at the prestigious Bell Telephone Lab in Holmdel, NJ.

John McCarthy was no slouch either, as he was the first to use the phrase "artificial intelligence," and the creator of the Lisp programming language family. He was a significant influence in the design of the ALGOL programming language. He also contributed significantly to the concept of computer timesharing, which makes modern computer networks possible. Minsky and McCarthy were also the founders of the MIT Media Lab, now known as the MIT Computer Science and Artificial Intelligence Lab.

Returning to the 1956 conference, McCarthy stated this now classic definition of AI, which as far as I know, remains the "gold standard" that most people use when asked to define AI:

> *It is the science and engineering of making intelligent machines, especially intelligent computer programs. It is related to the similar task of using computers to understand human intelligence, but AI does not have to confine itself to methods that are biologically observable.*

McCarthy used the phrase *human intelligence* in this definition, which I further explore a little later in this chapter. There were many other fundamental AI concepts set forth in this conference, which I cannot further explain in this book, but I urge interested readers to further explore.

The 1960s was a very progressive decade in terms of AI research. Arguably, the work of Newell and Simon in detailing the General Problem Solver algorithm stands out. This approach used both computer and human problem-solving techniques. Unfortunately, computer development was still evolving, and memory and speed capabilities to efficiently handle the algorithm's requirements were simply not present. (Remember Turing's warning that I earlier discussed.) The General Problem Solver project was eventually abandoned—not because it was theoretically incorrect, but because the hardware needed to implement it was simply not available.

Another significant AI contribution during this 1960s was Lofti Zadeh's introduction of fuzzy sets and logic, which were the foundation of the impressive AI branch known as *fuzzy logic*. Zadeh discussed how computers do not necessarily have to behave in a precise and discrete logical pattern, but instead take a more human-like fuzzy logic approach. I present an interesting fuzzy logic project in Chapter 5.

One unfortunate outcome from the ongoing research in the 1960s was the prediction that a computer could mimic a human brain. Of course, the computing power available to do fundamental research on how a human brain realistically functions was simply not available at that time. This led to much disappointment and disillusionment in the AI community.

The process of mimicking or somehow copying how the human brain works, and placing that functionality into a machine, has been termed as the classical AI approach. This has led to deep divisions within the AI community, where many researchers believe that machines should become intelligent in their own manner rather than mimicking human intelligence. The later approach has been termed *modern AI*.

There was considerable work in the late 1960s on how a computer could converse with a human by using natural language instead of computer code. One clever program created by Joseph Weisenbaum during this time was named ELIZA. While primitive by today's standards, it was still able to fool some users into thinking that they were conversing with another human instead of a machine. The ELIZA project brings up a very interesting topic regarding how one might determine if a machine has reached some level of "intelligence." One good answer lies in what is known as the Turing test, which I mentioned earlier. In a 1950 article in the *Journal of Computing Machinery and Intelligence*, Alan Turing discussed what he felt were sufficient conditions for considering a machine to have reached an intelligent state. He essentially argued that if a machine could successfully fool a knowledgeable human observer into thinking that he was having a conversation with another human instead of a machine, then the machine could be considered intelligent. Of course, the conversation would have had to done using a neutral communications channel to avoid the obvious clues of voice or appearance giving away the machine. Teletypes were the communication devices used in the 1950s to implement the neutral channel. The Turing test is still a reasonable benchmark, even considering today's technologies. One could even use highly effective modern voice recognition and synthesis technologies to further fool the observer. The Turing test is still controversial among philosophers and other interested parties who discuss the nature of intelligence.

In the 1970s, AI was slow to mature, due to the slow growth of computing technology. There was a lot of interest in natural language processing and image recognition and analysis, but unfortunately, the computers available to researchers were still quite limited and not up to these difficult tasks. It soon became apparent that there would have to be significant improvement in processing power before AI could really progress. In addition, there were also significant philosophical arguments against AI, including the famous "Chinese room" argument postulated by John Searle. Minsky argued against Searle's hypothesis, which only led to a lot of infighting and misdirection in ongoing research. Meanwhile, McCarthy argued for a modern AI approach, stating that human intelligence and machine intelligence are different and should be treated that way.

The 1980s showed considerable improvement in AI development due to the onset of the PC and many researchers taking on McCarthy's pragmatic approach. The advent of expert systems happened in this timeframe, which showed great promise and actual applications in the business and industrial/manufacturing sectors. I demonstrate several expert system applications in later chapters. The classic AI methodology continued; however, the modern approach was rapidly gaining acceptance, and perhaps more importantly, was used in many real-world situations. Coincidentally, there was a lot being done with robotics and real robot development at this time. AI research naturally gravitated to this area, because the areas seemed perfectly complementary. The age of practical AI had finally arrived and future developments came quickly, as the age of modern computing was also happening. It was about this time that the real impact of Moore's law became apparent. Moore's law refers to Gordon Moore, one of Intel's founders, who stated in 1965: "The number of transistors per square inch on integrated circuits has doubled every year since their invention."

This exponential growth in density seems to correlate nicely with the incredible improvement in computer performance, which is so sorely need for AI improvement and growth.

Significant milestones where reached in the 1990s, including the impressive win in 1997 by IBM's Deep Blue computer system over world grand-champion chess master, Garry Kasparov. Despite how impressive this win was, there was cold water thrown on this event. The stark reality of the win should be tempered by the following observation of McCarthy when he was asked specifically about a computer winning Go, a traditional Chinese board game:

> *The Chinese and Japanese game of Go is also a board game in which the players take turns moving. Go exposes the weakness of our present understanding of the intellectual mechanisms involved in human game playing. Go programs are very bad players, in spite of considerable effort (not as much as for chess). The problem seems to be that a position in* **Go** *has to be divided mentally into a collection of suppositions which are first analyzed separately followed by an analysis of their interaction. Humans use this in chess also, but chess programs consider the position as a whole. Chess programs compensate for the lack of this intellectual mechanism by doing thousands or, in the case of Deep Blue, many millions of times as much computation.*

This prescient analysis should assuage any reader's fear that computers are any nearer obtaining a human-level intellect featured in many science fiction movies, including *The Terminator* series, *2001: A Space Odyssey*, and the classic *War Games*. There is a long way to go and much more research to be completed before computing systems become truly intelligent. This is the subject of the next section.

Intelligence

Discussing the nature of intelligence is always a topic in beginning AI courses. Students most often wind up using circular reasoning when trying to come to grips with how to define what it is and how to recognize it. Exploring intelligence also usually ends in creating an almost endless list of questions, such as:

- Are mice intelligent?

- What does it mean for a machine to be intelligent?

- Are dolphins the smartest mammals in the sea?

- How would an extraterrestrial recognize intelligence on Earth?

One could continue ad infinitum with questions like these. Perhaps, on retrospect, just creating questions like these is a sure sign of intelligence. You can now see what I meant by circular reasoning. It turns out that agreeing to a common definition of intelligence is a difficult, if not impossible, action. There are dictionary definitions of intelligence, such as the following from *Meriam-Webster* online:

1. *a (1): the ability to learn or understand or to deal with new or trying situations : reason; also: the skilled use of reason (2): the ability to apply knowledge to manipulate one's environment or to think abstractly as measured by objective criteria (as tests), b Christian Science : the basic eternal quality of divine Mind, c: mental acuteness : shrewdness*

2. *a: an intelligent entity; especially : angel, b: intelligent minds or mind <cosmic intelligence>*

3. *the act of understanding : comprehension*

4. *a: information, news b: information concerning an enemy or possible enemy or an area; also: an agency engaged in obtaining such information*

5. *the ability to perform computer functions*

As you can readily see, the dictionary editors were widely diverse in trying to capture the definition of intelligence, including human behaviors, spiritual aspects, religion, and finally and somewhat interesting, a fifth-level definition of performing computer functions.

The online *Macmillan* dictionary offers a much more concise definition:

The ability to understand and think about things, and to gain and use knowledge

I am positive that if I went to other online dictionaries, I would see many other definitions, which is why trying to pin down intelligence is so hard. Consequently, not having an agreed standard regarding what intelligence is makes it nearly impossible to recognize it when it is happening on a consistent and agreed upon basis.

Intelligence is also related to both sensory inputs and motor or actuating outputs. Obviously, our brains are contained in our human bodies, which are also nicely equipped with five sensory systems—vision, hearing, taste, touch, and smell. These sensory systems are an integral part of our intelligence; however, it has been repeatedly demonstrated that there are still very intelligent human beings who have lost one or more of their sensory inputs. The human body is quite remarkable in its ability to compensate when a particular sensory system has been injured or destroyed. Likewise, human intelligence is also linked somewhat to our motor skills; however, I would argue not as much as the sensory inputs. Losing the ability to speak has not diminished the intellect and genius of Steven Hawking. Having the ability to walk, run, drive a car, or pilot an airplane gives individuals the opportunity to explore and understand their environment, and consequently, expand their knowledge and experiences, but not necessarily improve or expand their intelligence—unless you subscribe to the notion that knowledge and intelligence are synonymous.

It is only a small leap to study animals and consider whether or not they possess intelligence. Birds can fly and typically have much better vision than humans have. Does this mean that they possess intelligence beyond the human species, at least in those two areas? The answer is obviously unknowable, which leads to the following reasonable conclusion: animal and machine intelligence should simply be accepted for what it is and not be compared to human intelligence. Trying to make the latter comparison is simply like comparing apples and oranges; it is truly meaningless.

My goal in the foregoing discussion is to reiterate the premise of the modern approach to AI, in that machine intelligence should be considered by itself and not be compared to human intelligence. This is the underlying premise of the book, where projects explore machine advantages, but are neither expected to nor even desired to emulate or simulate human intelligence.

Strong AI vs. Weak AI, Broad AI vs. Narrow AI

There are additional descriptors that are commonly applied to AI, as you may have inferred from this section's title. AI work and research that attempts to simulate human reasoning to the maximum level possible is sometimes called *strong AI*. I would presume that proponents of the classical AI approach would also hardly endorse this terminology. This strong adjective contrasts sharply with the weak AI adjective that simply relates to getting practical AI systems to function effectively, without regard to the human analog. This approach is what I have referred to as the *modern approach*. I do not know how these strong and weak terms arose, but I suspect they exist to cast a prerogative shadow on the modern approach, which is unfortunate because both approaches are equally valid and deserving of equal importance and recognition. I have only introduced these terms so that you understand their significance if you happen to read about AI applications or projects. I do not use either term; instead, I just focus on the AI applications— regardless of their being strong or weak.

The other pair of terms I used in the section title are *broad* AI and *narrow* AI. Broad AI is concerned with general reasoning and not related to a specific task or application. I suppose that broad AI and strong AI would tend to have a natural bond, as both relate to the human context of reasoning and thinking. Narrow AI focuses on AI applied to specific tasks and it is not too generalized. However, there are exceptions, which tend to easily break the broad and narrow AI definitions. Google has developed systems that are excellent in predicting or characterizing how "things" should be described or arranged. Google applications exhibit both broad and narrow AI aspects regarding generalizations, as well as specific cataloging functions. Amazon, likewise, has intelligent agents, which tend to be excellent in both generalizations and making specific customer recommendations.

I close this section with Figure 1-3, which is a word cloud that I created using Mathematica running on a Raspberry Pi 3. This figure is a simply a graphical representation of the many different words that are commonly used with AI. Wikipedia was the source for all the words shown in the figure.

Figure 1-3. *A word cloud on artificial intelligence*

Reasoning

I repeatedly used the words *reason* and *reasoning* in the previous discussions. But what do they really mean and how are they related to AI? *Reasoning* describes creating or considering a reason. The word *reason* means to think about how things or ideas relate to what is known—or more simply, knowledge. A few reasoning examples help clarify the thoughts that I am attempting to convey.

- Learning is the process of building a new knowledge set based upon examining or discussing existing knowledge sets. *Sets* in this context are any data collections, whether or not based in reality.

- Use of language is the conversion of words, whether written or spoken into ideas and supportive relationships.

- Inference based on logic means deciding whether something is true based upon logical relationships.

- Inference based on evidence means deciding whether something is true based upon all the supportive available evidence.

- Natural language generation exists to satisfy communication goals and objectives using a given language.

- Problem solving is the process of determining how to achieve a set goal or an objective.

Any of these activities must necessarily involve reasoning to achieve a satisfactory end result. Please note that nowhere in the list do I limit the reasoning to only human beings. Some of these activities are certainty suitable to be implemented by machines, and in some cases, even by animals. There have been endless experiments that have satisfactorily demonstrated that animals can solve problems, especially if it involves getting to food.

There is a recent proliferation of voice-activated Internet devices, including Amazon's Alexa, Microsoft's Cortana, Apple's Siri, and Google's Home. These are either standalone devices or applications that are installed on smartphones. In any case, they are well equipped to recognize voice inquires, translate the inquiries into actionable Internet queries, and finally, relay the results to the user in a highly understandable format, usually as a well-spoken female voice. These devices/applications must use some level of reasoning to carry out their intended functions, even if to reply they do not understand the user's request.

AI Categories

Table 1-1 is a list that I created to show most of the categories that make up modern-day AI. I do not think it is comprehensive. There are likely some categories that have been inadvertently omitted. I did overtly omit some categories, such as the history and philosophy of AI, because they were not directly pertinent to the intent of this table.

Table 1-1. *Modern AI Categories*

Category	Brief Description
Affective computing	The study and development of systems and devices that can recognize, interpret, process, and simulate human affects.
Artificial immune systems	Intelligent, rule-based machine learning systems based primarily on the inherent principles and processes contained within vertebrate immune systems.
Chatterbot	A type of conversational agent or computer program designed to simulate an intelligent conversation with one or more human users through text or audio channels.
Cognitive architecture	A theory about the structure of the human mind. One of the main goals is to incorporate concepts from cognitive psychology into a comprehensive computer model.
Computer vision	An interdisciplinary field that deals with how computers can gain high-level understanding from digital images or videos.

(continued)

Table 1-1. (*continued*)

Category	Brief Description
Evolutionary computing	The use of evolutionary algorithms based on Darwinian principles from which the name is derived. These algorithms belong to a family of trial-and-error problem solvers and use metaheuristic or stochastic global methods to determine many solutions.
Gaming AI	AI used in games to generate intelligent behaviors, primarily in non-player characters (NPCs), often simulating human-like intelligence.
Human-Computer-Interface (HCI)	HCI researches the design and use of computer technology, focused on the interfaces between people (users) and computers.
Intelligent soft assistant or intelligent personal assistant (IPA)	A software agent that can perform tasks or services for an individual. These tasks or services are usually based on user input, location awareness, and the ability to access information from a variety of online sources. Examples of such an agent are Apple's Siri, Amazon's Alexa, Amazon's Evi, Google's Home, Microsoft's Cortana, the open source Lucida, Braina (application developed by Brainasoft for Microsoft Windows), Samsung's S Voice, and LG G3's Voice Mate.
Knowledge engineering	Refers to all technical, scientific, and social aspects involved in building, maintaining, and using knowledge-based systems.
Knowledge representation (KR)	Dedicated to representing information about the world in a form that a computer system can utilize to solve complex tasks, such as diagnosing a medical condition or having a dialog in a natural language.
Logic programming	A type of programming largely based on formal logic. Any program written in a logic programming language is a set of sentences in logical form, expressing facts and rules about some problem domain. Major logic programming language families include Prolog, answer set programming (ASP), and Datalog.
Machine learning (ML)	ML in the AI context provides computers the ability to learn without being explicitly programmed. Shallow and deep learning are two major subfields.
Multi-agent system (M.A.S.)	M.A.S. is a computerized system composed of multiple interacting intelligent agents within an environment.

(*continued*)

Table 1-1. (*continued*)

Category	Brief Description
Robotics	Robotics is the interdisciplinary branches of engineering and science that includes mechanical engineering, electrical engineering, computer science, AI, and others.
Robots	A robot is a machine, especially one programmable by a computer, which is capable of carrying out a complex series of actions autonomously.
Rule engines or systems	Rule-based systems are used to store and manipulate knowledge to interpret information in a useful way.
Turing test	The Turing test is a test, developed by Alan Turing in 1950, of a machine's ability to exhibit intelligent behavior equivalent to, or indistinguishable from, that of a human.

I will repeat that this table does not cover all modern AI research and activities, but it certainly highlights most of the important ones. I only demonstrate a few of the listed AI categories in this book, but even those should provide reasonable insight on how AI may be implemented using relatively simple computer resources.

At this point, I believe it is appropriate to discuss AI as it affects modern society in ways well beyond the scope of this book. I provide this brief discussion in hopes of enhancing my readers' knowledge and understanding of how AI affects us—one and all—in our daily lives.

AI and Big Data

Most readers have heard the term *big data*, but like most people, you may not have an appreciation of what it is and how it affects our modern society. There are many definitions of big data, just as there are many definitions of AI. The definition I like is rather simple: *a data collection characterized by huge volumes, rapid velocity, and great variety.*

The magnitude of the *huge volumes* can be characterized by saying it is typically measured in petabytes (PB), where one PB equals one million gigabytes (GB). That is truly a huge amount of data. The *rapid velocity* mentioned in the definition refers to how rapidly the data is generated or created. One need only look at Facebook to appreciate the rapidity of new content that is constantly being created by hundreds of millions of online users. Finally, the *great variety* phrase in the definition refers to the various data types that go into making up the huge data flows. This includes pictures, video, audio, as well as plain old text. An average photo uploaded to Facebook likely takes about four to five megabytes of storage. Multiply that by the multimillions of photos that are constantly uploaded, and you soon realize the nature of big data. So how does AI affect big data? The answer is that an AI learning system when applied to a big data set allows users to extract useful information from a huge and noisy input. Typical computer systems that can handle big data are composed of thousands of processors working together in a parallel fashion to greatly speed up the data reduction process often referred to as MapReduce. IBM's Watson computer is a prime example of such a system. It has implemented expert medical systems by using a rules-based engine and processing many thousands, if not millions, of medical records. The end result is a computer system that assists doctors in diagnosing illnesses and related maladies, which do not have obvious or relatable symptoms to known diseases.

Amazon's website is integrated with an impressive AI system that easily compiles a detailed profile of each potential or actual customer that repeatedly visits its site. It matches the customer's searches with those of other customers that have searched or inquired about similar products. It further tries to predict what might interest a site visitor based on their past searches and orders. All the data that the Amazon system uses is transactional, basically identifying what potentially interests its customers. This transactional data, which likely qualifies as big data, is the primary input into Amazon's AI computer systems. The output is the profile that I mentioned, but it may be also considered a set of characterizations attached to the potential or actual customer; for example, a resulting in a website suggestion may look like the following:

"You may be interested in Robert Heinlein's book *The Moon is a Harsh Mistress* because you have purchased the following books:"

- *Full Moon*

- *Star Wars: The Empire Strikes Back*

- *The Shawshank Redemption*

This list of seemingly unconnected books likely shows that the customer has an interest in the Moon, conflict in outer space, or injustice in a prison, all of which are touched in some fashion in Heinlein's book. (Incidentally, Heinlein's book received the Hugo Award for best science fiction novel in 1967.) Making this obscure connection between the customer's past book purchases and Heinlein's book content requires a significant computer analysis effort, as well as access to a huge database.

The biggest global user of big data analysis is the US government in the execution of the Global War on Terrorism (GWOT). The US National Security Agency (NSA) is at the forefront of detecting possible/likely terrorist attacks on the homeland. Its annual classified budget has been estimated at more than $15 billion, with the vast majority of it spent on collecting and analyzing all sorts of big data in the fight against GWOT. What it collects and how it conducts big data analysis is ultrasecret, but it is quite reasonable to assume that all appropriate AI techniques are used by the NSA experts, many of whom I expect are also experts at conducting secret AI research. This is not a conspiracy theory on my part, but simply what any reasonable layperson should expect.

This section concludes my introduction to AI, which although somewhat abbreviated, hopefully contained sufficient information to provide you with a reasonable background to start the study of specific AI concepts. This begins in the next chapter.

Summary

I began the chapter with an historical overview of AI that started in ancient times and proceeded to modern times. This shows that mankind has thought about making machines to accomplish intelligent actions for a very long time. It is only in very recent times that computers have been developed with the capabilities to implement intelligent actions

There was a brief discussion on the differences between the classic and modern approaches to AI development. In brief, the classic approach attempts to have computers mimic or simulate the human brain, whereas the modern approach simply takes advantage of a computer's inherent speed and processing power to implement AI on it. I also defined additional terms, such as broad AI and narrow AI and strong AI and weak AI.

The brief inspection of the nature of intelligence was presented to pique your curiosity and to think about how you might recognize if intelligence is present in machines or animals. A brief section on reasoning followed, which included some examples to help recognize reasoning when it is incorporated into AI applications.

I next presented a list of AI categories to help explain important and current AI R&D efforts. Only a few of the AI categories can be demonstrated in this book.

The chapter finished with a discussion on how AI influences modern society, especially when dealing with big data.

CHAPTER 2

▓ ▓ ▓

Basic AI Concepts

In this chapter, I introduce and explore the fundamental concepts that are crucial to AI.

It is very important to closely study these concepts to gain an appreciation and understanding of how AI functions at its most rudimentary level. It would indeed be difficult to proceed with more advanced AI projects without first doing this initial study. I only cover the concepts necessary to understand the projects in this book. Let's start with some foundational concept discussions.

Boolean Algebra

Boolean algebra was created by George Boole in 1847. It is an algebra in which variable values are the truth values—true and false, often denoted as 1 and 0, respectively. There are a few very basic Boolean operations, which are frequently used in AI expressions. These operations are listed for variables A and B, as follows:

- A AND B

- A OR B

- NEGATE A

- NEGATE B

The expression A AND B may also be represented by A * B where the * symbol represents the AND'ing operation. It is not a true analog to the general multiplication symbol used in ordinary algebra, but it is close enough that most people use it interchangeably. Similarly, the expression A OR B can be represented by A + B, where the same observation holds true for the normal + symbol used in regular algebra. You will shortly see that there is a situation where $1 + 1 = 1$ in Boolean algebra, but obviously is not true in non-Boolean algebra. The NEGATE or complement operation is *unary*, meaning it only uses one operand or variable; whereas AND and OR are binary, requiring two logical variables. The NEGATE operation has a formal symbol ($\neg$), but it is not widely used in programs. Instead, a bar placed over the symbol is commonly used in most in logical expressions, which is the one that I use.

Table 2-1 shows the output resulting from various A and B inputs for the operations I just mentioned. Note that I use the variable C to represent the output.

© Donald J. Norris 2017
D. J. Norris, *Beginning Artificial Intelligence with the Raspberry Pi*,
DOI 10.1007/978-1-4842-2743-5_2

Table 2-1. *Basic Boolean Operations*

Operation	Input Variables		Output Variable
	A	B	C
A * B	0	0	0
A * B	1	0	0
A * B	0	1	0
A * B	1	1	1
A + B	0	0	0
A + B	1	0	1
A + B	0	1	1
A + B	1	1	1
$\bar{A}$	0	-	1
$\bar{A}$	1	-	0

Logical symbols can easily be arranged to form both simple and complex Boolean algebraic expressions. For instance, the AND'ing operation may be expressed as follows:

$$C = A * B$$

It should not be hard to realize that far more complex expressions can be created by using more than two variables and combined using these basic operations. However, the important point to understand is that eventually all expressions resolve to a true or false, 1 or 0 output.

There are also three secondary operations used in Boolean algebra:

- EXCLUSIVE OR

- MATERIAL IMPLICATION

- EQUIVALENCE

I use two of these three operations in inference discussion (material implication and equivalence), but I do not specifically call them out by their Boolean algebra names. In AI, there is a lot of overlap among the different subfields that go into overall AI technology; hence, it is not unusual to use concepts present in one subfield that uses a specific name that also exists in another subfield with a different name or reference. This differentiation should not bother you as long as you grasp the underlying concepts.

Some Additional Boolean Laws

It is also important that you understand some more basic Boolean algebra laws, because they are used at various times to combine logical expressions used in many of the chapters. They are briefly described here.

This is an example of De Morgan's law:

$$\overline{(A * B)} = \overline{A} + \overline{B}$$

$$\overline{(A + B)} = \overline{A} * \overline{B}$$

This is an example of associativity:

$$(A * B) * C = A * (B * C)$$

$$(A + B) + C = A + (B + C)$$

This is an example of commutativity:

$$A * B = B * A$$

$$A + B = B + A$$

This is an example of distributivity:

$$A * (B + C) = (A * B) + (A * C)$$

$$A + (B * C) = (A + B) * (A + C)$$

Inference

Inference is part of the reasoning process introduced in Chapter 1. This reasoning process consists of moving from an initial premise or statement of fact to a logical conclusion. Inference is ordinarily divided into three categories.

- *Deduction*: The derivation of a logical conclusion based on premises known or assumed to be true using the laws and rules of logic.

- *Induction*: Making a universal conclusion based upon specific premises.

- *Abduction*: Reduction of premises to the optimal explanation.

I use the inference deduction category for the following discussion, as it is the best fit for the topic of expert systems, which is introduced shortly.

There is a Latin phrase, *modus ponens*, which means *"the way that affirms by affirming."* It represents the fundamental rule for deductive inference. Using logic terms, this rule may be stated as "P implies Q, and P is asserted to be true, so therefore Q must be true." This rule dates to antiquity and has been used by logicians throughout the ages, up to and including the modern era. The rule may be broken into two sections. The first is a conditional claim that is traditionally stated in the form of *if ... then.* The second part is the *consequent* of the conditional claim; that is, the logical statement following the *then.* The conditional claim for the general rule consists of two premises: that *P implies Q* and *P is true. P* is also known as the antecedent of the conditional claim. The consequent is obviously *Q is true.* The application of this simple *modus ponens* rule in AI is known as *forward chaining,* which is a key element in expert systems. I discuss it in the next section.

Expert Systems

An *expert system* is a computer program designed to use facts present in a specific problem domain. It then develops conclusions about those facts in a way analogous to a human expert reasoning with the same facts and reaching similar conclusions. Such a program or expert system would need access to all the facts in the domain, as well as be programmed with a set of rules that a human expert would follow regarding those facts and drawing conclusions from the same facts. Sometimes this expert system is known as a *rules-based* or *knowledge-based system.*

The first, large-scale expert system able to perform at a human-expert level was named MYCIN. It was used as an intelligent aide for doctors in their diagnosis of blood-borne infections. MYCIN incorporated about 450 rules. It was capable of creating correct diagnoses on a level comparable to an inexperienced doctor. The set of rules used in MYCIN was created based on interviews with a large number of experts in the field, who in turn relied on their own experiences and knowledge. To a large extent, the rules captured real-world data and knowledge beyond what was in medical textbooks and standard procedures. The rules used in MYCIN were in the same format I introduced earlier:

```
if (conditional claim) then (consequent)
```

The following is an example:

```
if (bacteria in blood) then (septicemia)
```

Incidentally, septicemia is a very serious blood-borne illness and must be treated immediately.

The conditional claim, which I will now simply shorten to the word *condition* may be complex by combining it with other conditions using the logical operators introduced in the Boolean algebra section. I will also use the word *conclusion* instead of *consequent,* because it is more commonly used in expert system design.

The following are some general formats for complex rules:

- if (condition1 and condition2) then (conclusion)

- if (condition1 or condition2) then (conclusion)

- if ((condition1 or condition2) and condition3) then (conclusion)

It is not hard to imagine that the MYCIN rules created were fairly complex, based upon the problem domain and all the variables or conditions present in that domain. The tools and techniques developed for MYCIN were later used in other expert systems.

Would there ever be a case where different conclusions could be reached given the same set of facts or conditions? The answer is definitely *yes*, and that is where conflict resolution enters the picture.

Conflict Resolution

Conflict results when rules are applied using the given conditions, and several different conclusions are created, but only one conclusion is required. This conflict must somehow be resolved. The conflict resolution answer can be provided in several ways, as described in the following list.

- *Highest rule priority*: Every rule in the expert system is assigned a priority or a number. The conclusion reached by the highest priority rule is the one selected. There also must be some sort of tiebreaker procedure in these situations.

- *Highest condition priority*: Every condition in the expert system is assigned a priority or number. The conclusion reached by a rule that contains the highest priority condition(s) is the one selected. There also must be some sort of tiebreaker procedure in these situations.

- *Most specific priority*: The conclusion created by the rule that used the most conditions is the one selected.

- *Recent priority*: The most recent conclusion created by a rule created is the one selected.

- *Context-specific priority*: The expert system rules are divided into groups of which only one to a few are active or used at any given time. A selected conclusion must be generated from one of the active rule groups.

Deciding which conflict resolution approach to employ really depends upon the nature of the expert system. It very well might require applying different approaches and evaluating which one performs the best. And, of course, there is always the default decision to not use any conflict resolution and simply present all conclusions to the human users and let them decide.

Rules may also be combined in a hierarchical manner to create a "reasoned" approach that reflects how a human expert would function with a given set of conditions. The following example should help clarify how rule combinations function. I chose to use a phantom quarterback (QB) playing in the National Football League (NFL) as my virtual expert. Suppose the situation is that the QB's team is at a third down, with seven yards to gain for a first down. It is a reasonable conclusion that an expert QB would be selecting a pass play to gain the needed yardage, because a seven-yard run gain on a third down has a low probability of success, at least in the NFL.

The QB's next concern is the defense's setup, because it materially affects the pass type selected. The pass type may also be changed if the QB detects that the defense will likely blitz, meaning they are sending one or two additional pass rushers to stop the QB. Blitzing almost always places the defense in a one-on-one or man-to-man coverage, increasing the probability of a successful pass play. An actual blitz would normally have the QB try a long yardage pass play. When a blitz is shown but not executed, the QB often tries for a shorter screen pass play, which normally results in a short yardage gain.

The scenario that I just described can be divided into planning and action phases. The planning phase starts when the team's lineup against each other. The action phase starts when the offense's center snaps the football to the QB. These two phases translate into layers when a hierarchical rule structure is generated. The following is a reasonable set of hierarchical rules for this football scenario.

The following are the layer 1 rules:

```
if (third down and long yardage to gain) then (pass play planned)
if (blitz suspected) then (long yardage pass planned)
```

These are the layer 2 rules:

```
if (blitz happens) then (execute long yardage pass play)
if (blitz does not happen) then (execute screen pass play)
```

These rules are obviously simplified, because in reality, the QB has other options, depending on his own athletic abilities—such as holding on to the football and trying to run for a first down on his own. The rules shown in layer 1 are independent of each other, while the rules shown in layer 2 are totally dependent, meaning that either one will be executed or "fired," but never both. Finally, the rule set is dynamic in the sense that the conditions are not determined until moments before any rules are fired. This differs sharply from most routine expert systems, where the conditions are fixed and completely available before being applied to the rule set.

Backward Chaining

The process of firing rules to generate conclusions, which in turn are then used as conditions in following rules, is forward chaining. Forward chaining is the normal way expert systems work. However, it is sometimes very useful and important to begin with the conclusions and try to deduce which conditions were needed to produce that end-point conclusion. This process is known as *backward chaining*, which is often used to verify that the systems work as intended and to ensure that improper or "wrong" conclusions are never reached. Such verification is especially important in expert systems that are employed in safety critical systems, such as control systems used in land, sea, or air vehicles.

Backward chaining can also be used to determine if any more rules need to be developed to prevent untended or strange conclusions from being reached by using a specific set of input conditions.

At this point, you should have a sufficient amount of background information to tackle a beginning AI project using a Raspberry Pi. This project entails installing the SWI Prolog language on a Raspberry Pi, and subsequently using it to make queries from a small knowledge base. But first, a few words about the Raspberry Pi configuration used to work with Prolog.

Raspberry Pi Configuration

I connected to a Raspberry Pi running in a standalone setup using a headless or SSH connection. My client computer is a MacBook Pro, which I use for all my manuscript production. It also allowed me to easily capture screenshots of the terminal window controlling the Raspberry Pi. I find this connection type to be very efficient; it allows me full access to the Raspberry Pi and to all the files on my Mac. Everything displayed in the terminal window can be duplicated in a monitor connected directly to the Raspberry Pi, if this is the way you choose to run your own system. Of course, file manipulation on the Raspberry Pi has to be done through a command line, rather than through drag/drop/click—as is the case on a Mac.

Introduction to SWI Prolog

The AI language Prolog was initially created by mix of Scottish, French, and Canadian researchers from the 1960s to the early 1970s. It has been around a long time, considering how quickly modern computer languages are generated. Originally, the project's purpose was to make deductions from French text extracted through automated means. This effort involved natural language processing, development of computer algorithms, and logical analysis. The name *Prolog* comes from a combination of three French words: *PROgrammation en LOGique.*

Prolog is considered a declarative programming language because it uses a set of facts and rules called a *knowledge base.* A Prolog user can address queries or questions to the knowledge base, which are knowns as *goals.* Prolog responds with an answer to the goal(s) using logical deduction, as discussed in the inference section. Often, the answer is simply true or false, but it could be numerical, or even textual, depending upon how the goal was expressed.

Prolog is also considered a symbolic language, totally devoid of any connection to hardware or specific implementations. Prolog is often used by people with minimal computer knowledge, due to its level of abstraction. Most users do not need any prior computer programming experience to effectively use Prolog—at least at its most basic levels, as you will shortly experience.

From its start, Prolog was considered by the AI community as a shining example of what could be achieved by using symbols with AI. The language is essentially reasoning and logical processes, with the concepts of thinking and intelligence. While fairly simple from the outset, Prolog has become increasing complex as researchers add additional features and capabilities to the language. In my humble opinion, this has been both good and bad for the promotion of the language. Once quite simple and attractive to non-AI users, it has become quite complex and daunting to beginners in AI. However, do not fear: I keep things quite straightforward in the following Prolog demonstrations. However, be aware that you are only seeing the very tip of the "iceberg" when it comes to Prolog's capabilities.

The computational power necessary to run Prolog has changed dramatically from the 1970s, when the equivalent of a supercomputer was necessary, compared to today, when a $35 single-board computer can easily and more quickly process Prolog queries.

Installing Prolog on a Raspberry Pi

The following instructions enable you to install a very capable and useful Prolog version, named SWI Prolog, on a Raspberry Pi. SWI is the acronym for *social science informatics*, as expressed in the Dutch language. SWI Prolog's website is at www.swi-prolog.org. I urge you to take a look at this site because it contains a lot of useful tutorials and other key data.

To start the SWI Prolog installation, you first need to update your Raspian distribution. I assume that most readers are using the latest distribution, named Jessie, which was available from the Raspberry Pi Foundation at the time this book was written.

The first command you need to execute is the one that updates the Rasperry Pi Linux distribution:

```
sudo apt-get Update
```

The update should only take a few minutes to complete. Afterward, you are ready to install SWI Prolog. Enter the following:

```
sudo apt-get install swi-prolog
```

This command installs the SWI Prolog language along with all the required dependencies necessary for it to run on a Raspberry Pi. This installation takes several minutes or longer, depending on the Raspberry Pi model that you are using.

To test if you had a successful installation, simply enter the following:

```
swipl
```

You should see the following text appear on the monitor:

```
pi@raspberrypi:~ $ swipl
Welcome to SWI-Prolog (Multi-threaded, 32 bits, Version 6.6.6)
Copyright (c) 1990-2013 University of Amsterdam, VU Amsterdam
SWI-Prolog comes with ABSOLUTELY NO WARRANTY. This is free software,
and you are welcome to redistribute it under certain conditions.
Please visit http://www.swi-prolog.org for details.

For help, use ?- help(Topic). or ?- apropos(Word).

?-
```

The prompt is ?–, which means that Prolog is awaiting your input. Assuming that you see this opening screen, you are set to start experimenting with Prolog, which is the subject of the next section.

Initial Prolog Demonstration

As I stated, you need a knowledge base to query Prolog. The knowledge base I use comes straight from a SWI Prolog tutorial that is located on their website. This knowledge base concerns the sun, planets, and a moon. The knowledge base is just a text file that should be put in the Raspberry Pi's home directory. I created this text file using the default nano editor. I highly recommend that you also use nano; however, you certainly could use other text editors if you so desire. You should not use Microsoft Word or similar powerful word editors unless you ensure that all hidden formatting is excluded from the text file. Any hidden formatting causes the Prolog program to generate an error, so you would not be able to use that knowledge base.

The following is a listing of the knowledge base, which is named `satellites.pl`, and located in the `pi` directory.

```
%% a simple Prolog knowledge base

%% facts
orbits(earth, sun).
orbits(saturn, sun).
orbits(titan, saturn).

%% rules
satellite(X) :- orbits(X, _).
planet(X) :- orbits(X, sun).
moon(X) :- orbits(X, Y), planet(Y).
```

There are a few things that you should know about this knowledge base. Comments are started these symbols: %%. Comments are for human readers; they are ignored by the Prolog interpreter. Case counts in the file (meaning x and X) are not the same symbol. Facts and rules are always terminated with a period '.'.

You must use the `consult` command to force Prolog to use a knowledge base. In this situation, the command is with the name of the knowledge base without the `.pl` extension as the command argument:

```
?- consult(satellites).
```

This is a shorthand version of the `consult` command:

```
?- [satellites].
```

You can now start making queries, or setting goals, once the knowledge base is in place. The following is a simple query that asks if the Earth is a satellite of the sun:

```
?- satellite(earth).
```

The Prolog response is *true* because one of the facts in the knowledge base is that the Earth orbits the sun, and one of the rules is that a satellite is defined as any symbol that orbits the sun. Of course, the symbol used for this rule is the text "earth". Figure 2-1 shows five queries that involve satellites, planets, and a moon.

```
pi@raspberrypi:~ $ swipl
Welcome to SWI-Prolog (Multi-threaded, 32 bits, Version 6.6.6)
Copyright (c) 1990-2013 University of Amsterdam, VU Amsterdam
SWI-Prolog comes with ABSOLUTELY NO WARRANTY. This is free software,
and you are welcome to redistribute it under certain conditions.
Please visit http://www.swi-prolog.org for details.

For help, use ?- help(Topic). or ?- apropos(Word).

?- [satellites].
% satellites compiled 0.00 sec, 7 clauses
true.

?- satellite(sun).
false.

?- satellite(earth).
true.

?- satellite(titan).
true.

?- planet(titan).
false.

?- moon(titan).
true.

?- halt.
pi@raspberrypi:~ $ █
```

Figure 2-1. Prolog knowledge base queries

Technically, moons also orbit the sun because their planets orbit the sun, but that can quickly become confusing, so it is left to the reader to ponder. Notice also that a halt. command is the last of the interactive Prolog entries shown in Figure 2-1. This command causes Prolog to stop and return control to the default operating system (OS) prompt.

It should be obvious that many additional facts can be added to the knowledge base to encompass more of the solar system. Additional rules can also be easily added to cover behaviors other than determining planet, satellite, and moon status. This flexibility is one of the inherent powers that Prolog possesses to handle more complex and comprehensive knowledge bases.

It should now also be obvious that through its knowledge bases, Prolog is a natural way to implement an expert system. One such system is thoroughly examined in the chapter devoted to expert systems. Now it is time to shift focus to discuss the approach fuzzy logic takes with AI.

Introduction to Fuzzy Logic

I start this section with the obvious point that there is nothing fuzzy or imprecise with the theory behind fuzzy logic (FL), which is so named because it goes well beyond a core concept in traditional logic that a statement is either true or false (also called a *binary decision*). In FL, a statement can be partially true or false. There can also be probabilities attached to a statement, such as *There is a 60 percent chance that the statement is true*. FL reflects reality in the sense that human beings not only make binary decisions but also decide things based on gradations. When you adjust the temperature in your shower, it is not just hot or cold but more likely warm or slightly cool. When driving, you likely adjust the speed of your car to the nominal traffic flow, which could easily be a little above the posted limit; you are not just speeding or stopped. These decisions—based on magnitude or gradations—are all around us. FL helps capture this decision making within AI. The following example should shed more light on what FL is and how it functions.

Example of FL

Let's go back to the shower example to illustrate how FL works. I'll start with some extreme ranges for the water temperature: the coldest it can be is 50°F and the hottest is 150°F. The total temperature range is a convenient 100°F, which I arranged to ease the calculations. Of course, either extreme would not be acceptable for normal showers. Now let's take a percentage of the range and see what happens. Let's say that the shower temperature is set at 40% of the range. That would make the actual shower temperature a cozy 90°F, well within the comfort zone of most people. This simple method of relating a percentage to an actual temperature is the start of a process called *fuzzification*, where real-world conditions are associated with FL values, or temperatures to percentages in this case. The following set of conditions applies to the fuzzification of the shower temperature example:

- 50°F becomes 0%, 60°F becomes 10%, and so forth, until 150°F becomes 100%

- Every 1°F difference is precisely 1% within the extremes

It is also very easy to create a simple equation relating percentages with temperatures:

Percentage = (T – 50) where T is °F and in the range 50 to 150.

Once a real-world value has been fuzzified, it can then be passed on to a set of rules to be evaluated. These rules are exactly the same as I described in the expert system discussion, which only reinforces the integration of various technologies within AI. These FL models are sometimes called *fuzzy inference systems*.

However, the general *modus ponens* form of *if (condition) then (conclusion)* must be modified a bit to accommodate FL. What this means is that the following rules might apply in a traditional logic arrangement:

```
if (water temp is cold) then (turn on water heater)
if (water temp is hot) then (turn off water heater)
```

They can be replaced with a simpler FL compatible rule:

```
if (water is hot) then (turn on water heater)
```

But wait a moment! At first glance, this rule makes no sense. It seems to say if the water is hot, turn on the water heater. That is because you are thinking about it in the traditional sense of either true/false or on/off. Now, rethink the condition about *water is hot from* not being either true or false, but to a fuzzified percentage value ranging from 0 to 100%, and you should start to realize that the conclusion part of *turn on water heater* also changes to a percentage, but in reverse manner. For instance, if the *water is hot* condition is only 10% true, then the *turn on water heater* conclusion might be 90% of its maximum value, and the water heater would be working at nearly maximum capacity. However, if the *water is hot* condition is 90% true, then the *turn on water heater* conclusion might be 10% of its maximum value, and the water heater would essentially be turned off. It does take a bit of effort to realign your thinking regarding FL and how it is applied within a rules system, but I guarantee it is well worth the effort.

Rules may be combined in a similar way that was shown in the expert systems discussion. Let's suppose that the hot water heating system has been installed in an energy distribution grid where there are different kilowatt-hour (kw-hr) usage rates for different times during the day. There could be a modified rule that accounts for the different energy utility costs, such as the following:

```
if (water is hot and kw-hr rate is high) then (turn on water
heater)
```

Now, what is the combined conditional value given that the fuzzified water temperature has been assigned a value of 45% and the fuzzified energy cost is valued at 58%? It turns out that under FL rule construction, the minimum percentage is carried forward when an and operator is used in the conditional expression. In this example, that value is 45%. In a similar manner, the maximum percentage is carried forward when an or operator is used in a conditional expression. You might be wondering what the final fuzzified value is in a complex expression that includes both and and or operators. The answer is that the final and minimum value is used because the and operator takes precedence over the or operator per the laws of logical combination, as described earlier in this chapter.

Defuzzification

Defuzzification is the process in which the numerical conclusions from multiple rules are combined to produce a final, overall resultant value. The simplest and most straightforward procedure is simply to average all the conclusions to produce a single number. This approach would be fine if all the rules had equal importance, but that is often not the case. Importance assigned to a rule is done through a weighting factor; for example, suppose there are four rules, each weighted with different values, as shown in Table 2-2.

Table 2-2. *Weighted Rules Example*

Rule No.	Weighting	Conclusion Value	Conclusion Value * Weight
1	2	74	148
2	4	37	148
3	6	50	300
4	8	22	176

The combined or defuzzified value is equal to the sum of all the conclusion values, multiplied by the respective rule weights, divided by the sum of all the rule weights. This is shown in the following:

Defuzzified value = $(148 + 148 + 300 + 176)/(2 + 4 + 6 + 8) = 772/20 = 38.6$
This defuzzified value is also known as the *weighted average*.

Conflict resolution is often not an issue with FL rules application because the weighting values invoke a prioritization to the rules.

I demonstrate a comprehensive FL example in Chapter 5, at which point I also introduce the concept of fuzzy sets with regard to the specific FL project. I felt it would make more sense if you saw a fuzzy set applied to a real-word example, rather than read an abstract discussion. Let's now turn our attention to the problem-solving area.

Problem Solving

Up until this point in the AI discussion, all the various questions/decisions regarding the problem domain have been carefully detailed in a comprehensive set of rules. That is not the case when it comes to the general topic of problem solving. Consider the classic example of knowing your starting and finishing points in your car's GPS system. There are usually many ways to travel between two points, excluding the trivial case of going between two points on an isolated, desert highway. This is the type of problem that AI is very good at solving, often in a fast and efficient manner.

Let's set up a scenario to examine the various facets of how to solve this problem. Consider a road trip between Boston and New York City. There are a variety of ways to make this trip. There are many paths between Boston and New York, because it is a heavily populated corridor with many towns and cities between the two locations. There will be some common-sense guidelines applied, including that any town or city on the path may be visited only once in a trip. It would not make much sense to repeatedly loop through a specific town or city during a trip. The key realistic points to consider in making the trip's path selections are the costs that are manifested: travel time, path length, fuel costs, tolls and traffic density, which are actual or anticipated delays. These costs are often dependent because a longer path will increase fuel expenses, but not necessarily travel time because an alternate path could use a super highway, on which the car maintains a higher consistent speed, as compared to traveling through backroads and going through many small towns. But, a super highway can be congested, reducing overall speed, and there may even be tolls to add to the misery.

The first approach in determining the optimal path is called the *breadth-first search*.

Breadth-First Search

The breadth-first approach starts by considering all possible paths between Boston and New York City, and computing and accumulating the total costs incurred while progressing through the various paths. This brute-force approach is both time-consuming and memory intensive because the computer must keep track of all the costs for perhaps thousands of paths before deciding on the optimal one. Of course, the algorithm might streamline the search by automatically excluding all secondary roads and sticking solely to the interstate highways. The typical cost that most modern vehicle GPS systems optimize is path length, but not always. Sometimes minimizing the travel time is a priority goal; it all depends upon the requirements given to the GPS system's software developers. There are other ways to conduct a path search.

Depth-First Search

In a depth-first search, one path is followed from start to finish, and its total cost is calculated. Then, another path is followed and its cost is calculated. Next, the two costs are compared and the more expensive one is rejected. Then, another path is considered and a cost comparison is done. This process continues until all possible paths have been considered. This approach minimizes memory requirements because only the most recent and least expensive path is retained. The real problem with this type of search is that it can take a long time to complete computationally, especially if there is a poor choice made for the first path. Search algorithms often only slightly change an initial path and then compute its cost. It doesn't take much imagination to recognize that it could take a long time before a good path is finally discovered.

The next search improves a lot on this search approach.

Depth-Limited Search

The depth-limited search is much like the depth-first search, except only a limited number of towns and cities are selected before a cost is determined. The cost comparison is made when the selection number is reached and the least expensive path is retained. This approach is based on the realistic assumption that if the path starts out less expensive than a competing path, it most likely remains so. No path search algorithms that I am aware of search in broadly different directions to unexpectedly increase the cost by including a path with a radical detour from the preferred direction. Selecting the appropriate depth number is the main concern with this algorithm. Too few, and you could easily miss the optimal path, but with too many, it starts resembling the depth-first search in terms of computational load. A depth limit of 10 to 12 is reasonable.

Bidirectional Search

The bidirectional search is a variant of the depth-limited search designed to greatly improve on the latter's computational efficiency. The path examined in a bidirectional search is first split in two, with two searches then conducted: one in the backward direction to the start point and other in the forward direction toward the finish point. These two new bifurcated search paths are both depth-limited, so only a preselected number of towns and cities will be transverse. Cost comparisons are made in the same manner done in the depth-limited search, in which the least expensive path is retained. The thought process behind this search algorithm is that splitting a path and examining two sections is a more efficient approach in quickly determining the lower cost path. It also eliminates the issue with a poor initial path selection that is present in a regular depth-limited search.

Other Problem-Solving Examples

There are many other situations where path searching can be applied. Solving a maze is one excellent example, in which a bidirectional path search makes short work of negotiating even the most complex maze. Search algorithms can even be applied to a Rubik's Cube solution, where the ultimate goal is to change each of the cube's side to a solid color.

Playing a game of chess is completely different from the path-search-problem domain. This is because there is an intelligent opponent in the game, who is actively countering moves and whose goal is to ultimately achieve a checkmate position. This new dynamic is not present in a traveler's path search problem, where all the path routes are static and unchanging. In chess, a computer cannot simply examine all the future available moves, because they are dependent on the next move that the opponent makes—and the number of potential moves is literally astronomical. Instead, the computer is set up to incorporate deep machine learning, which is a portion of the next section's discussion.

Machine Learning

Machine learning was first defined in 1959 by MIT professor Arthur Samuel, a recognized pioneer in both computer science and artificial intelligence. Professor Samuel stated in part, "machine learning as a field of study that gives computers the ability to learn without being explicitly programmed." What he was essentially driving at is that computers can be programmed with algorithms that can learn from input data and then make consequent predictions based on that same data. This means that learning algorithms can be completely divorced from any preprogrammed or static algorithms and be free to make data-driven decisions or predictions by building models based on the input data.

Machine learning is used in a many modern applications, including e-mail spam filters, optical character recognition (OCR), textual search engines, computer vision, and more.

Implementing machine learning may be easier than you realize if you consider an expert system. In a traditional expert system, there are a series of rules generated by interviewing experts, which are then "fired" using input conditions. What if a machine could take one or more of those rules and slightly modify them, and subsequently try to use the conclusions generated by the modified rules? If the new modified rules improved upon the final conclusion, then they would be retained and perhaps awarded with somewhat higher priorities than older rules, similar to what is done with conflict resolution. On the other hand, if the conclusions reached using the modified rules were less optimal, then they would be rejected and replaced with additional new rule modifications. If this was a continual process, could it not be said that the computer is indeed learning? Answering this type of question has been somewhat of a contentious area within the AI community.

There are a variety of ways to implement machine learning. I discuss a few of them in the following sections. However, I think it would be prudent to review some fundamental concepts (prediction and classification) regarding learning, as it will be applied in this area.

Prediction

Prediction is how you determine a new output value using specific input with a model that relates the output to the input. Perhaps the simplest predictor is a sloped straight line going through the origin of an x-y graph. This is easily modeled by the following equation and is shown graphically in Figure 2-2.

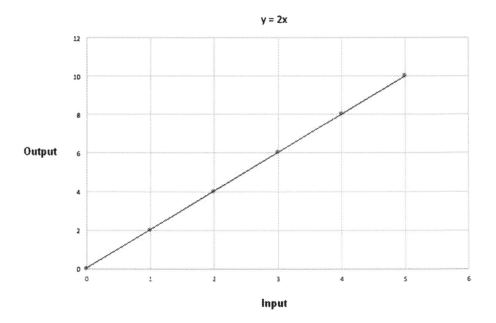

Figure 2-2. *Graph of* $y = 2x$

There are a several hidden constraints using this predictor. First, is the allowed range of input values. In Figure 2-2, there are five output values plotted that match the five corresponding input values ranging between 0 and 10. Normally, you could assume that the input values were not restricted to this same range, but models in the real world could have restrictions, such as only non-negative numbers are allowed. In addition, while the equation is linear within the plotted zone, there is no guarantee that a real-world model wouldn't become non-linear if input values exceeded a certain value.

As you have probably determined from the brief introduction, useful prediction is only as good as the model employed in the prediction. Realistic models are typically much more complex than a simple straight-line equation, because modeling real-world behavior is a complex matter. Now it is time to consider classification, which is as equally important as prediction.

Classification

I begin the classification discussion by stating a hypothetical situation where it is import to classify a select species of mushroom. Note, the mushrooms discussed are pure fiction, so any mycologists (fungi experts) in my readership need not respond. Assume there are two mushroom types: one delicious and non-poisonous, and the other poisonous and obviously inedible. They look almost identical; however, the edible variety is larger and less dense, whereas the poisonous variety is smaller and denser. There are two parameters or input values used to classify these mushroom types: weight in grams and the crown (or cap) circumference in millimetres (mm). Density is a derived parameter, which can be determined, if needed, from the two basic measurements of weight and circumference. Figure 2-3 is an x-y scatter plot of a selection of both mushroom types.

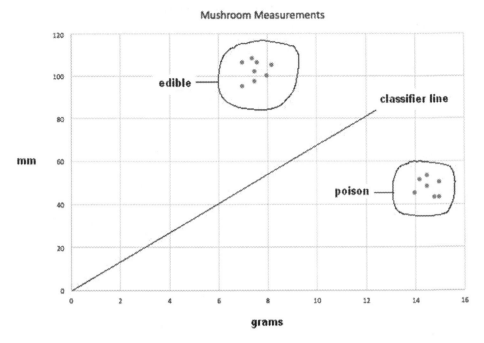

Figure 2-3. *Mushroom scatter plot*

In Figure 2-3, I encircled all the data points for both mushroom types, and I placed a sloped dividing line, labeled *classification line*. This line clearly divides the two groups, as you can easily see, but the problem remains as to how to best analytically determine the diving line. The line equation is precisely the same form shown in Figure 2-1, with a generalized form of

$$y = mx$$

where *m* is the slope. Let's try *m* = 2 for an initial value and see what happens. Figure 2-4 shows the result.

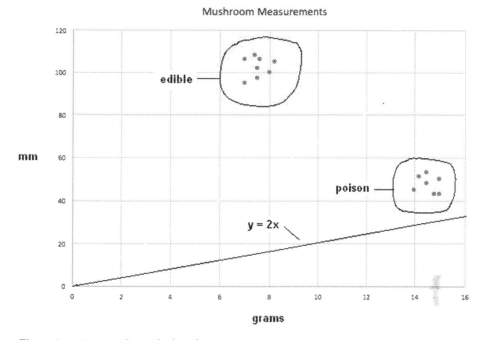

Figure 2-4. *Scatter plot with classification line y = 2x*

Clearly, this is not a satisfactory result, as both data point clusters are on the same side of the line, which proves that this particular choice for *m* cannot serve as a useful classifier. What is needed is a precise way of determining *m* other than using a blind manual trial-and-error approach. This approach is the start of a machine learning process.

I first need to establish what is known as a *training data set*, which will be used to assess how well the classifier function works. This data is simply a data point from each cluster, as shown in Table 2-3.

Table 2-3. *Training Data*

Data Point #	Grams (x)	mm (y)	Mushroom type
1	15	50	poisonous
2	8	100	edible

Substituting the x value for data point 1 into the equation $y = 2x$ yields a value of 30 for y instead of 100, which is the true or target value. The difference of +20 is known as the *error value*. It must be minimized to achieve a workable classifier. Increasing the classifier line slope is the only way to minimize the error. Let's use the symbol Δ to represent a change in the slope, ϵ for the error, and y_t for the desired target value. The error thus becomes

$$\epsilon = y_t - y$$

Expand the preceding equation with the assumption that Δ assumes a value that allows y_t to be reached yields the following:

$$\epsilon = y_t - y = (m + \Delta)x - mx$$

Expanding and collecting terms yields the following:

$$\epsilon = y_t - y = mx + \Delta x - mx$$

$$\epsilon = y_t - y = \Delta x$$

The very simple final expression for the error term is simply the Δ value times the input value, which makes complete sense if you reflect on it for a while. Rearranging the last equation and solving for Δ yields

$$\Delta = \epsilon / x$$

Plugging in the initial trial values yields a Δ value of

$$\Delta = 20/15 = 1.3333$$

The new value for m is now 1.3333 + 2, or 1.3333, and the revised classifier line equation is consequently

$$y = 3.3333x$$

Plugging in the previous value for the x training value, or 15, now yields the desired target value of 50. Figure 2-5 shows the revised classifier line on the scatter plot.

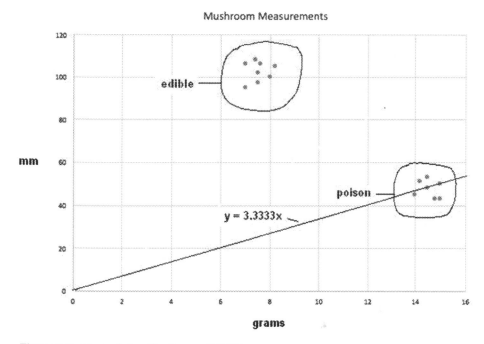

Figure 2-5. *Revised classifier line y = 3.3333x*

Further Classification

While the revised classifier line has improved the classification somewhat there are still poisonous mushrooms data points either on or above the line, which still makes this classifier line unsatisfactory.

Now, let's use data point number 2 with this revised classifier line and see what results. Using the value $x = 8$ yields a y value of 26.664. Now, the actual y data point value is 100, which means that $\epsilon = 100 - 26.664 = 73.336$. A newly revised m value can be calculated as follows:

$$m = 73.336 / 8 + 3.333 = 12.5$$

Plugging in the training value x, which is 8, now yields the desired target value of 50. Figure 2-6 shows the newly revised classifier line on the scatter plot.

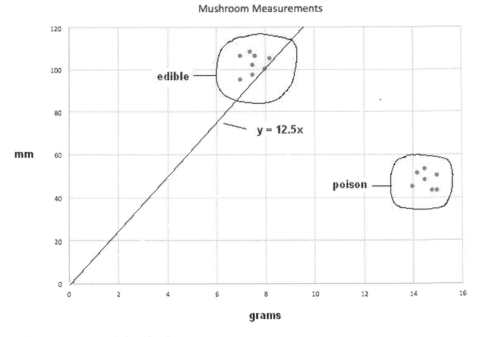

Figure 2-6. *Revised classifier line y = 12.5x*

While this newly revised classifier line does separate all the edible mushrooms from the poisonous ones, it is unsatisfactory: there could still be some edible mushrooms falsely rejected because they fell slightly below the line. Now there exists a larger problem, however, because all the training points have been exhausted. If I went back and reused the previous point number 1, it would return to the $y = 3.3333x$ classifier line. This is because the procedure does not consider the effects of any previous data points; that is, there is no memory. A way around this is to introduce the concept of a learning rate that moderates the revisions so that they do not jump to the extremes, which is what is happening at present.

The standard symbol used in AI for learning rate is η (the Greek letter Eta). The learning rate is a simple multiplier used in the equation for Δ:

$$\Delta = \eta \epsilon / x$$

Setting η = 0.5 is a reasonable start, if only one-half the update is applied. For the initial data point, the new Δ = 0.5 * 1.333 = 0.667. The new classifier line is therefore $y = 2.667x$. I am not going to show the scatter plot line for this change, but suffice it to say, it is slightly worse than the original revision. That's OK because the next revision should be considerably better.

For data point 2, the new classifier line is $y = 6.25x$, using the new η learning rate. Figure 2-7 shows the resulting scatter plot for this new classifier line.

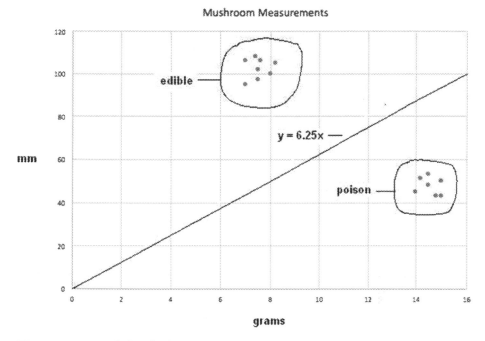

Figure 2-7. *Revised classifier line y = 6.25x*

Figure 2-7 reveals an excellent classifier line that properly separates the two mushroom types, minimizing the likelihood of a false classification.

It is now time to introduce the very fundamental concept of a *neural network*, which is essential for implementing practical machine learning.

Neural Networks

The concept of neural networks can be traced back to a 1943 research article by McCulloch and Pitts, which focused on neurocomputing. I first mentioned these pioneering researchers in Chapter 1. This article shows that simple neural networks could, in principle, compute any arithmetic or logical function. To understand a neural network, you must understand the key element in a biological neural network, which is the neuron. Figure 2-8 is a diagram of a human neuron.

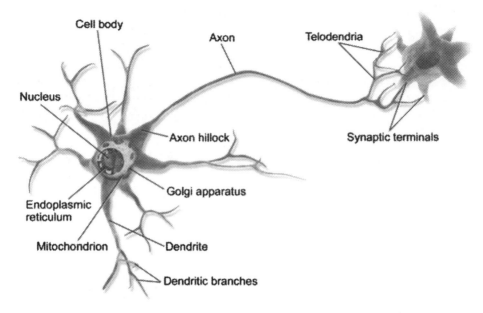

Figure 2-8. Diagram of a human neuron (Source: Wikipedia)

Figure 2-9 is a sketch of pigeon brain neurons, created in 1899 by Spanish neuroscientist Santiago Ramón y Cajal. Dendrites and terminals are clearly shown in the figure.

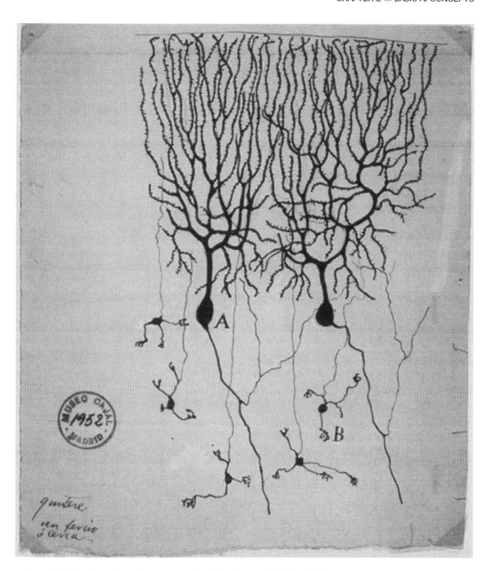

Figure 2-9. *Pigeon brain neurons sketch (Source: Wikipedia)*

The question now becomes *Why is the human brain so much more capable of successfully undertaking intelligent tasks when compared to modern computers?* One answer is that a mature human brain is estimated to have over 100 billion neurons. The precise functioning is still unknown. To get an idea of the inherent capabilities of such a large number of neurons, you can simply consider the capabilities of a simple earthworm, which has only 302 neurons, yet is still capable of doing tasks that would baffle large-scale computers.

Examining how a single neuron functions helps explain how a network of them can be created to solve AI problems. The output signal from a neuron can either cause an excitation or an inhibition to a neuron immediately connected to it. When a neuron sends an excitation signal to the connected neuron, it is added to all the other inputs that neuron is concurrently receiving, and when the combined excitation of all the inputs reaches a preset level or threshold, that neuron will fire. The firing does not depend on the level of any given input; it only matters that the threshold be exceeded to initiate a firing. Figure 2-10 shows a time trace of a typical neuron electrical signal.

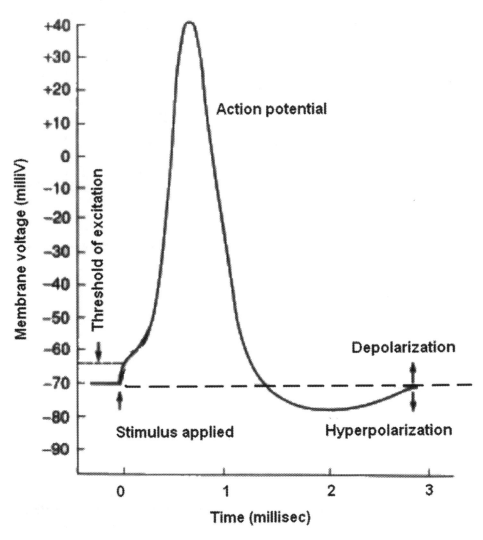

Figure 2-10. *Firing neuron time trace*

As you can see in Figure 2-10, the peak voltage is only 40 millivolts and total pulse time duration is approximately 3 milliseconds (ms). Most neurons have one axon, so the delay between stimulus input and excitation output in a given neuron is only 3 ms. It is interesting to try to relate this to human reaction time. The fastest human reaction time ever verified is 101 ms, with the average being approximately 215 ms. This is the total time that it takes to progress from a sensory input, such as sight, to a motor actuation, such as a mouse click. Assume that it takes 10 ms to send a signal from the eyes to the appropriate neurons in the brain; perhaps 20 ms to send a nerve signal from the neurons controlling finger-muscle action and 40 ms for muscle activation itself. This leaves about 145 ms for total brain-processing time. That time duration limits the longest chain of neurons to about 14 to 15 in length. That number implies there must be a huge number of short parallel neuron chains interoperating to accomplish the tasks of interpreting a visual signal, recalling the appropriate action to take, and then sending nerve control signals to the fingers to do a mouse click. And all of these tasks are done dynamically while still doing the background autonomic things necessary to stay alive.

The neuron's excitation action can be roughly modeled by using a step function, as shown in Figure 2-11.

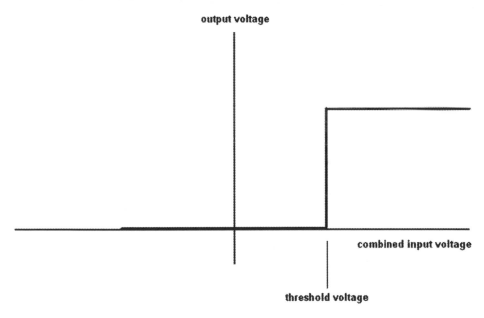

Figure 2-11. *Step function*

In nature, nothing is ever as sharp and defined as a step function, especially for biological functions. AI researchers have adopted the sigmoid function as more realistically modeling the neuron threshold function. Figure 2-12 shows the sigmoid function.

sigmoid function

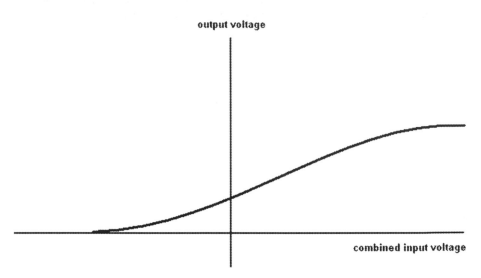

Figure 2-12. *Sigmoid function*

The sigmoid function analytic expression is

$y = 1/(1 + e^{-x})$, where e = math constant 2.71828...

When $x = 0$, then $y = 0.5$, which is the y axis intercept for the sigmoid function. This function is used as the threshold function for our neuron model. Consider Figure 2-13 a very basic neuron model with three inputs ($x1$, $x2$, and $x3$) and one output (y).

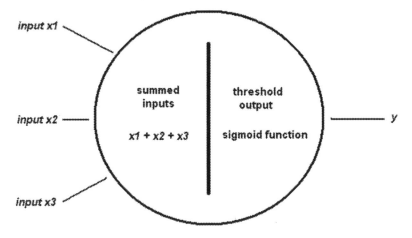

Figure 2-13. *Basic three-input neuron model*

The basic model is useful, but it is not the complete answer because neurons must be connected to a network to function as a learning entity. Figure 2-14 shows a simple neural network made up of three neuron layers, labeled *input, hidden*, and *output*, respectively.

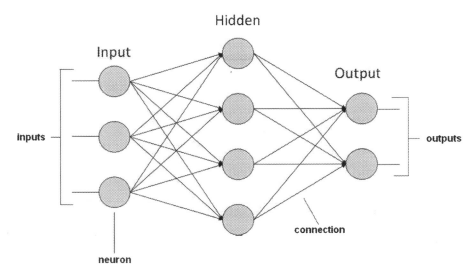

Figure 2-14. *Example neural network*

The next obvious question is *How does this network learn?* The easiest way is to adjust the weights of the connections. This means adjusting the amplitude or strength from an output to an input. Thus, a high weight means a given connection is emphasized more, whereas a low weight is de-emphasized. Figure 2-15 shows weights assigned to each of the neuron, or node, connections. They are shown as $w_{n,m}$, where n is the source node number and m is the destination node number.

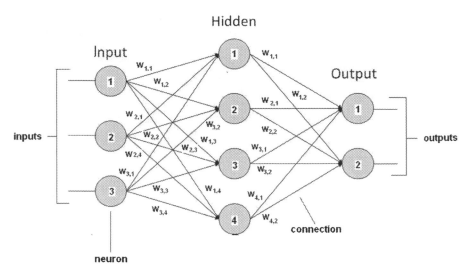

Figure 2-15. *Neural network with weighted interconnections*

At this point, I defer any further discussion until the neural network chapter, in which I assign actual weights and demonstrate an actual learning system. The primary purpose of the discussion to this point is to prepare you for the neural network implementation.

Shallow Learning vs. Deep Learning

You may have heard the terms *shallow* and *deep* applied to machine learning. The term *shallow* seems to imply that somewhat trivial and lightweight learning is going on, whereas *deep* implies the opposite. In actuality, shallow learning and deep learning are only subjective adjectives applied to neural networks, based upon the number of layers implemented in the network. There really isn't a formal definition separating shallow from deep learning, because the effectiveness of a particular neural network is determined by many factors, one of which is the number of layers in the network. The point in stating this is because I am not really worried about whether a particular neural network is classified as shallow or deep, but I am concerned about its effectiveness in performing at the desired requirements and standards.

Evolutionary Computing

There is a rapidly evolving AI field called *evolutionary computing*. It is inspired by the theory of biological evolution, but uses algorithms grounded on population-based trial-and-error problem solvers. In turn, these problem solvers use metaheuristic techniques, meaning they rely on statistical and probabilistic approaches rather than strict deterministic, analytical techniques. In broad terms, an evolutionary computing problem starts with an initial set of candidate solutions, which are subsequently tested for optimality. If they are found to be suboptimal, the solutions are altered by only a small random amount and then retested. Every new generation of candidate solutions is improved by removing the less desired solutions determined from the previous generation. A biological analog is when a population is subjected to natural selection and mutations. This results in the population gradually evolving to increase overall fitness to meet environmental conditions. For evolutionary computing, the analogous process is to optimize the algorithm's pre-selected fitness function. In fact, evolutionary computation is sometimes used by researchers in evolutionary biology for experimental procedures to study common processes.

Evolutionary computing can be used in other AI areas. If you recall, I alluded to an evolutionary computing approach when I stated that a machine could take one or more of those rules and slightly modify them, and subsequently try to use the conclusions generated by the modified rules. It would likely be a difficult but solvable problem to create a candidate set of expert rules subjected to the evolutionary screening process.

A very popular subset of evolutionary computing is known as *genetic algorithms*, which I briefly introduce in the next section.

Genetic Algorithms

A genetic algorithm (GA) starts with a population of candidate solutions, as mentioned in the evolutionary computing introduction. These solutions in the GA jargon are called *individuals*, *creatures*, or **phenotypes**. They are used in an optimization procedure to find improved solutions. Every candidate solution has a set of properties known as *chromosomes*, or *genotypes*, which can be altered or mutated. It is also traditional to represent candidate solutions as a string of binary digits, 1s and 0s. The evolutionary process follows, where every individual in a randomly generated candidate solution is evaluated regarding fitness. The more "fit" individuals are stochastically selected from the population. Those individuals' genomes are further modified to form the next generation. This next generation is then iteratively used in the GA until one of two things happens. First, the maximum number of iterations is reached and the process is terminated, whether or not an optimal solution is found. Second, a satisfactory fitness level is achieved prior to reaching the maximum iteration limit.

A typical GA requires

- A genetic representation compatible with the problem domain

- A fitness function that can effectively evaluate the solution

Binary digits, or bits, are the most common way candidate solutions are generated. There are other forms and structures, but using bits seems by far the most popular way that GA is done in modern AI. Usually, there is a fixed size to the bit string, which makes it easy to perform what are known as *crossover operations*. These operations, along with others, are imperative to complete the generational modifications and mutations.

If this explanation is as clear as mud, do not be dismayed. I assure you that a GA demonstration in a later chapter will clarify this subject to the point where you may even wish to experiment with some GA algorithms. Readers who wish to further explore GA may go to `https://intelligence.org` to read some interesting articles.

This introduction to GA brings this basic AI concepts chapter to an end. You should already feel somewhat prepared to take on the demonstrations and projects presented in the remaining chapters. But be forewarned: there is new AI material presented in the project chapters, because it is simply impossible to cover it all in one chapter.

Summary

The primary purpose of this chapter was to introduce and discuss some basic AI concepts that will be demonstrated in the project chapters. I began with a brief overview of Boolean logic and associated logical operations, as these are frequently used in AI expressions. The remainder of the chapter provided an overview of the following:

- Inference, expert systems, and conflict resolution as it pertains to implementing an expert system

- The installation of SWI Prolog on a Raspberry Pi

- A Prolog demo, which is my program of choice to implement an expert system when required for a project

- A simple example of fuzzy logic to help clarify the underlying concepts

- A series of sections on machine learning

- Neural networks (NN), which are modeled after biological brain neurons

- Evolutionary computing that features genetic algorithms

CHAPTER 3

■ ■ ■

Expert System Demonstrations

This chapter contains several expert systems demonstrations, all of which have been run on a Raspberry 3 standalone desktop configuration. The first demonstration, Demo 3-1, is a very simple one—designed to show you how to get started using Prolog on the Raspberry Pi. I have included some discussion on how to use both the command line and GUI trace functions that are very useful in debugging a Prolog program. The second demonstration, Demo 3-2, is somewhat more complex, in which the program asks the user some questions about an unknown animal and then tries to reach a conclusion based on the answers to the questions.

The complexity rises with the next expert program, Demo 3-3, which implements a tic-tac-toe game. I provide some detailed discussion on how the tic-tac-toe program functions in order to provide some insight into predicates and how they are used in a Prolog program. The next demonstration, Demo 3-4, should help diagnosis whether you are suffering with a cold or the flu. It is only a demonstration; it should not be substituted for a visit to the doctor's office. Demo 3-5 couples the results from the Prolog expert system to the actual activation of Raspberry Pi GPIO pins. I show you how to install and use a library named PySWIP, which allows Prolog commands to be called and executed within a Python program.

All of these demonstrations should also run on earlier Raspberry models, but at a somewhat slower pace. For Demo 3-5, you need some additional parts, which are described in Table 3-1.

Table 3-1. *Parts Lists*

Description	Quantity	Remarks
Pi Cobbler	1	40-pin version, either T or DIP form factor acceptable
solderless breadboard	1	860 insertion points with power supply strips
jumper wires	1 package	
LED	2	
220Ω resistor	2	1/4 watt

© Donald J. Norris 2017
D. J. Norris, *Beginning Artificial Intelligence with the Raspberry Pi*,
DOI 10.1007/978-1-4842-2743-5_3

These parts are readily available from a number of online sources, including Adafruit Industries, MCM Electronics, RS Components, Digikey, and Mouser.

I start the expert system demonstrations with a simple database, in which I use the trace command to illustrate how Prolog resolves user goals or queries.

Demo 3-1: Office Database

The following program and discussion are based largely on a very clear tutorial from the MultiWingSpan website on tracing with Prolog. The following listing is the Prolog database, which is aptly named office.pl.

```
/*office program */
adminWorker(black).
admnWorker(white).

officeJunior(green).

manager(brown).
manager(grey).
supervises(X,Y) :- manager(X), adminWorker(Y).
supervises(X,Y) :- adminWorker(X), officeJunior(Y).
supervises(X,Y) :- manager(X), officeJunior(Y).
```

The database is quite simple: only five facts regarding office roles and three rules regarding who supervises whom. Figure 3-1 shows an interactive Prolog session where I have queried Prolog regarding various office members' roles and who they supervise. The queries are very straightforward, but not very revealing about how Prolog reaches conclusions.

Figure 3-1. *Interactive Prolog session*

An important debugging tool available in Prolog is the `trace` command. Trace allows you to view all the goals as they are executed in a sequence in a Prolog query. You can also view any "backtracking" that happens when a goal fails. Tracing is turned on by this command:

```
?- trace.
```

Prolog will respond with:

```
true.
```

When finished with tracing, you turn it off using this command:

```
?- notrace.
```

Prolog will respond with:

```
true.
```

The trace command is among more than 20 debugging commands that are implemented in SWI Prolog. Covering all the various ways of using the Prolog debugging tools would likely take a separate book by itself. My intention is only to illustrate some straightforward debugging measures that should help you understand how Prolog functions with a database.

The following is a command-line trace session using the office database that I just presented. Figure 3-2 is a complete screenshot of the tracing session.

Figure 3-2. *Office database tracing session*

Table 3-2 is a line-by-line commentary on the tracing session shown in Figure 3-2. You should note that the SWI Prolog debugger supports six standard ports, which are named Call, Exit, Redo, Fail, Exception, and Unify. You see some of these ports in the following commentary, as they represent which actions the Prolog interpreter is taking with regard to the database facts and rules. You also see a number in parenthesis following the port name. This is the current clause line number that is being processed from the database.

Table 3-2. *Line-by-Line Trace Session Commentary*

Prolog dialog/trace output	Commentary
swipl	Start SWI-Prolog
[office].	Load the office database. This form is shorthand for the consult function.
trace.	Start the tracing.
supervises(Who, green).	The user input query to determine who supervises employee green.
Call: (6) supervises(_G2345, green) ? creep	Prolog finds the first rule for supervises(X,Y) and instantiates Y to match green, as stated in the query. The word creep appears when you press Enter. It means that Prolog has been instructed to move to the next instruction. Prolog memory reference _G2345 is for the X argument, which is henceforth named Who.
Call: (7) manager(_G2345) ? creep	Prolog tries to satisfy the first subgoal of the rule. It tries manager(X).
Exit: (7) manager(brown) ? creep	brown is found as a manager. Prolog next tests whether this leads to a solution. The word Exit reflects the fact that Prolog has found a solution to its last call. It sets X to brown.
Call: (7) adminWorker(green) ? creep	If brown manages green, green must be an adminWorker.
Fail: (7) adminWorker(green) ? creep	Since green is not an adminWorker, the second subgoal of the rule cannot be satisfied.
Redo: (7) manager(_G2345) ? creep	Prolog backtracks to the first subgoal and resumes where it left off with manager(X).
Exit: (7) manager(grey) ? creep	Prolog finds grey and instantiates X to this new value.
Call: (7) adminWorker(green) ? creep	Prolog again tests whether or not green is an adminWorker.
Fail: (7) adminWorker(green) ? creep	Once again, it fails. This means the rule cannot provide a solution.
Redo: (6) supervises(_G2345, green) ? creep	Prolog backtracks to the initial rule and proceeds with processing the top-level goal.
Call: (7) adminWorker(_G2345) ? creep	This time, Prolog looks for an adminWorker as the supervisor. (The second rule.)
Exit: (7) adminWorker(black) ? creep	Prolog finds black and instantiates X to this new value.

(continued)

Table 3-2. (*continued*)

Prolog dialog/trace output	Commentary
`Call: (7)` `officeJunior(green) ? creep`	Prolog checks if the second subgoal is now satisfied.
`Exit: (7)` `officeJunior(green) ? creep`	`green` is an `officeJunior`, and consequently, the second subgoal is satisfied.

`Exit: (6)`
`supervises(black, green) ?`
`creep`
	The top-level goal is satisfied.

The statement `Who = black.` in the figure is not part of the trace but is the Prolog response that is displayed in response to the initial query, `supervises(Who, green)`.

The word `creep` that is shown on all of the trace lines appears after you press the Enter key. It just indicates that Prolog is proceeding to the next line of the trace. There is a lot of additional information available regarding the `trace` command. Simply type the following to find out more about trace and its capabilities:

`?- help(trace).`

You should also note that trace does not work on Prolog's built-in functions. You have to rely on Prolog's extensive documentation to learn about those functions.

SWI Prolog also provides a debugging graphical user interface (GUI) in addition to the command-line version that I just demonstrated. Figure 3-3 shows the command-line session used to invoke the GUI using the same database and query in the previous example.

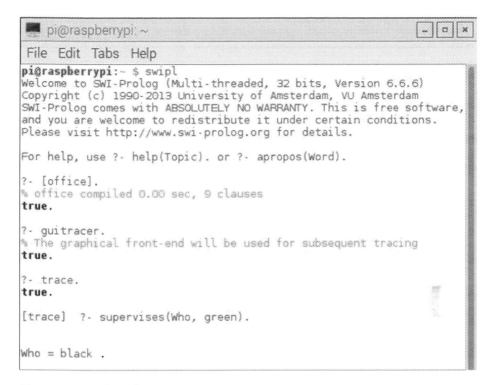

Figure 3-3. *Invoking the GUI tracer*

The only difference between the command line and GUI invocations is that the guitracer. command is entered right after the consult command. Prolog returns this statement:

```
% The graphical front—end will be used for subsequent tracing
true.
```

However, no GUI is displayed until you actually enter the trace. command and then enter a goal, which in this example is supervises(Who, green). From this point on, all the user tracing and debugging actions take place in the GUI dialog screen, which is shown in Figure 3-4.

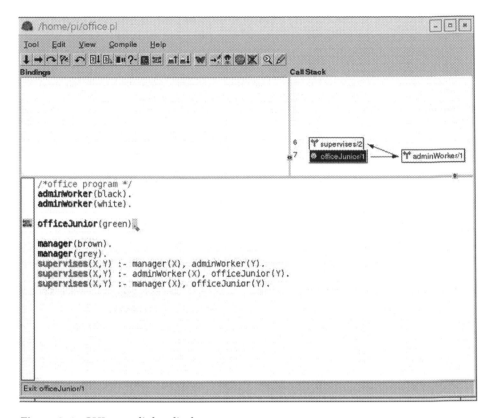

Figure 3-4. *GUI trace dialog display*

You must repeatedly click the right-facing arrow located in the upper left-hand portion of the toolbar in order to step through all the Prolog operations detailed in Table 3-2. Figure 3-4 actually shows the state of the Prolog sequence at the following step, excerpted from Table 3-2.

`Call: (7)` `officeJunior(green) ? creep`	Prolog checks if the second subgoal is now satisfied.

A graphical representation of the call stack is also shown in the upper right-hand pane of the GUI display. Many Prolog users prefer the GUI representation to the command-line version, but you can be assured that either version does precisely the same tracing actions.

You can stop the GUI trace by using a command similar to the command-line version:

```
?- noguitracer.
```

The next expert system demonstration is a classic game that is presented to most beginning AI students.

Demo 3-2: Animal Identification

This expert system is an animal identification game that is the Prolog version of a Lisp program originally presented in *The Handbook of Artificial Intelligence Vol 4*, a book edited by Barr, Cohen and Feigenbaum (Addison-Wesley, 1990). It is a relatively simple program that tries to identify the animal that you are thinking about from a choice of seven:

- cheetah

- tiger

- giraffe

- zebra

- ostrich

- penguin

- albatross

The program is set up to ask a series of questions in an endeavor to determine the animal. I suggest you try the program before I discuss how it works. You need only enter a yes or no to answer the questions. Your responses can even be shortened to y or n. Enter the following

```
?- go.
```

after you load the program.

The following is a listing of the Prolog animal script.

```
/* animal.pl
   animal identification game.

     start with ?- go.      */

go :- hypothesize(Animal),
      write('I guess that the animal is: '),
      write(Animal),
      nl,
      undo.

/* hypotheses to be tested */
hypothesize(cheetah)   :- cheetah, !.
hypothesize(tiger)     :- tiger, !.
hypothesize(giraffe)   :- giraffe, !.
hypothesize(zebra)     :- zebra, !.
hypothesize(ostrich)   :- ostrich, !.
hypothesize(penguin)   :- penguin, !.
hypothesize(albatross) :- albatross, !.
hypothesize(unknown).                  /* no diagnosis */
```

```
/* animal identification rules */
cheetah :- mammal,
           carnivore,
           verify(has_tawny_color),
           verify(has_dark_spots).
tiger :- mammal,
         carnivore,
         verify(has_tawny_color),
         verify(has_black_stripes).
giraffe :- ungulate,
           verify(has_long_neck),
           verify(has_long_legs).
zebra :- ungulate,
         verify(has_black_stripes).

ostrich :- bird,
           verify(does_not_fly),
           verify(has_long_neck).
penguin :- bird,
           verify(does_not_fly),
           verify(swims),
           verify(is_black_and_white).
albatross :- bird,
             verify(appears_in_story_Ancient_Mariner),
             verify(flys_well).

/* classification rules */
mammal     :- verify(has_hair), !.
mammal     :- verify(gives_milk).
bird       :- verify(has_feathers), !.
bird       :- verify(flys),
              verify(lays_eggs).
carnivore :- verify(eats_meat), !.
carnivore :- verify(has_pointed_teeth),
             verify(has_claws),
             verify(has_forward_eyes).
ungulate :- mammal,
            verify(has_hooves), !.
ungulate :- mammal,
            verify(chews_cud).

/* how to ask questions */
ask(Question) :-
    write('Does the animal have the following attribute: '),
    write(Question),
    write('? '),
    read(Response),
    nl,
```

```
( (Response == yes ; Response == y)
  ->
  assert(yes(Question)) ;
  assert(no(Question)), fail).

:- dynamic yes/1,no/1.

/* How to verify something */
verify(S) :-
   (yes(S)
    ->
    true ;
    (no(S)
     ->
     fail ;
     ask(S))).

/* undo all yes/no assertions */
undo :- retract(yes(_)),fail.
undo :- retract(no(_)),fail.
undo.
```

This program is interesting because it tries to verify properties to draw conclusions. The answers to the questions are also briefly stored for future reference. When a question is asked and answered with a yes, then the answer is recorded by asserting the clause yes(question) and succeeding; otherwise, the answer is recorded by asserting the clause no(question) and failing. The yes answers are recorded because a later no answer to a different question while trying to verify the same hypothesis could cause the entire hypothesis to fail; whereas the same yes answer could have led to a successful verification of a different hypothesis later in the process. Recording answers is the way the program avoids asking the same question twice. Conditions specified in a question are verified by checking if the yes(question) is in the memory and has succeeded or the no(question) is stored and has failed. If neither check is true, then ask(question) is done.

Figure 3-5 shows a sample interactive session with this program, in which I went through several question-and-answer runs.

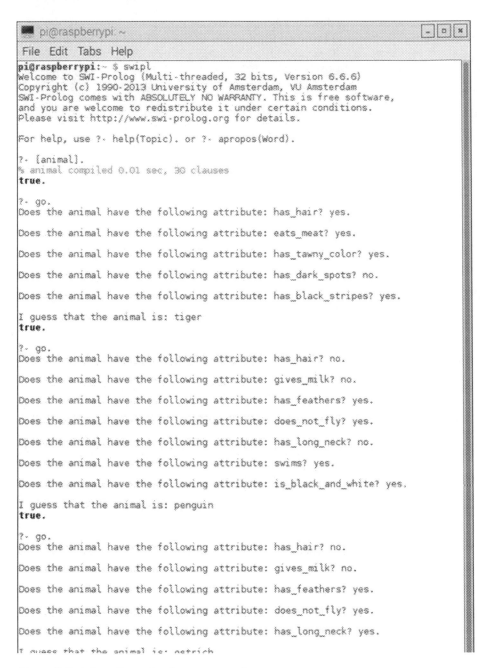

Figure 3-5. *Interactive animal program session*

I did determine that the program will draw an erroneous conclusion regarding carnivores based on the addition of a rule that classifies carnivores solely on having pointed teeth, claws, and forward-facing eyes. Figure 3-6 shows the interactive session in which I answered no to the question asking if the animal eats meat and yes to the questions on teeth, claws, and eyes.

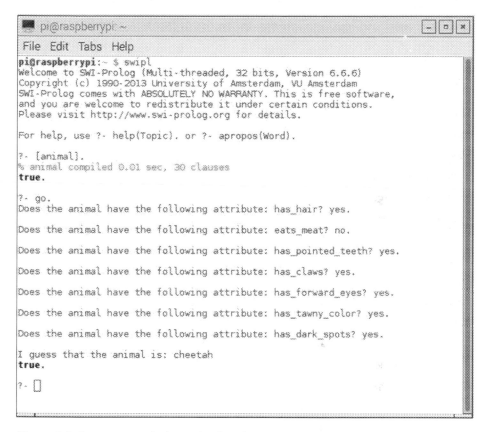

Figure 3-6. *Incorrect conclusion animal session*

This behavior in this particular expert system simply points out that incorrect results can be reached if the rules are not consistent with the real-world models on which they are based. By definition, carnivores are meat eaters, even though I deliberately answered no to that question. In the next demonstration, I get away from big cats and birds to a much more benign, yet interesting expert system.

Demo 3-3: tic-tac-toe

Tic-tac-toe, as it's known in the United States, or noughts and crosses in other lands, is a delightful game often played quite effectively by very young children. It may also be implemented by an expert system. The following listing is a straightforward tic-tac-toe program named tictactoe.pl, which may be played against the computer by entering the following:

```
?- playo.
```

There is also a self-play option in which the computer plays against itself. That option always ends with X winning. To initiate self-play enter this:

```
?- selfgame.
```

The tictactoe.pl listing follows:

```
% A tic-tac-toe program in Prolog.   S. Tanimoto, May 11, 2003.
% Additional comments   D. J. Norris, Jan, 2017.
% To play a game with the computer, type
% playo.
% To watch the computer play a game with itself, type
% selfgame.

% Predicates that define the winning conditions:

win(Board, Player) :- rowwin(Board, Player).
win(Board, Player) :- colwin(Board, Player).
win(Board, Player) :- diagwin(Board, Player).

rowwin(Board, Player) :- Board = [Player,Player,
Player,_,_,_,_,_,_].
rowwin(Board, Player) :- Board = [_,_,_,Player,Player,
Player,_,_,_].
rowwin(Board, Player) :- Board = [_,_,_,_,_,_,Player,Player,
Player].

colwin(Board, Player) :- Board = [Player,_,_,Player,_,_,
Player,_,_].
colwin(Board, Player) :- Board = [_,Player,_,_,Player,_,_,
Player,_].
colwin(Board, Player) :- Board = [_,_,Player,_,_,Player,_,_,
Player].

diagwin(Board, Player) :- Board = [Player,_,_,_,Player,_,_,_,
Player].
diagwin(Board, Player) :- Board = [_,_,Player,_,Player,_,
Player,_,_].
```

```
% Helping predicate for alternating play in a "self" game:

other(x,o).
other(o,x).

game(Board, Player) :- win(Board, Player), !, write([player,
Player, wins]).
game(Board, Player) :-
  other(Player,Otherplayer),
  move(Board,Player,Newboard),
  !,
  display(Newboard),
  game(Newboard,Otherplayer).

% These move predicates control how a move is made

move([b,B,C,D,E,F,G,H,I], Player, [Player,B,C,D,E,F,G,H,I]).
move([A,b,C,D,E,F,G,H,I], Player, [A,Player,C,D,E,F,G,H,I]).
move([A,B,b,D,E,F,G,H,I], Player, [A,B,Player,D,E,F,G,H,I]).
move([A,B,C,b,E,F,G,H,I], Player, [A,B,C,Player,E,F,G,H,I]).
move([A,B,C,D,b,F,G,H,I], Player, [A,B,C,D,Player,F,G,H,I]).
move([A,B,C,D,E,b,G,H,I], Player, [A,B,C,D,E,Player,G,H,I]).
move([A,B,C,D,E,F,b,H,I], Player, [A,B,C,D,E,F,Player,H,I]).
move([A,B,C,D,E,F,G,b,I], Player, [A,B,C,D,E,F,G,Player,I]).
move([A,B,C,D,E,F,G,H,b], Player, [A,B,C,D,E,F,G,H,Player]).

display([A,B,C,D,E,F,G,H,I]) :- write([A,B,C]),nl,
write([D,E,F]),nl,
 write([G,H,I]),nl,nl.

selfgame :- game([b,b,b,b,b,b,b,b,b],x).

% Predicates to support playing a game with the user:

x_can_win_in_one(Board) :- move(Board, x, Newboard),
win(Newboard, x).

% The predicate orespond generates the computer's (playing o)
reponse
% from the current Board.

orespond(Board,Newboard) :-
  move(Board, o, Newboard),
  win(Newboard, o),
  !.
orespond(Board,Newboard) :-
  move(Board, o, Newboard),
  not(x_can_win_in_one(Newboard)).
```

```
orespond(Board,Newboard) :-
  move(Board, o, Newboard).
orespond(Board,Newboard) :-
  not(member(b,Board)),
  !,
  write('Cats game!'), nl,
  Newboard = Board.
```

```
% The following translates from an integer description
% of x's move to a board transformation.
```

```
xmove([b,B,C,D,E,F,G,H,I], 1, [x,B,C,D,E,F,G,H,I]).
xmove([A,b,C,D,E,F,G,H,I], 2, [A,x,C,D,E,F,G,H,I]).
xmove([A,B,b,D,E,F,G,H,I], 3, [A,B,x,D,E,F,G,H,I]).
xmove([A,B,C,b,E,F,G,H,I], 4, [A,B,C,x,E,F,G,H,I]).
xmove([A,B,C,D,b,F,G,H,I], 5, [A,B,C,D,x,F,G,H,I]).
xmove([A,B,C,D,E,b,G,H,I], 6, [A,B,C,D,E,x,G,H,I]).
xmove([A,B,C,D,E,F,b,H,I], 7, [A,B,C,D,E,F,x,H,I]).
xmove([A,B,C,D,E,F,G,b,I], 8, [A,B,C,D,E,F,G,x,I]).
xmove([A,B,C,D,E,F,G,H,b], 9, [A,B,C,D,E,F,G,H,x]).
xmove(Board, N, Board) :- write('Illegal move.'), nl.
```

```
% The 0-place predicate playo starts a game with the user.
```

```
playo :- explain, playfrom([b,b,b,b,b,b,b,b,b]).
```

```
explain :-
  write('You play X by entering integer positions followed by a
  period.'),
  nl,
  display([1,2,3,4,5,6,7,8,9]).
```

```
playfrom(Board) :- win(Board, x), write('You win!').
playfrom(Board) :- win(Board, o), write('I win!').
playfrom(Board) :- read(N),
  xmove(Board, N, Newboard),
  display(Newboard),
  orespond(Newboard, Newnewboard),
  display(Newnewboard),
  playfrom(Newnewboard).
```

Figure 3-7 shows one of the games that I played against the computer.

Figure 3-7. *Game played against the computer*

You should notice that the program displayed `Cats game!` at the end of rounds, which is tic-tac-toe terminology for a tie game.

I also initiated a self-game in which the computer played against itself. Figure 3-8 shows that result. It always ends with X winning, as I mentioned earlier.

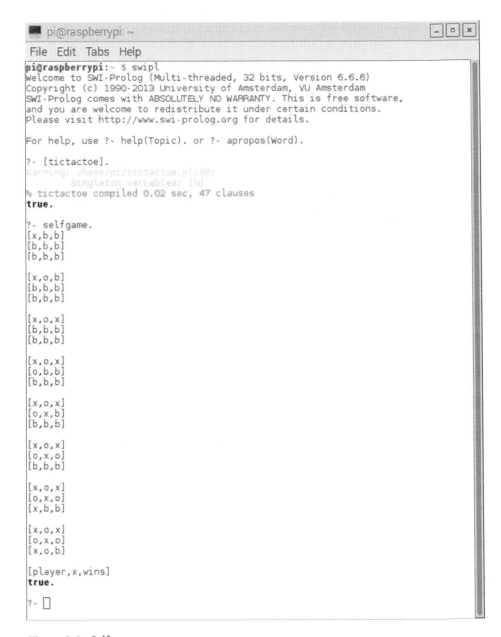

Figure 3-8. Self-game

At this point, I discuss the inner workings of the tic-tac-toe program, now that you have seen how it runs. There are three rules or predicates that define winning: by row, by column, or by diagonal. The following is one of the generalized win predicates:

```
win(Board, Player) :- rowwin(Board, Player).
```

Next, there are three ways of winning: by row or by column, and two by diagonal. The following predicate is one way of winning by completing the top row:

```
rowwin(Board, Player) :- Board = [Player,Player,
Player,_,_,_,_,_,_].
```

Similar predicates are generated for the other rows, columns, and diagonals, as you can see by reviewing the code.

There are nine move predicates that control how a move is made, which corresponds to each of the nine board positions.

The predicate, as follows, controls how the human player interacts with the game:

```
x_can_win_in_one(Board) :- move(Board, x, Newboard),
win(Newboard, x).
```

Similarly, the series of orespond predicates control how the computer interacts with the game.

Finally, there are nine predicates named xmove that ensure only legal moves can be made. They also translate the internal game position representations from A, B, C, … to the corresponding displayed positions 1, 2, 3, … .

The next expert system demonstration deals with a situation that we all occasionally encounter: determining whether we have a cold or the flu.

Demo 3-4: Cold or Flu Diagnosis

This example is a very basic medical-diagnosis expert system in which you answer a few questions and the system tries to determine whether you are suffering from the flu or a much more benign cold.

▓ **Caution**   This expert system is in *no* way a substitute for a real doctor's advice and consultation. If you are really sick, please go to your doctor. Do not rely on this program for a trusted diagnosis.

The following program is named flu_cold.pl.

```
% flu_cold.pl
% Flu or cold identification example
% Start with ?- go.

go:- hypothesis(Disease),
     write('I believe you have: '),
     write(Disease),
     nl,
     undo.

% Hypothesis to be tested
hypothesis(cold):- cold, !.
hypothesis(flu):- flu, !.

% Hypothesis Identification Rules
cold :-
        verify(headache),
        verify(runny_nose),
        verify(sneezing),
        verify(sore_throat).
flu :-
        verify(fever),
        verify(headache),
        verify(chills),
        verify(body_ache).

% Ask a question
ask(Question) :-
    write('Do you have the following symptom: '),
    write(Question),
    write('? '),
    read(Response),
    nl,
    ( (Response == yes ; Response == y)
      ->
      assert(yes(Question)) ;
      assert(no(Question)), fail).
```

```
:- dynamic yes/1,no/1.

% Verify something
verify(S) :- (yes(S) -> true ;
              (no(S)  -> fail ;
              ask(S))).

% Undo all yes/no assertions
undo :- retract(yes(_)),fail.
undo :- retract(no(_)),fail.
undo.
```

As noted in the comments, you start the program with this:

```
?- go.
```

The symptoms are then presented one after the other. Just answer with either a yes. or no. (alternatively, you can use the single letters y. or n.). Do not forget to enter the period at the end of the response; otherwise, Prolog will not recognize your entry. If you select a combination of symptoms that are not inclusive to either one of the hypotheses, then Prolog will simply show a fail because it cannot match your entries with the known facts.

Figure 3-9 shows a sample session that I conducted with this expert system. I selected symptoms for the flu, a cold, and finally, some for the no-match case.

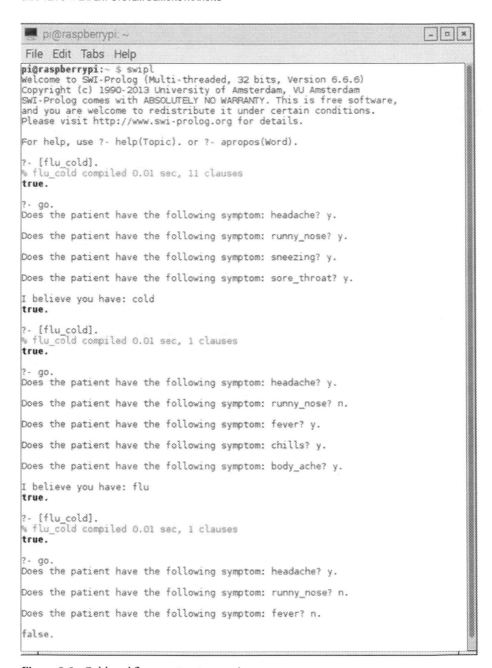

Figure 3-9. Cold and flu expert system session

The next demonstration is the last one in the chapter. It involves another simple expert system—but with a twist, because the system controls several Raspberry Pi GPIO outputs.

Demo 3-5: Expert System with Raspberry Pi GPIO Control

Until now, I have shown you expert systems that could be run on any PC or Mac with a compatible version of Prolog. This demonstration differs because I show you how to directly control some general-purpose input/out (GPIO) pins with Prolog—something that is not generally possible on a regular PC.

To be totally honest, it is simply not possible to directly control a GPIO pin using a Prolog command; but it is possible if you combine Prolog with the Python language. This combination is made possible by a great program named PySWIP, which allows Prolog commands to be called and executed within a Python program. There is also a great Python application program interface (API) named RPi.GPIO, which easily facilitates GPIO pin control. Next, I describe how to install the PySWIP application and set up the RPi.GPIO API, which are both prerequisites for this expert system demonstration.

Installing PySWIP

PySWIP was created by Yuce Tekol as a bridge program between Prolog and Python. He provided it to the community as GPL open source software. The program is not part of the Raspian repositories and therefore cannot be installed using the apt package manager. To install it, you must use the pip program. If you do not have pip already installed on your Raspberry Pi, use the following command to install it:

```
sudo apt-get install python-pip
```

Once pip is installed, you can then use it to install PySWIP with this command:

```
sudo pip install pyswip
```

There is one additional step that must be done for Python to recognize Prolog, and that is to create a symlink between the original shared library name and the latest one. Just enter this next command to create the link:

```
sudo ln -s libswipl.so /usr/lib/libpl.so
```

You should next enter the following Python commands in an interactive Python session to test if the PySWIP installation was successful:

```
>>> from pyswip import Prolog
>>> prolog = Prolog()
>>> prolog.assertz("father(michael,john)")
>>> prolog.assertz("father(michael,gina)")
>>> list(prolog.query("father(michael,X)"))
```

The following line is the Prolog response to the preceding command:

```
[{'X': 'john'}, {'X': 'gina'}]
```

```
>>> for soln in prolog.query("father(X,Y)"):
```

Ensure that you indent the next line. I used four spaces.

```
...        print soln["X"], "is the father of", soln["Y"]
...
```

Press the Backspace and Enter keys to execute the for statement. The Python interpreter should then display the following:

```
michael is the father of john
michael is the father of gina
```

If you see these two lines, you can be assured that Python and Prolog are working fine together, courtesy of the PySWIP bridge program. Figure 3-10 shows this test done with a Raspberry Pi.

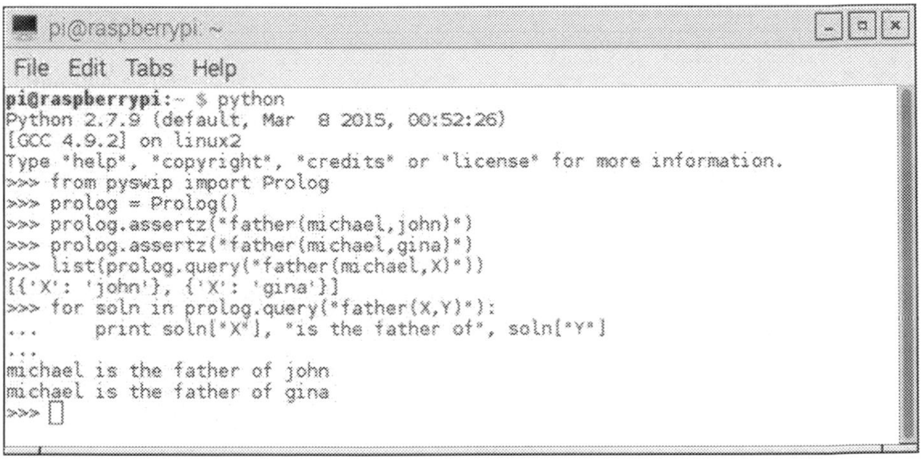

Figure 3-10. *Prolog and Python compatibility test*

It is now time to discuss the hardware setup, which uses the Python/Prolog expert system.

Hardware Setup

I used a T-form Pi Cobbler accessory to extend the Raspberry Pi GPIO pins so that they can be easily used with a solderless breadboard in this setup. Figure 3-11 is a Fritzing diagram, which shows the setup with two LEDs and two current-limiting resistors.

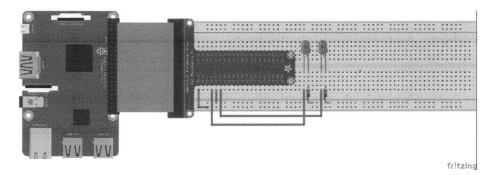

Figure 3-11. *Fritzing diagram*

The LEDs are connected to GPIO pins #4 and #17, with the 220Ω current-limiting resistors connected to ground. Thus, the LEDs light when the pins are set to a high value, which is 3.3V for the Raspberry Pi. The LED series resistor sets the maximum current flow to approximately 12 ma, which is well within the 25 ma current limit for any given Raspberry Pi GPIO pin.

Figure 3-12 shows the Raspberry Pi physical setup with the T Pi Cobbler, solderless breadboard, LEDs, and other components.

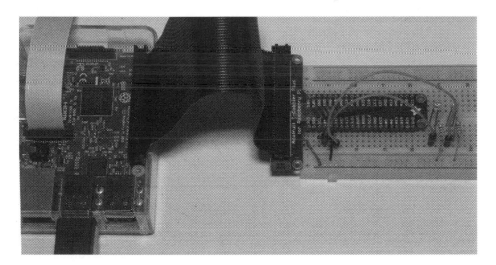

Figure 3-12. *Raspberry Pi physical setup*

You should next set up the RPi.GPIO API to control the LEDs with Python.

Rpi.GPIO Setup

This discussion focuses on how the RPi.GPIO API is used in a Python program. These setup steps must be included in every Python program that needs to control GPIO pins. I demonstrate the setup in an interactive session, but you should realize that the same statements must be included in a regular program script.

The RPi.GPIO API is now included with all standard Raspian Linux distributions. You should be all set if you are using the latest Jessie Raspian distribution. The first step is to import the API, as follows:

```
>>> import RPi.GPIO as GPIO
```

From this point on, all references to the API simply use the GPIO name. Next, you have to select the appropriate pin-numbering scheme. There are two variations in the Raspberry Pi pin-numbering scheme:

- GPIO.BOARD: The board numbers that follow the physical pin numbers on the P1 header, which contains all the GPIO pins.

- GPIO.BCM: The numbering scheme used by the chip manufacturer, BROADCOM, or BCM.

The pin numbers on the Pi Cobbler follow the BCM scheme, so that is what I used. You establish which numbering scheme to use with this statement:

```
>>> GPIO.setmode(GPIO.BCM)
```

Next, the two selected pins must be set from the default input mode to the output mode, which is done using these two statements:

```
>>> GPIO.setup(4, GPIO.OUT)
>>> GPIO.setup(17, GPIO.OUT)
```

Now, everything should be established to switch the pins high or low. By default, they are set to a low state upon boot-up. These next two statements should turn on the two LEDs:

```
>>> GPIO.output(4, GPIO.HIGH)
>>> GPIO.output(17, GPIO.HIGH)
```

If the LEDs did not light up, you should double-check the orientation of the LEDs in the breadboard. Every standard LED has two "legs," one of which is slightly shorter than the other. The shorter leg is connected to one lead of the resistor, whose other lead is connected to ground. Try switching the orientation of the LED and see if it turns on. You will not harm the LED by switching the orientation. Also, double-check that you are connected to pins 4 and 17, and that you have selected the correct numbering scheme. I have found that when something does not work as expected, it is usually a connection issue or a simple mistake in the setup.

Turning off the LEDs is accomplished using these statements:

```
>>> GPIO.output(4, GPIO.LOW)
>>> GPIO.output(17, GPIO.LOW)
```

An expert system is now ready to be created to control the LEDs.

Expert System with LED Control

I decided to essentially use the same simple Prolog script that was used to verify the PySWIP installation. However, the program was restructured a bit to take advantage of the Python way of using functions. That is the reason for using the PySWIP Functor function near the start of the program. This program is named LEDtest.py, which is run by entering the following:

```
python LEDtest.py
```

The LEDtest.py listing follows.

```
# LEDtest.py by D. J. Norris  Jan, 2017
# Uses Prolog with Python type functions

import time
import RPi.GPIO as GPIO
from pyswip import Functor, Variable, Query, call

# Setup GPIO pins
GPIO.setmode(GPIO.BCM)
GPIO.setup(4, GPIO.output)
GPIO.setup(17, GPIO.output)

# Setup Python like functions for Prolog statements
assertz = Functor("assertz", 1)
father = Functor("father", 2)

# Add facts to a dynamic database
call(assertz(father("michael","john")))
call(assertz(father("michael", "gina")))

# Setup an iterative query session
X = Variable()
q = Query(father("michael",X))
while q.nextSolution():
    print "Hello, ", X.value
```

```
if str(X.value) == "john": # LED #4 on if john is michael's
child
    GPIO.output(4,GPIO.HIGH)
    time.sleep(5)
    GPIO.output(4,GPIO.LOW)
if str(X.value) == "gina": # LED #17 on if gina is
michael's child
    GPIO.output(17,GPIO.HIGH)
    time.sleep(5)
    GPIO.output(17,GPIO.LOW)
```

Figure 3-13 shows the program output. What cannot be shown is that LEDs were lit for five seconds each, indicating that the two queries were successfully run.

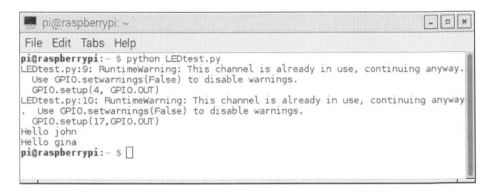

Figure 3-13. *Program output*

At this point, you are probably wondering how this demonstration can be put to a practical use with a Raspberry Pi. That answer will have to be deferred for several chapters until I cover a fuzzy logic project, which uses an embedded expert system with some GPIO pins controlling a heating and cooling system (HVAC).

Summary

There were five expert systems demonstrated in this chapter. They ranged from an extremely simple one with only a few facts and rules, to a much more complicated one that implemented the tic-toe-toe game.

The final demonstration showed you how to combine Python with Prolog so that Raspberry Pi GPIO pins could be controlled.

CHAPTER 4

Games

This chapter is all about games. But the games I discuss are not the multi-million-dollar video blockbusters that are currently saturating the marketplace. Instead, they are the much simpler games that have been around for a very long time; some for thousands of years. But even in these simple games, AI has had an impact. The games discussed in this chapter traditionally involve two human opponents, but the modern varieties involve one human playing against a computer. That's where the AI comes in: to provide some randomness and competition to the human player such that playing the game does not quickly become boring and trivial.

Each demonstration presents several iterations for which you will need some additional parts, as detailed in the Table 4-1.

Table 4-1. *Parts Lists*

Description	Quantity	Remarks
Pi Cobbler	1	40-pin version, either T or DIP form factor acceptable
solderless breadboard	1	860 insertion points with power supply strips
jumper wires	1 package	
LED	3	
220Ω resistor	3	1/4 watt
16 × 4 LCD display	1	Adafruit p/n 198 or equivalent You can also use a 16 × 2 LCD
10k Ω potentiometer	1	Included with LCD display
push button switches	4	Tactile, suitable for use with a solderless breadboard

The first game to be demonstrated is that old-time favorite we all have played: rock-paper-scissors.

© Donald J. Norris 2017
D. J. Norris, *Beginning Artificial Intelligence with the Raspberry Pi*,
DOI 10.1007/978-1-4842-2743-5_4

Demo 4-1: Rock-Paper-Scissors

Here are the rules for the human-to-human rock-paper-scissors game, in case you have not played it for a while. Each opponent clenches his or her fist, counts to three, and then displays one of the following hand signals:

- Flat hand: paper

- Fist: rock

- Two fingers in a V: scissors

Winning is determined as follows:

- The same signal from each opponent is a tie.

- Rock dulls a scissor, so the rock sign wins.

- Paper covers a rock, so the paper sign wins.

- Scissors cut paper, so the scissor sign wins.

There are only nine possible combinations, including three ways to tie. Each opponent has three ways to win, as described, which leads to the nine possible combinations.

The following Python program named prs.py is a straightforward implementation of the rock-paper-scissors game. This program does not use any Prolog statements demonstrated in the previous chapter, but instead relies on standard Python if ... else statements. These statements have the same effect as the *if <condition> then <conclusion>* discussed in the section on inference.

prs.py listing

```
# prs.py
from random import randint

# List the input options
inputList = ["paper", "rock", "scissors"]

# Random computer pick
computer = inputList[randint(0,2)]

# Initially set player = False
player = False

while player == False:

    player = raw_input("paper, rock, scissors?")
    if player == computer:
        print("Tie!")
    elif player == "rock":
```

```
        if computer == "paper":
            print("You lose ", computer, "covers", player)
        else:
            print("You win ", player, "dulls", computer)
    elif player == "paper":
        if computer == "scissors":
            print("You lose ", computer, "cuts", player)
        else:
            print("You win ", player, "covers", computer)
    elif player == "scissors":
        if computer == "rock":
            print("You lose ", computer, "dulls", player)
        else:
            print("You win ", player, "cuts", computer)
    else:
        print("Invalid input. Please reenter")

    # Reset player = False to continue looping
    player = False

    computer = inputList[randint(0,2)]
```

Figure 4-1 shows several rounds that I conducted with the Raspberry Pi.

Figure 4-1. *Rock-paper-scissors game play*

I do want to comment on one aspect of this program, which is especially directed to those readers who are not too comfortable with writing Python programs. The `elif` command is a contraction of the words `else if` and is used as part of a nested `if ... else` structure, which implements the game logic. The game logic can also be portrayed in a tree diagram, as shown in Figure 4-2.

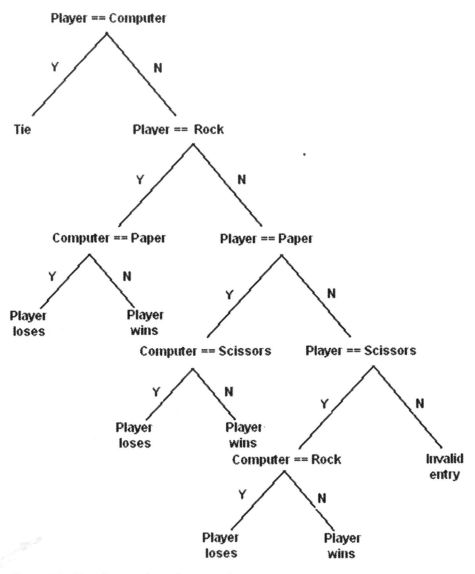

Figure 4-2. *Tree diagram for rock-paper-scissors game*

I think you can appreciate the symmetry of the logic as depicted in the figure. Note that there are six leafs or end points, which show where the player either wins or loses. This matches exactly with the six win/loss combinations I mentioned earlier.

Believe or not, there is some underlying strategy, which can be invoked when playing this game against a human opponent. To understand the competitive strategy, I must first assign some values to the game outcomes. Let's assume the following reasonable point assignment for each outcome:

- Win = 2 points

- Tie = 1 point

- Loss = 0 points

Table 4-2 shows, on average, what the expected player values should be for a long run of consecutive play.

Table 4-2. *Averaged Player Outcomes*

		Opponents' Move			Averaged Player Score
		paper	rock	scissors	
Player's Move	paper	1	2	0	1
	rock	0	1	2	1
	scissors	2	0	1	1

The averaged player score should not surprise you, as over the long run (assuming random choices by each opponent), the expected scores or values should be equally divided over all the possible outcomes. But now, let's add a twist to the normal approach and take advantage of a human trait. This trait or behavior involves random number selection. If you asked someone to select three random numbers from 1 to 10, odds would favor that they might answer 7, 4, and 8, or some similar variation. They could easily answer 5, 5, and 5, which would have satisfied the request, but using the word *random* obviously biases behavior. Let's assume now that your opponent selected rock in the last round. It is more likely than not that he will not select rock again for the next round. The averaged expected values table can now be modified, as shown in Table 4-3.

Table 4-3. *Modified Averaged Expected Values*

		Opponent's Move			Averaged Player Score
		paper	rock	scissors	
Player's Move	paper	1	-	0	0.5
	rock	0	-	2	1
	scissors	2	-	1	1.5

Clearly, there is a best move on the player's part based on the opponent's previous move, which is based on normal human behaviors. However, it is not too hard to program in a check routine to avoid providing the human player a competitive advantage. The code would be something like the following; but note that I just used the index integer values and not the equivalent string values.

```
if computer == lastMove & won == 0:
    computer = player + 1
    if computer > 3:
        computer = 1
```

lastMove and won are new integer variables representing the computer's previous selection and whether it won, respectively. I did not incorporate this code into the current program because I just wanted to demonstrate the classic game design.

My next iteration of the rock-paper-scissors game eliminates keyboard entry and the screen display, and replaces them with push buttons and LEDs.

Rock-Paper-Scissors Game with Switches and LEDs

I thought it would both be fun and interesting to change the game play on the Raspberry Pi to use push button switches to select the sign and have LEDs indicate a win, lose, or tie for the game. In this project, I also introduce how the Raspberry Pi handles interrupts using the Python language. There is one caveat to this program. It must be started using the following command-line entry:

```
python prs_with_LEDs_and_Switches.py
```

The Raspberry Pi system now needs to be set up. The Fritzing diagram is shown in Figure 4-3.

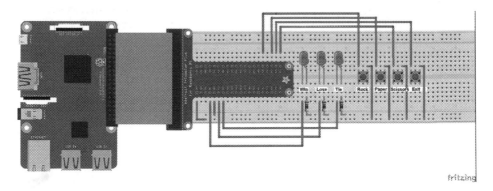

Figure 4-3. *Fritzing diagram for rock-paper-scissors game machine*

Figure 4-3 is an extension of Figure 3-11, which was used in an expert system demonstration. I added one additional LED and four push button switches to the circuit. The additional LED was connected to pin 27, while the push buttons were connected to pins 12, 16, 20, and 21.

The physical Raspberry Pi setup is shown in Figure 4-4. Notice that I put labels near the LEDs and push buttons to help the user determine what the LEDs indicate and which sign a particular push button enables. The fourth push button exits the program when pushed.

Figure 4-4. *Physical Raspberry Pi setup*

The push buttons act as inputs that momentarily provide a high level of 3.3V to the pin when pushed. Each of the input pins is also set up to be in a pull-down mode, where an internal resistor at the pin input is connected to ground. This prevents an indeterminate floating state from being applied to the pin. In such a state, a floating pin could "see" voltages ranging from tens of millivolts to as high as two volts, which could trigger a false high on the pin. The actual float voltage is highly variable and dependent on the local potential field surrounding the pin. Connecting a pull-down resistor avoids all that nasty trouble. And the good news is that the pull-down resistor is actually configured via a software command, which I discuss after I show you the following code listing.

prs_with_LEDs_and_Switches.py

```
import RPi.GPIO as GPIO
import time
from random import randint

# Setup GPIO pins
# Set the BCM mode
GPIO.setmode(GPIO.BCM)
```

```
# Outputs
GPIO.setup( 4, GPIO.OUT)
GPIO.setup(17, GPIO.OUT)
GPIO.setup(27, GPIO.OUT)

# Ensure all LEDs are off to start
GPIO.output( 4, GPIO.LOW)
GPIO.output(17, GPIO.LOW)
GPIO.output(27, GPIO.LOW)

# Inputs
GPIO.setup(12, GPIO.IN, pull_up_down = GPIO.PUD_DOWN)
GPIO.setup(16, GPIO.IN, pull_up_down = GPIO.PUD_DOWN)
GPIO.setup(21, GPIO.IN, pull_up_down = GPIO.PUD_DOWN)
GPIO.setup(20, GPIO.IN, pull_up_down = GPIO.PUD_DOWN)

global player
player = 0

# Setup the callback functions
def rock(channel):
    global player
    player = 1  # magic number 1 = rock, pin 12

def paper(channel):
    global player
    player = 2  # magic number 2 = paper pin 16

def scissors(channel):
    global player
    player = 3  # magic number 3 = scissors pin 21

def quit(channel):
    exit()      # pin 20, immediate exit from the game

# Add event detection and callback assignments
GPIO.add_event_detect(12, GPIO.RISING, callback=rock)
GPIO.add_event_detect(16, GPIO.RISING, callback=paper)
GPIO.add_event_detect(21, GPIO.RISING, callback=scissors)
GPIO.add_event_detect(20, GPIO.RISING, callback=quit)

# computer random pick
computer = randint(1,3)

while True:

    if player == computer:
        # This is a tie condition
```

```
        GPIO.output(27,GPIO.HIGH)
        time.sleep(5)
        GPIO.output(27, GPIO.LOW)
        player = 0
elif player == 1:
    if computer == 2:
        # Player loses, paper covers rock
        GPIO.output(17,GPIO.HIGH)
        time.sleep(5)
        GPIO.output(17, GPIO.LOW)
        player = 0
    else:
        # Player wins, rock dulls scissors
        GPIO.output(4,GPIO.HIGH)
        time.sleep(5)
        GPIO.output(4, GPIO.LOW)
        player = 0
elif player == 2:
    if computer == 3:
        # Player loses, scissors cuts paper
        GPIO.output(17,GPIO.HIGH)
        time.sleep(5)
        GPIO.output(17, GPIO.LOW)
        player = 0
    else:
        # Player wins, paper covers rock
        GPIO.output(4,GPIO.HIGH)
        time.sleep(5)
        GPIO.output(4, GPIO.LOW)
        player = 0
elif player == 3:
    if computer == 1:
        # Player loses, rock dulls scissors
        GPIO.output(17,GPIO.HIGH)
        time.sleep(5)
        GPIO.output(17, GPIO.LOW)
        player = 0
    else:
        # Player wins, scissors cuts paper
        GPIO.output(4,GPIO.HIGH)
        time.sleep(5)
        GPIO.output(4, GPIO.LOW)
        player = 0

# another random pick for the computer
computer = randint(1,3)
```

One thing that you should immediately notice is that I only used numbers to represent the signs in this game version. There is no need for actual string names because the LEDs show the result of the round and the push buttons are already clearly labeled. However, I did identify what these "magic" numbers represent by using comments with the code listing. I use the magic to represent any number that is used to represent something else. Without a comment or other identifying means, it does become a magic trick to figure what an isolated number in a program is supposed to represent. Unfortunately, more than a few developers still resort to using magic numbers in their programs—a practice I highly suggest you avoid unless you comment them, but then they are no longer magic.

The logic in the preceding program is exactly the same as what was presented in the first version of the program. Yet, there are big differences in the input and outputs, which now use push buttons and LEDs. I will discuss the LED output first since you have already seen it in the expert system demonstration. The pin number scheme is first selected, which is still going to BCM because it matches the T Pi Cobbler pin designations. The pins selected to be outputs are set up next. Those pins are 4, 17, and 27, which represent win, lose, and tie, respectively. That's all that's needed to preconfigure the outputs. Turning on an output is done using this command:

```
GPIO.output(n, GPIO.HIGH)  # where n = pin number
```

You should also notice that I followed each LED output command with this command:

```
time.sleep(5)
```

This forces the Python interpreter to pause for five seconds, which allows the user to easily recognize which LED is lit. Without a pause, the LED will light and extinguish so quickly that you could never see it. That condition would likely puzzle a lot of new programmers who expect to see a lit LED, but never do. The program was probably functioning as desired but the new programmer neglected the reality of a real-time clock cycle, such that the LED stayed on for only microseconds—far too brief a time to detect with the human eye.

Now on to the input pins and the interrupt discussion.

Interrupts

There are two principal ways to handle pin inputs: polling and interrupts. Polling, as the name suggests, simply periodically checks on a pin state. It must be implemented in a loop to work. The following code snippet shows a way to check on a pin status:

```
if GPIO.input(n):             # where n = pin number
    print('Input was HIGH')
else:
    print('Input was LOW')
```

Polling is much slower than using interrupts, because all the code in a loop must be executed. It is possible to miss a button press if the program takes a relatively long time to complete each loop, especially if there are any pause statements in the loop.

Interrupts, on the other hand, are practically immediate, independent of what is going on in the main program, looping or not. Interrupts take advantage of a hardware subsystem contained within the ARM microprocessor called the *interrupt controller*. Figure 4-5 is a very simplified diagram of an interrupt controller that has three interrupt sources: a push button, a serial input, and a clock input. The push button interrupt source is pertinent in this project.

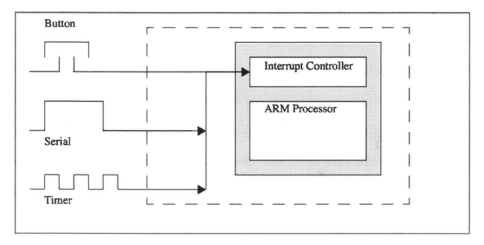

Figure 4-5. *Interrupt controller*

Figure 4-6 is a logic flow diagram that clearly shows the sequence of actions when an interrupt occurs.

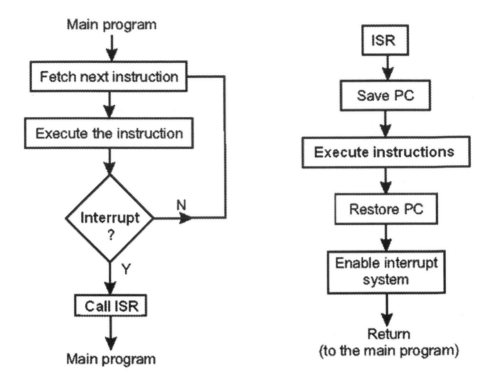

Figure 4-6. Interrupt logic flow diagram

Normally, the microprocessor fetches and executes one instruction after another while running the main program. When an interrupt occurs, which I will now call an *event* to conform to the Python language terminology, a jump is made to an interrupt service routine (ISR), as shown in Figure 4-6. And just to further confuse you, ISRs are known as *callback functions* in Python. The interrupt controller automatically saves the address of the next executable instruction, as well as several other parameters, which is known as *saving the processor state*. The callback function is run next, and when that is completed, the interrupt controller reloads the processor state and resumes exactly from the point it was when interrupted. All of this action only takes microseconds to complete and is much faster than polling.

There are several steps that must be done in Python to set up interrupts. First, the appropriate pin to receive the interrupt must be set up. I will use the rock push button as an example. This next statement sets pin 12 as an input with a pull-down resistor configured for the reasons I discussed earlier:

```
GPIO.setup(12, GPIO.IN, pull_up_down = GPIO.PUD_DOWN)
```

Next, the interrupt source must be identified and linked to a callback function. The following statement does it for the rock-signal push button:

```
GPIO.add_event_detect(12, GPIO.RISING, callback=rock)
```

Finally, the callback function must be defined. For the rock signal, this function is

```
def rock(channel):
    global player
    player = 1  # magic number 1 = rock, pin 12
```

Notice, that the word channel must be used as an argument in the function definition. This is just a peculiarity of the Python language.

Also notice that I used the word global in the function definition, which specifies that the player variable was global or available to all portions of the program, whether or not it was in the function or the main program. I normally do not like to use globals because they break the object-oriented principle of encapsulation, but in this case, it seemed appropriate to minimize code duplication and to increase program efficiency. You also need to identify player as a global in the main program.

The last new program feature is the exit push button, which causes it to immediately quit the Python interpreter. This is the callback function:

```
def quit(channel):
    exit()        # pin 20, immediate exit from the game
```

Everything else in the program is straightforward or was discussed previously.

There is no screenshot that I can show of this program running because the inputs are manual push button activations and the outputs are LEDs being lit. I can just assure you that everything functioned as anticipated.

The next game that I discuss is Nim.

Demo 4-2: Nim

Nim is game of mathematical strategy in which two players take turns removing items from a common heap. In each turn, a player may remove one, two, or three items. The objective of the game is to avoid being the player removing the last item, although there are Nim variants in which you win by removing the last item.

Various Nim-style games have been played since ancient times, often using pebbles as the heap. Nim has also been called *pebble pickup*, *last pebble*, and in recent times, *sticks*, or *pick-up sticks*. Although not really known as a fact, Nim is thought to have originated in China because it closely resembles the game *Tsyan-shizi*, or "picking stones." In European history, Nim dates back to the beginning of the 16th century. The actual name of *Nim* name is attributed to Harvard University Professor Charles Bouton, who is recognized as the creator game theory during the early 1900s.

I will first demonstrate a Python version of Nim in a two-person game. I simply describe it as "naive Nim," in which there is no AI but simply innate player intelligence.

naive_nim.py listing

```
sticks = 21
max_picks = 3

while (sticks != 0):
    pick1 = 0
    pick2 = 0

    pick1 = int(raw_input("Player 1 pick: "))
    while pick1 > max_picks or (sticks - pick1) <= 0:
        print "You cannot pick more than 3 or reduce sticks to
        zero or less"
        pick1 = int(raw_input("Player 1 pick: "))
    sticks =  sticks - pick1
    print "remaining sticks = ", sticks
    if sticks == 1:
        print 'Player 1 Wins!'
        exit()

    pick2 = int(raw_input("Player 2 pick: "))
    while pick2 > max_picks or (sticks - pick2) <= 0:
        print "You cannot pick more than 3 or reduce sticks to
        zero or less"
        pick2 = int(raw_input("Player2 pick: "))
    sticks = sticks - pick2
    print "remaining sticks = ", sticks
    if sticks == 1:
        print 'Player 2 Wins!'
        exit()
```

Figure 4-7 shows two rounds that I played: pick1 and pick2. Notice that I added some validation checks, which ensured that no more than three sticks were picked and that any pick did not reduce the stick total to zero or less.

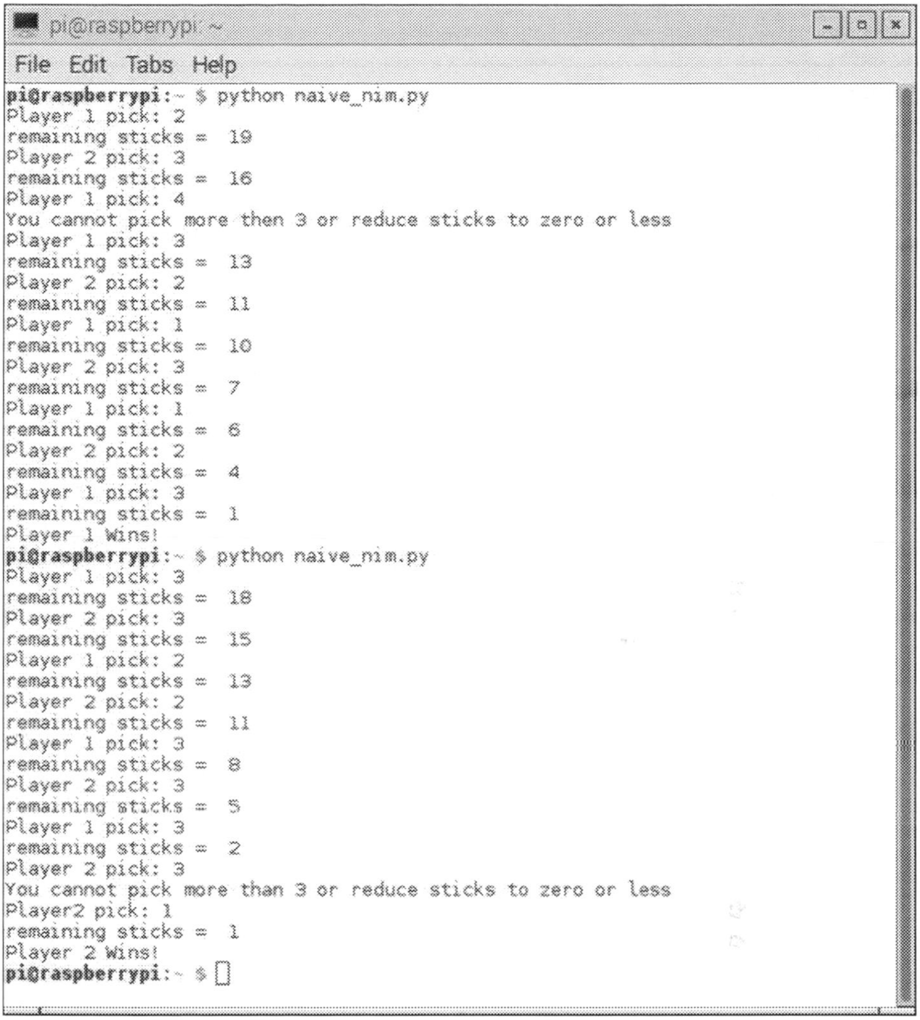

```
■ pi@raspberrypi: ~                                          [ - ][ □ ][ × ]
File  Edit  Tabs  Help
pi@raspberrypi:~ $ python naive_nim.py
Player 1 pick: 2
remaining sticks = 19
Player 2 pick: 3
remaining sticks = 16
Player 1 pick: 4
You cannot pick more then 3 or reduce sticks to zero or less
Player 1 pick: 3
remaining sticks = 13
Player 2 pick: 2
remaining sticks = 11
Player 1 pick: 1
remaining sticks = 10
Player 2 pick: 3
remaining sticks = 7
Player 1 pick: 1
remaining sticks = 6
Player 2 pick: 2
remaining sticks = 4
Player 1 pick: 3
remaining sticks = 1
Player 1 Wins!
pi@raspberrypi:~ $ python naive_nim.py
Player 1 pick: 3
remaining sticks = 18
Player 2 pick: 3
remaining sticks = 15
Player 1 pick: 2
remaining sticks = 13
Player 2 pick: 2
remaining sticks = 11
Player 1 pick: 3
remaining sticks = 8
Player 2 pick: 3
remaining sticks = 5
Player 1 pick: 3
remaining sticks = 2
Player 2 pick: 3
You cannot pick more than 3 or reduce sticks to zero or less
Player2 pick: 1
remaining sticks = 1
Player 2 Wins!
pi@raspberrypi:~ $ []
```

Figure 4-7. *Two rounds of Nim play*

Now it is time to add some AI to the Nim game by implementing a computer opponent.

nim_computer.py listing

```python
import random
print "NIM GAME"

player1 = raw_input("Enter your name: ")
player2 = "Computer"
howMany = 0
```

```python
gameover=False
global stickNumber
stickNumber = 21

def moveComputer():
    removedNumber = random.randint(1,3)
    global stickNumber
    while (removedNumber < stickNumber) or (stickNumber <= 4):
        if stickNumber >= 5:
            stickNumber -= removedNumber
            return stickNumber
        elif (stickNumber == 4) or (stickNumber == 3) or
        (stickNumber == 2):
            stickNumber = 1
            return stickNumber

def moveHuman():
    global stickNumber
    global howMany
    stickNumber -= howMany
    return stickNumber

def humanLegalMove():
    global howMany
    global stickNumber
    legalMove=False
    while not legalMove:
        print("It's your turn, ",player1)
        howMany=int(input("How many sticks do you want to
        remove?
        (from 1 to 3) "))
        if  howMany>3 or howMany<1:
            print("Enter a number between 1 and 3.")
        else:
            legalMove=True
    while (howMany >= stickNumber):
        print("The entered number is greater than or equal to
        the number of sticks remaining.")
        howMany=int(input("How many sticks do you want to
        remove?"))
        return howMany

def checkWinner(player):
    global stickNumber
    if stickNumber == 1:
        print(player," wins.")
        global gameover
```

```
                  gameover = True
                  return gameover

def resetGameover():
      global gameover
      global stickNumber
      gameover = False
      stickNumber = 21
      howMany = 0
      return gameover

def game():
      while gameover == False:
          print("It's ",player2,"turn. The number of sticks left:
          ", moveComputer())
          checkWinner(player2)
          if gameover == True:
              playAgain()
          humanLegalMove()
          print("The number of sticks left: ", moveHuman())
          checkWinner(player1)
          if gameover == True:
              playAgain()

def playAgain():
      answer = raw_input("Do you want to play again?(y/n)")
      resetGameover()
      if answer=="y":
          game()
      else:
          print("Thanks for playing the game")
          exit()

game()
playAgain()
```

Figure 4-8 shows two rounds of Nim played against the computer.

```
▬ pi@raspberrypi: ~                                    [-][□][x]
File  Edit  Tabs  Help
pi@raspberrypi:~ $ python nim_computer.py
NIM GAME
Enter your name: Don
("It's ", 'Computer', 'turn. The number of sticks left: ', 19)
("It's your turn, ", 'Don')
How many sticks do you want to remove?(from 1 to 3) 3
('The number of sticks left: ', 16)
("It's ", 'Computer', 'turn. The number of sticks left: ', 13)
("It's your turn, ", 'Don')
How many sticks do you want to remove?(from 1 to 3) 2
('The number of sticks left: ', 11)
("It's ", 'Computer', 'turn. The number of sticks left: ', 8)
("It's your turn, ", 'Don')
How many sticks do you want to remove?(from 1 to 3) 3
('The number of sticks left: ', 5)
("It's ", 'Computer', 'turn. The number of sticks left: ', 2)
("It's your turn, ", 'Don')
How many sticks do you want to remove?(from 1 to 3) 1
('The number of sticks left: ', 1)
('Don', ' wins.')
Do you want to play again?(y/n)y
("It's ", 'Computer', 'turn. The number of sticks left: ', 18)
("It's your turn, ", 'Don')
How many sticks do you want to remove?(from 1 to 3) 2
('The number of sticks left: ', 16)
("It's ", 'Computer', 'turn. The number of sticks left: ', 15)
("It's your turn, ", 'Don')
How many sticks do you want to remove?(from 1 to 3) 2
('The number of sticks left: ', 13)
("It's ", 'Computer', 'turn. The number of sticks left: ', 10)
("It's your turn, ", 'Don')
How many sticks do you want to remove?(from 1 to 3) 2
('The number of sticks left: ', 8)
("It's ", 'Computer', 'turn. The number of sticks left: ', 6)
("It's your turn, ", 'Don')
How many sticks do you want to remove?(from 1 to 3) 3
('The number of sticks left: ', 3)
("It's ", 'Computer', 'turn. The number of sticks left: ', 1)
('Computer', ' wins.')
Do you want to play again?(y/n)n
Thanks for playing the game
pi@raspberrypi:~ $ []
```

Figure 4-8. *Two rounds of computer vs. human play*

Figure 4-8 demonstrates that the program functions as designed when each opponent enters a valid stick number. While it is impossible for the computer to enter an invalid number, the same is not true for a human. In addition, the program must guard against an entry that would reduce the number of sticks to zero or less. Figure 4-9 shows these safeguards in action when I attempted to enter a number greater than three, or to reduce the stick total to zero.

```
pi@raspberrypi: ~                                              [-][□][×]

File  Edit  Tabs  Help

pi@raspberrypi:~ $ python nim_computer.py
NIM GAME
Enter your name: Don
("It's ", 'Computer', 'turn. The number of sticks left: ', 20)
("It's your turn, ", 'Don')
How many sticks do you want to remove?(from 1 to 3) 3
('The number of sticks left: ', 17)
("It's ", 'Computer', 'turn. The number of sticks left: ', 14)
("It's your turn, ", 'Don')
How many sticks do you want to remove?(from 1 to 3) 4
Enter a number between 1 and 3.
("It's your turn, ", 'Don')
How many sticks do you want to remove?(from 1 to 3) 3
('The number of sticks left: ', 11)
("It's ", 'Computer', 'turn. The number of sticks left: ', 10)
("It's your turn, ", 'Don')
How many sticks do you want to remove?(from 1 to 3) 1
('The number of sticks left: ', 9)
("It's ", 'Computer', 'turn. The number of sticks left: ', 8)
("It's your turn, ", 'Don')
How many sticks do you want to remove?(from 1 to 3) 2
('The number of sticks left: ', 6)
("It's ", 'Computer', 'turn. The number of sticks left: ', 4)
("It's your turn, ", 'Don')
How many sticks do you want to remove?(from 1 to 3) 2
('The number of sticks left: ', 2)
("It's ", 'Computer', 'turn. The number of sticks left: ', 1)
('Computer', ' wins.')
Do you want to play again?(y/n)y
("It's ", 'Computer', 'turn. The number of sticks left: ', 19)
("It's your turn, ", 'Don')
How many sticks do you want to remove?(from 1 to 3) 3
('The number of sticks left: ', 16)
("It's ", 'Computer', 'turn. The number of sticks left: ', 14)
("It's your turn, ", 'Don')
How many sticks do you want to remove?(from 1 to 3) 2
('The number of sticks left: ', 12)
("It's ", 'Computer', 'turn. The number of sticks left: ', 11)
("It's your turn, ", 'Don')
How many sticks do you want to remove?(from 1 to 3) 3
('The number of sticks left: ', 8)
("It's ", 'Computer', 'turn. The number of sticks left: ', 5)
("It's your turn, ", 'Don')
How many sticks do you want to remove?(from 1 to 3) 1
('The number of sticks left: ', 4)
("It's ", 'Computer', 'turn. The number of sticks left: ', 3)
("It's your turn, ", 'Don')
How many sticks do you want to remove?(from 1 to 3) 3
The entered number is greater than or equal to the number of sticks remaining.
How many sticks do you want to remove?2
('The number of sticks left: ', 1)
('Don', ' wins.')
Do you want to play again?(y/n)n
Thanks for playing the game
pi@raspberrypi:~ $ □
```

Figure 4-9. *Validation or "sanity" checks*

What is not evident in Figures 4-8 and 4-9 is my addition of a small amount of AI to the program. Normally, the computer entry for each turn is determined by the following statement:

```
removedNumber = random.randint(1,3)
```

This statement generates a random number between one and three, inclusively. Normally, this is OK for a naive approach; however, I did not wish to give too much of an unfair advantage to the human player when the stick count was four or lower. Therefore, I added the following code to the moveComputer function:

```
elif (stickNumber == 4) or (stickNumber == 3) or
(stickNumber == 2):
            stickNumber = 1
            return stickNumber
```

This ensures that the computer wins the round as it emulates the exact human behavior expected if a human player was presented with two, three, or four remaining sticks.

There is more to the Nim game competitive strategy that you should know. Let's assume that six sticks are left and it is your turn. According to game theory, your best option would be to remove the exact number of sticks that satisfies the following equation:

$n \bmod 4 = 1$ where n is the remaining sticks number *after* your turn.

The *mod* operator in the equation represents integer remaindering division. For instance, 8 *mod* 3 would equal 2 because 3 divides twice into 8 with a remainder of 2. So basically, you discard the dividend and keep the remainder for integer division. Table 4-4 shows all of your possible moves with six sticks still in the heap.

Table 4-4. *Competitive Strategy for Six Sticks in the Heap*

Possible Move	Remaining Sticks (*n*)	*n* mod 4
1	5	1
2	4	0
3	3	3

Thus, according to game theory, your optimal move is to remove one stick. You don't have to be a gaming expert to understand this choice. Remember your opponent can only remove one, two, or three sticks. Therefore, after the opponent removes the sticks, there can only be two, three, or four sticks remaining. You are then guaranteed a win because you can remove the appropriate amount to have one remaining.

The human player has a distinct advantage in this particular game because the computer always randomly selects a stick removal number until there are four or less sticks remaining in the heap. Therefore, you should always try to have the computer's second-to-last move be with six sticks. I have removed this advantage in the next demonstrated Nim version in the following section.

Nim with LCD and Switches

This Nim version uses push button switches to enter the number of sticks to be removed. It uses an LCD to display when the human player should press a push button and to show the number of remaining sticks. The push buttons are connected to Python callback functions, as was done with the automated rock-paper-scissors (rps) game version. In fact, I used a very similar push button circuitry in the prs game. I did have to change the pins used with the push buttons to accommodate the LCD display interconnections. The LEDs in the prs game are no longer needed because they are replaced by the 16 × 2 LCD display.

The Fritzing diagram for the automated Nim setup is shown in Figure 4-10.

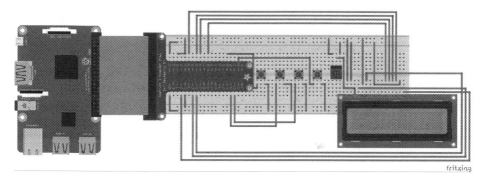

Figure 4-10. *Fritzing diagram for the automated Nim game*

There are obviously too many wiring connections in this setup than can be properly shown in a Fritzing diagram. Therefore, I have provided both a schematic showing the LCD-to-Pi Cobbler interconnections and a pin list showing all the system interconnections. Figure 4-11 is the LCD module–to–Pi Cobbler schematic.

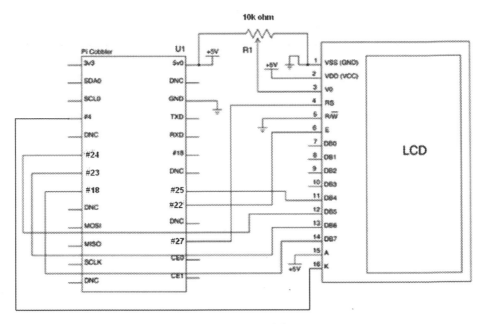

Figure 4-11. *Schematic of Pi Cobbler–to–LCD module*

Table 4-5 is the pin list detailing all the board interconnections. Note that the LCD pin designations start at 1 at the left and go to 16 at the far right for the LCD orientation, as shown in the Fritzing diagram. The potentiometer is oriented "upside-down," which places the pins on top. The left pin connects to ground, the middle pin to LCD pin 3, and the right pin connects to 5V.

Table 4-5. *Pin List for Wiring Interconnections*

From	To	Remarks
LCD pin 1	ground	
LCD pin 2	5V	Vcc
LCD pin 3	middle lead - potentiometer	Contrast adjustment Vo
LCD pin 4	RasPi pin 27	Register select
LCD pin 5	ground	Read/Write (R/W)
LCD pin 6	RasPi pin 22	Enable (Clock)
LCD pin 7	-	no connection (Bit 0)
LCD pin 8	-	no connection (Bit 1)
LCD pin 9	-	no connection (Bit 2)

(continued)

Table 4-5. (*continued*)

From	To	Remarks
LCD pin 10	-	no connection (Bit 3)
LCD pin 11	RasPi pin 25	Bit 4
LCD pin 12	RasPi pin 24	Bit 5
LCD pin 13	RasPi pin 23	Bit 6
LCD pin 14	RasPi pin 18	Bit 7
LCD pin 15	5V	Backlight LED anode
LCD pin 16	RasPi pin 4	Backlight LED cathode
left lead potentiometer	ground	
middle lead potentiometer	LCD pin 3	
right lead potentiometer	5V	
stick button 1, left side	RasPi pin 12	
stick button 1, right side	3.3V	
stick button 2, left side	RasPi pin 13	
stick button 2, right side	3.3V	
stick button 3, left side	RasPi pin 19	
stick button 3, right side	3.3V	
exit button, left side	RasPi pin 20	
exit button, right side	3.3V	

There are a lot of jumpers to connect in this setup, so be especially carefully when wiring the solderless breadboard. I recommend that you use a separate power rail for the 5V supply that should be located on the top of the breadboard if you are using a horizontal orientation for the board. Pay particular attention that you do *not* connect any 5V source to a Raspberry Pi input because it will surely destroy that input pin. The GPIO inputs are strictly limited to a maximum level of 3.3V, anything higher will burn out that input pin and likely cause further damage to the Raspberry Pi core.

Figure 4-12 shows the complete physical setup with each of the push buttons' functions labeled.

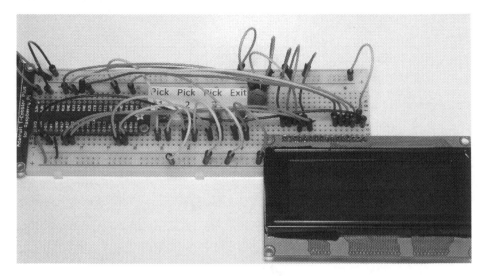

Figure 4-12. *Physical setup for the automated Nim game*

The program that controls this hardware is named automated_nim.py. It is based on the previous program, except all the inputs are now accomplished with callback functions and an LCD display is used to show the game status. I felt it was appropriate to first discuss how the LCD display functions with the Raspberry Pi before actually getting into the main program.

LCD Display

I will first acknowledge that most of the material in this section is based on a very good Adafruit tutorial by Tony DiCola available at `https://learn.adafruit.com/ character-lcd-with-raspberry-pi-or-beaglebone-black/overview`.

Inexpensive 16 × 2 or 16 × 4 LCDs with 16 connector pins are most likely using a Hitachi HD44780 controller or a generic equivalent. The LCD uses a parallel interface, meaning that you need multiple wires from the Raspberry Pi to control it. This setup uses only four data pins and two control pins. This configuration is known as the *LCD nibble input mode.* The other mode is where a full byte, or eight bits, is transferred each time there is a new character input to the LCD. Obviously, the nibble mode is slower than the byte mode, but for this application, the speed difference is not apparent. The Raspberry Pi is only sending data to the display; it is not reading any data. This means that that you do not have to be concerned about any 5V pulses being sent to the more sensitive Raspberry Pi input pins that only have a 3.3V maximum voltage input, as I mentioned earlier.

The register select pin #4 on the 16-pin LCD header has two uses. When pulled low, the Raspberry Pi can send control commands to the LCD, such as change to a designated character position or clear the screen. This is mode is referred to as *writing to the instruction or command register.* When the register select pin is set high, the LCD controller goes into a data mode and accepts data to display on the screen.

The read/write pin #5 is grounded, because only data is to be written to the LCD for this setup.

The enable pin #6 is toggled as necessary to write data to the input registers that eventually display on the screen.

After you wire the LCD, push button switches, and potentiometer, you need to load a special Python library that allows the LCD display to work with the Raspberry Pi. This library was created by the clever folks at Adafruit, who have a lot of libraries to support all sorts of devices and sensors. The procedure I go through next is also applicable to loading most other specialty Adafruit libraries.

Loading the Adafruit LCD Library

You need the Git application to load the library because Adafruit uses github.com to store all of its libraries. Enter the following commands to install Git:

```
sudo apt-get update
sudo apt-get install git
```

Once Git is installed, you can now download the LCD library. This download process is called *cloning*. It results in new directory named Adafruit_Python_CharLCD created in your home directory. Enter this command:

```
sudo git clone git://github.com/adafruit/Adafruit_Python_CharLCD
```

The newly created directory contains all the required files for the next step, which is to set up the library. The setup process is long and involved; however, there is a simple setup script provided to automate the whole process. Enter the following commands to set up the library:

```
cd Adafruit_Python_CharLCD
sudo python setup.py install
```

Figure 4-13 shows the beginning and ending of the install process. Overall, there are more than 70 separate actions taking place in the installation, including downloading and building multiple dependencies.

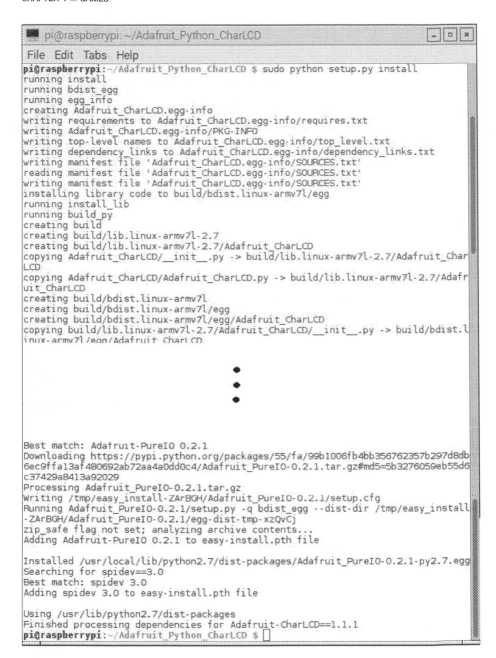

Figure 4-13. *LCD library installation script execution*

Now, you should test the both the hardware and the software installations to verify that everything is working properly.

LCD Test

The test program named char_lcd.py should be located in the examples subdirectory of the Adafruit_Python_CharLCD directory that was created after the Git clone operation completed. Go to the examples directory and enter this command:

```
python char_lcd.py
```

If everything is wired correctly, and all the libraries are installed properly, you should see the display as shown in Figure 4-14.

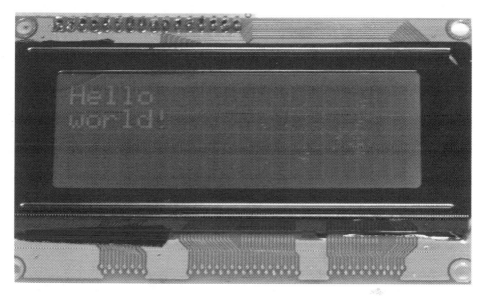

Figure 4-14. *Result of running the char_lcd.py program*

If you do not see this display, please recheck all the wiring because it is pretty easy to misplace a jumper insertion point or connect to the wrong pin on the Pi Cobbler or LCD module. As I mentioned earlier, most faults are normally wiring or interconnection mistakes.

Assuming that the LCD test was successful, it is now time to consider the main Nim program.

automated_nim.py

This program has been substantially changed from the previous Nim program because of the need to incorporate callback functions and LCD display routines. I have also incorporated some AI logic into the program: the computer opponent now uses the game theory *n mod 4 = 1* equation to help in its stick selection, in addition to using the random number generator when the optimal pick is not achievable.

automated_nim.py listing

```
!/usr/bin/python

# import statements
import random
import time
import Adafruit_CharLCD as LCD
import RPi.GPIO as GPIO

# Start Raspberry Pi configuration
# Raspberry Pi pin designations
lcd_rs        = 27
lcd_en        = 22
lcd_d4        = 25
lcd_d5        = 24
lcd_d6        = 23
lcd_d7        = 18
lcd_backlight =  4

# Define LCD column and row size for a 16x4 LCD.
lcd_columns = 16
lcd_rows    =  4

# Instantiate an LCD object
lcd = LCD.Adafruit_CharLCD(lcd_rs, lcd_en, lcd_d4, lcd_d5,
lcd_d6, lcd_d7, lcd_columns, lcd_rows, lcd_backlight)

# Print a two line welcoming message
lcd.message('Lets play nim\ncomputer vs human')

# Wait 5 seconds
time.sleep(5.0)

# Clear the screen
lcd.clear()

# Setup GPIO pins
# Set the BCM mode
GPIO.setmode(GPIO.BCM)

# Inputs
GPIO.setup(12, GPIO.IN, pull_up_down = GPIO.PUD_DOWN)
GPIO.setup(13, GPIO.IN, pull_up_down = GPIO.PUD_DOWN)
GPIO.setup(19, GPIO.IN, pull_up_down = GPIO.PUD_DOWN)
GPIO.setup(20, GPIO.IN, pull_up_down = GPIO.PUD_DOWN)
```

```python
# Create the global variables
global player
player = ""
global humanTurn
humanTurn = False
global stickNumber
stickNumber = 21
global humanPick
humanPick = 0
global gameover
gameover = False

# Set up the callback functions
def pickOne(channel):
    global humanTurn
    global humanPick
    humanPick = 1
    humanTurn = True

def pickTwo(channel):
    global humanTurn
    global humanPick
    humanPick = 2
    humanTurn = True

def pickThree(channel):
    global humanTurn
    global humanPick
    humanPick = 3
    humanTurn = True

def quit(channel):
    lcd.clear()
    exit()        # pin 20, immediate exit from the game

# Add event detection and callback assignments
GPIO.add_event_detect(12, GPIO.RISING, callback=pickOne)
GPIO.add_event_detect(13, GPIO.RISING, callback=pickTwo)
GPIO.add_event_detect(19, GPIO.RISING, callback=pickThree)
GPIO.add_event_detect(20, GPIO.RISING, callback=quit)

# random selection for the players
playerSelect = random.randint(0,1)
if playerSelect:
    humanTurn = True
    lcd.message('Human goes first')
    time.sleep(2)
    lcd.clear()
```

```python
else:
    humanTurn = False
    lcd.message('Computer goes first')
    time.sleep(2)
    lcd.clear()

# The AI portion
def computerMove():
    global stickNumber
    global humanTurn

    if (stickNumber-1) % 4 == 1:
        computerPick = 1
    elif (stickNumber-2) % 4 == 1:
        computerPick = 2
    elif (stickNumber-3) % 4 == 1:
        computerPick = 3
    else:
        computerPick = random.randint(1,3)

    if stickNumber >= 4:
        stickNumber -= computerPick
    elif (stickNumber==4) or (stickNumber==3) or
    (stickNumber==2):
        stickNumber = 1
    humanTurn = True

# The human portion
def humanMove():
    global humanPick
    global humanTurn
    global stickNumber
    while not humanPick:
        pass
    while (humanPick >= stickNumber):
        lcd.message('Number selected\n')
        lcd.message('is >= remaining\n')
        lcd.message('sticks')
    stickNumber -= humanPick
    humanTurn = False
    humanPick = 0
    lcd.clear()

def checkWinner():
    global gameover
    global player
    global stickNumber
```

```
        if stickNumber == 1:
            msg = player + ' wins!'
            lcd.message(msg)
            time.sleep(5)
            gameover = True

def resetGameover():
    global gameover
    global stickNumber
    gameover = False
    stickNumber = 21
    return gameover

# This module controls the overall game play
def game():
    global player
    global humanTurn
    global gameover
    global stickNumber
    while gameover == False:
        if humanTurn == True:
            lcd.message('human turn\n')
            msg = 'sticks left: ' + str(stickNumber) + '\n'
            lcd.message(msg)
            humanMove()
            msg = 'sticks left: ' + str(stickNumber)
            lcd.message(msg)
            time.sleep(2)
            checkWinner()
            lcd.clear()
        else:
            lcd.message('computer turn\n')
            computerMove()
            msg = 'sticks left: ' + str(stickNumber)
            lcd.message(msg)
            time.sleep(2)
            checkWinner()
            lcd.clear()

    if gameover == True:
            lcd.clear()
            playAgain()

# As the name suggests; play again?
def playAgain():
    global humanPick
    lcd.message('Play again?\n')
    lcd.message('1 = y, 2 = n')
```

```
    # This loop is needed to idle while waiting for a button
    press
    while humanPick == 0:
        pass
    if humanPick == 1:
        lcd.clear()
        resetGameover()
        game()
    elif humanPick == 2:
        lcd.clear()
        lcd.message('Thanks for \n')
        lcd.message('playing the game')
        time.sleep(5)
        lcd.clear()
        exit()

# This function call kicks off the game play
game()
```

I believe you will find that defeating the computer in this program is quite difficult, which differs sharply from the earlier, more naive Nim program. Figure 4-15 is a photograph of the LCD screen captured while I was playing a round with the computer.

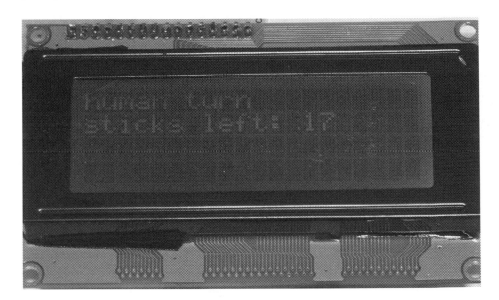

Figure 4-15. *LCD display during round play*

This automated Nim program is the final project in this chapter. There are more Python games readily available in the Jessie Linux distribution that you may wish to investigate. They can be found in the main X window GUI that is shown in Figure 4-16.

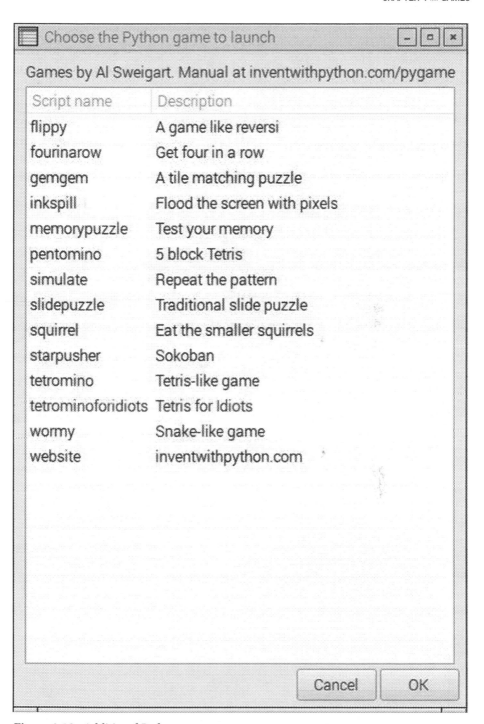

Figure 4-16. *Additional Python games*

These games are curtesy of Al Sweigert, whose website is at `www.inventwithpython.com`. At this website, you may freely download a 347-page e-book entitled *Making Games with Python & Pygame*, in which Al describes, in detail, how the games listed in Figure 4-16 function. It is highly recommended for those readers interested in taking the next step in Python game development beyond what I have discussed in this chapter.

Summary

Fairly simple game programs written in the Python language were the focus of this chapter. I presented several versions of two games—rock-paper-scissors and Nim—that progressed from relatively naive versions to more sophisticated versions incorporating AI into the computer opponent.

One of goals of this chapter was to show how fairly straightforward AI concepts can be implemented into classic game play where a human player opposes a computer program.

Another incidental goal was to demonstrate some hardware and software technology that included Python interrupts and to show how to use an LCD display with the Raspberry Pi.

CHAPTER 5

■ ■ ■

Fuzzy Logic System

This chapter is an extension of the fuzzy logic (FL) concepts first introduced in Chapter 2. I demonstrate two fuzzy logic projects. The first one deals with a common situation that we all occasionally encounter: how to compute a tip for a meal at a restaurant. The second demonstration is more complex and involves implementing a control system that uses FL as part of its control technology. Both demonstrations use Python with the pyFuzzy add-in library, which incorporates FL into the Python language. There are also a number of new FL topics that I need to discuss. I incorporate these new topics with the FL tipping demonstration to provide a better framework for the new concepts.

Before I begin the basic fuzzy logic system (FLS) section, it is important that you set up the Raspberry Pi so that you can load and run the FL demonstration programs.

Parts List

For the last demonstration, you need the parts listed in Table 5-1.

Table 5-1. *Parts List*

Description	Quantity	Remarks
Pi Cobbler	1	40-pin version, either T or DIP form factor acceptable
solderless breadboard	1	860 insertion points with power supply strips
jumper wires	1 package	Available from many sources
LED	3	Commodity item available from many sources
220Ω resistor	3	1/4 watt

Software Installation

First, you need Python 2.7, which should already be installed as part of the Jessie Linux distribution. You also need the numpy, scipy, matplotlib, and skfuzzy packages, which implement FL with Python and the plotting functions that create the visualizations.

© Donald J. Norris 2017
D. J. Norris, *Beginning Artificial Intelligence with the Raspberry Pi*,
DOI 10.1007/978-1-4842-2743-5_5

Enter the following commands at the command line to install the numpy, scipy, and matplotlib software:

```
sudo apt-get update
sudo apt-get install python-numpy
```

■ **Note** numpy may already be installed, so all that you see when this command is run is that the latest version is installed.

```
sudo apt-get install python-scipy
sudo apt-get install python-matplotlib
```

The skfuzzy software is somewhat more complex to install. You need to clone the software from the GitHub website; however, you need the Git application to do this. So install Git by entering this command:

```
sudo apt-get install git
```

Once Git is installed, you then need to clone the software by using this command:

```
sudo git clone https://github.com/scikit-fuzzy/scikit-fuzzy.git
```

The cloning operation automatically unzips all the skfuzzy software into a new subdirectory named scikit-fuzzy, located in the home directory. Enter the following commands to set up skfuzzy:

```
cd scikit-fuzzy
sudo python setup.py install
```

You will see a lot of dialog scroll by as the skfuzzy installation is in progress. After this installation, you should be all set to execute fuzzy Python scripts.

Basic FLS

Figure 5-1 shows all four of the principal components that make up a basic FLS.

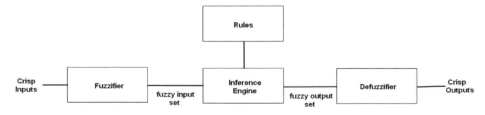

Figure 5-1. *Block diagram for a basic FLS*

These are the principal FLS components:

- *Fuzzifier*: The process in which a crisp set of input data is collected and converted to a fuzzy set using fuzzy linguistic variables, fuzzy linguistic terms, and membership functions.

- *Rules*: The expert knowledge collected and codified into the inference engine.

- *Inference engine*: Inferences are generated based upon a set of rules applied to the input fuzzy set.

- *Defuzzifier*: Crisp outputs are created based on the fuzzy set output from the inference engine.

Figure 5-1 may also be expressed as a series of steps or a logical algorithm that implements the FL process. I use this generic algorithm, shown in Table 5-2, to implement all of the chapter's FLS demonstration projects.

Table 5-2. *FL Algorithm*

Step #	Name	Description
1	Initialization	Define linguistic variables and terms
2	Initialization	Construct membership functions
3	Initialization	Build rule set
4	Fuzzification	Convert crisp input data into fuzzy set using membership functions
5	Inference	Evaluate fuzzy set according to rule set
6	Aggregation	Combine results from each rule evaluation
7	Defuzzification	Convert fuzzy set to crisp output values

Initialization: Define Linguistic Variables and Terms

The linguistic variables that I just introduced are values that represent the inputs and outputs of the system. They are not typically numerical values but instead are usually words, or even sentences, from a natural language, such as English. Linguistic variables are also decomposed into a set of linguistic terms.

Demo 5-1: Using FL to Calculate a Tip

In a tipping scenario, there are a number of input variables that go into the decision about how much to tip the server after completing a restaurant meal. Let us consider two primary inputs: *food quality* and *service quality*.

I do realize that many people, when determining a tip, differentiate the quality of the food from the quality of the service because the server has no control over food quality or preparation other than ensuring that the meal is still hot when served at the table. For this demonstration, however, I consider food quality as a valid input.

The only output variable is the *tip amount*, which is a percentage of the total bill.

Now, it is important to develop some linguistic terms that are appropriate to this situation.

Perhaps the easiest and most obvious way to classify food quality is to use the following terms:

- *great*

- *decent*

- *bad*

Likewise, classifying service quality uses these terms:

- *amazing*

- *acceptable*

- *poor*

The tip amount is also subject to fuzzy linguistic terms. These are the terms used for the tip amount:

- *low*

- *medium*

- *high*

▪ **Note**   From now on, I italicize linguistic variables to help differentiate them from ordinary words or terms.

There must be a numerical scale for users to rate both the service quality and the food quality. A scale of 0 to 10 is fine for most people, where 0 is the worst and 10 is the best. The tip output must also have a numerical scale. This is set at 0 to 26 to represent a suitable scale for normal tipping percentages. All of these numerical scales represent the crisp or non-fuzzy inputs or outputs to the membership functions, which are discussed in the next section.

Initialization: Construct Membership Functions

Membership functions are used in both FL fuzzification and defuzzification steps. These functions map non-fuzzy input values to fuzzy linguistic variables for fuzzification, and map fuzzy variables to non-fuzzy output values for defuzzification. Essentially, a membership function quantifies linguistic terms. Figure 5-2 shows the food quality membership function.

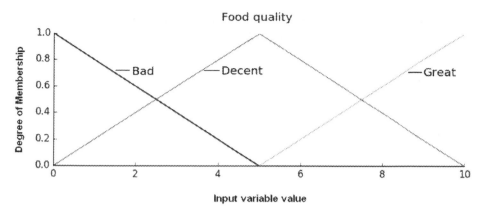

Figure 5-2. *Food quality membership function*

Figure 5-3 shows the service quality membership function.

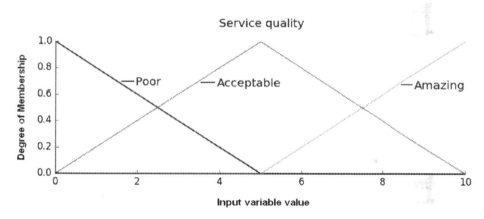

Figure 5-3. *Service quality membership function*

Finally, Figure 5-4 shows the tip amount membership function.

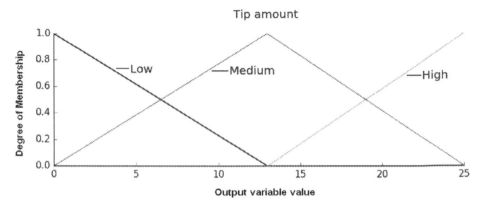

Figure 5-4. *Tip amount membership function*

I chose to use triangular shapes for the *decent, acceptable,* and *medium* linguistic terms. I use open-ended trapezoid shapes for the extremis *bad, great, poor, amazing, low,* and *high* terms. There are shapes other than triangular that are commonly used for membership functions, including

- Gaussian

- trapezoidal

- singleton

- piecewise linear

- sinusoidal

- exponential

The selection of an appropriate membership function shape is often based on the user's experience. I sometimes use the following analogy to help people understand membership functions. Suppose that you interviewed a large group of people on their preferences in determining an appropriate amount to tip, given the quality of the food and the service. As most of my readers understand, the resulting distribution of tip values is Gaussian, or normal in shape, which is the likely outcome of randomly interviewing large numbers of people. Any point on a Gaussian curve is the group probability for the corresponding measure of food and service quality. It is perfectly possible to use a Gaussian distribution shape as the membership function, as shown in Figure 5-5.

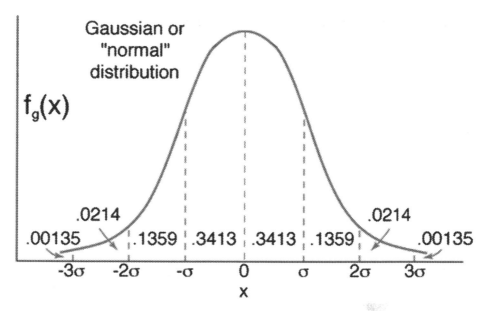

Figure 5-5. *Gaussian membership function*

The only problem with using this shape is that you are now dealing with the underlying mathematics behind the Gaussian curve, which rapidly becomes messy and cumbersome when trying to use it in an FL application. A normalized Gaussian equation is of the following form:

$$f(x) = ae^{-(x-b)^2/2c^2}$$ where a, b, and c are generalized parameters

The Gaussian curve is mostly likely a better model of human behavior and choice for this example, but using it is not worth the effort, as the AI concepts can be well understood using the much simpler triangular shape for the membership curves.

Membership Function Visualization

The main Python program also contains the code shown in Figures 5-2, 5-3, and 5-4, which should help greatly in understanding the membership functions. The following code segment generates these figures when the overall program is executed:

```
# Visualize the membership functions
fig, (ax0, ax1, ax2) = plt.subplots(nrows=3, figsize=(8, 9))

ax0.plot(x_qual, qual_lo, 'b', linewidth=1.5, label='Bad')
ax0.plot(x_qual, qual_md, 'g', linewidth=1.5, label='Decent')
ax0.plot(x_qual, qual_hi, 'r', linewidth=1.5, label='Great')
ax0.set_title('Food quality')
ax0.legend()
```

```
ax1.plot(x_serv, serv_lo, 'b', linewidth=1.5, label='Poor')
ax1.plot(x_serv, serv_md, 'g', linewidth=1.5, label='Acceptable')
ax1.plot(x_serv, serv_hi, 'r', linewidth=1.5, label='Amazing')
ax1.set_title('Service quality')
ax1.legend()

ax2.plot(x_tip, tip_lo, 'b', linewidth=1.5, label='Low')
ax2.plot(x_tip, tip_md, 'g', linewidth=1.5, label='Medium')
ax2.plot(x_tip, tip_hi, 'r', linewidth=1.5, label='High')
ax2.set_title('Tip amount')
ax2.legend()

# Turn off top/right axes
for ax in (ax0, ax1, ax2):
    ax.spines['top'].set_visible(False)
    ax.spines['right'].set_visible(False)
    ax.get_xaxis().tick_bottom()
    ax.get_yaxis().tick_left()

plt.tight_layout()
```

▓ **Note**   This code segment listing needs additional initialization before it can be run. That additional code is shown in the next code segment listing.

Initialization: Build Rule Set

An FLS also requires an expert system to generate the appropriate control actions based upon the fuzzified input variables. This expert system is of the form *if <condition> then <conclusion>*, which was discussed in Chapter 2. The following are the rules implemented for this FLS demonstration:

- if the food is *bad* or the service is *poor*, then the tip will be *low*

- if the service is *acceptable*, then the tip will be *medium*

- if the food is *great* or the service is *amazing*, then the tip will be *high*

These three rules apply to both the input variables and the output variable. I discuss how the rules are applied after the fuzzification section discussion, which is next. Fuzzification is step 4 in the FLS algorithm.

Fuzzification: Convert crisp input data a into fuzzy set using membership functions.

The membership function shapes and the rules for generating an appropriate tip percentage are set. The next thing is to show you how to fuzzify the crisp food and service ratings. The procedure is exactly the same for each of these crisp variables, because I chose the same membership function shapes for each one. That choice can vary and it is often common to have distinct and separate member functions in an FLS for different crisp variables.

The word *fuzzification* refers to the action of converting a crisp set of input data to a fuzzy set using fuzzy linguistic variables and terms along with membership functions. The actual fuzzification takes place in a set of functions that depend upon the following code segment, which creates the input and output variable ranges and the membership functions:

```
import numpy as np
import skfuzzy as fuzz
import matplotlib.pyplot as plt

# Generate universe variables
#   * food quality and service on subjective ranges, 0 to 10
#   * tip has a range of 0 to 25 in units of percentage points
x_qual = np.arange(0, 11, 1)
x_serv = np.arange(0, 11, 1)
x_tip  = np.arange(0, 26, 1)

# Generate fuzzy membership functions
qual_lo = fuzz.trimf(x_qual, [0, 0, 5])
qual_md = fuzz.trimf(x_qual, [0, 5, 10])
qual_hi = fuzz.trimf(x_qual, [5, 10, 10])
serv_lo = fuzz.trimf(x_serv, [0, 0, 5])
serv_md = fuzz.trimf(x_serv, [0, 5, 10])
serv_hi = fuzz.trimf(x_serv, [5, 10, 10])
tip_lo  = fuzz.trimf(x_tip,  [0, 0, 13])
tip_md  = fuzz.trimf(x_tip,  [0, 13, 25])
tip_hi  = fuzz.trimf(x_tip,  [13, 25, 25])
```

To test the algorithm, let's assume that the food quality was valued at 6.5 and the service at 9.8. The following code segment calculates the six degrees of membership for each input variable and membership function:

```
qual_level_lo = fuzz.interp_membership(x_qual, qual_lo, 6.5)
qual_level_md = fuzz.interp_membership(x_qual, qual_md, 6.5)
qual_level_hi = fuzz.interp_membership(x_qual, qual_hi, 6.5)

serv_level_lo = fuzz.interp_membership(x_serv, serv_lo, 9.8)
serv_level_md = fuzz.interp_membership(x_serv, serv_md, 9.8)
serv_level_hi = fuzz.interp_membership(x_serv, serv_hi, 9.8)
```

The fuzz.interp_membership(a, b, c) function is part of the skfuzzy library that you installed earlier. This is an interpolation function that uses the membership function range (a) and linear shape (b) along with the crisp input value (c) to calculate the degree of membership for that particular group.

It is time to apply the rules once the degree of membership values has been determined. This is step 5 of the algorithm or inference.

Inference: Evaluate Fuzzy Set According to Rule Set

Applying the *if … then* inferential rules is rather easy because all you must do is focus on how the linguistic terms are related. For instance, this is rule 1:

> if the food is *bad* or the service is *poor*, then the tip will be *low*

The conjunction between the *bad* and *poor* linguistic terms is the or operator. In fuzzy logic, using an or operator is equivalent to selecting the maximum of the two membership values representing the respective linguistic terms. If you refer back to Figures 5-2 and 5-3, you quickly see that there are no intersections with either the *bad* and *poor* membership functions for the assumed crisp input variable values, so the result of applying this rule must be 0. Connecting the combined *bad* and *poor* linguistic terms to the *low* tip membership function is trivial because the value is still 0 more than the universe of applicable values.

Applying rule 2 is a bit different. This is rule 2:

> If the service is *acceptable*, then the tip will be *medium*.

In this case, only the service membership function is considered for input. Referring back to Figure 5-3, you see that applying a crisp input variable value of 9.8 to the *acceptable* membership group results in a degree of membership of approximately 0.02. The and operator is then applied to the *acceptable* service and *medium* tip membership functions, which results in the minimum operation being applied to both membership functions. This minimum operation effectively "flattops" the membership functions, resulting in a new shape, as shown in Figure 5-6. Note also that the input range has been expanded to accommodate the tip value range, which is 2.5 times the input service range. Notice also that the slopes of the lines at the ends of the membership function are lessened due to the expanded x-axis scale.

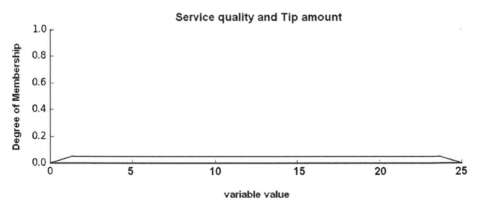

Figure 5-6. *Service and tip membership functions after rule 2 is applied*

Rule 3 is the last to be applied:

If the food is *great* or the service is *amazing*, then the tip will be *high*.

The or operation is applied for rule 3, just as it was for rule 1. But in this case, there are definite intersections with the *great* and *amazing* membership functions. Figure 5-7 shows both the food and the service membership functions after being flattop but before being combined.

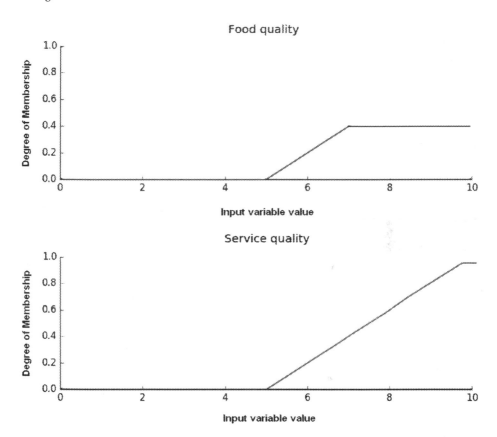

Figure 5-7. *Flattop food and service membership functions*

Figure 5-8 shows the *great, amazing,* and *high* membership functions combined. It should not be a big surprise that the shape is roughly the same as the unmodified membership functions because the or operation commands the maximum value and the two unmodified membership shapes are exactly the same. The shape also remains unchanged after the combined membership function is "anded" with the *high* tip membership function, although the range of x-axis values changes to 0 to 25 to accommodate the tip range, as done with the previous rule, and the flattop region expands a bit due to the x-axis expansion.

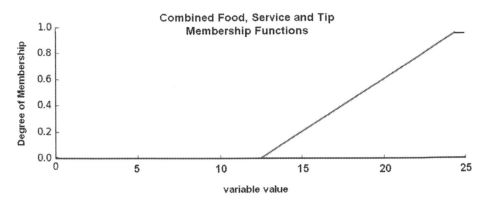

Figure 5-8. *Combined great, amazing, and high membership functions*

The following code segment applies the rules and combines the membership functions:

```
# Apply rule 1
# The 'or' operator means to take the maximum by using the
'np.max' function

active_rule1 = np.fmax(qual_level_lo, serv_level_lo)

# Next, flattop the corresponding output
# Combine with low tip membership function using `np.fmin`

tip_activation_lo = np.fmin(active_rule1, tip_lo)  # Removed
entirely to 0

# Rule 2  connects acceptable service to medium tipping
# No flat topping needed as there is only one input membership
function
# However, the tip membership must be combined using an 'and'
or 'np.fmin' function

tip_activation_md = np.fmin(serv_level_md, tip_md)

# Rule 3 connects amazing service or great food with high
tipping

active_rule3 = np.fmax(qual_level_hi, serv_level_hi)
tip_activation_hi = np.fmin(active_rule3, tip_hi)
```

At this point, all the rules have been applied to the output membership functions. It now remains to combine them all. In FL terminology, this is known as *aggregation*, which is step 6 in the FLS algorithm.

Aggregation: Combine Results from Each Rule Evaluation

Aggregation is normally done using the maximum operator. The following statement does the aggregation:

```
# Aggregate all three output membership functions together

aggregated = np.fmax(tip_activation_lo, np.fmax(tip_
activation_md, tip_activation_hi))
```

Figure 5-9 shows the final combined membership functions after the aggregation is complete.

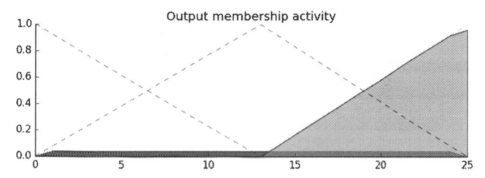

Figure 5-9. *Membership functions after aggregation*

There is only one more step in the FLS algorithm: defuzzification.

Defuzzification: Convert Fuzzy Set to Crisp Output Values

Defuzzification is the process where we return from the fuzzy world to the real world and create an output that can be acted upon, which in this case is a tip percentage. There are a variety of mathematical techniques available for defuzzification, including

- centroid

- bisector

- mean

- smallest of maximum

- largest of maximum

- weighted average

123

Figure 5-10 demonstrates how values for each method are chosen using an arbitrary aggregation membership function.

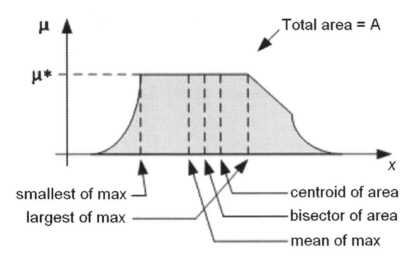

Figure 5-10. *Various defuzzification methods*

Centroid defuzzification is the most commonly used method because it is very accurate. It calculates the center of the area under the curve of membership function. This can require significant computational processing for complex membership functions. The centroid equation is

$$z_0 = \int \mu_i(x)x\,dx / \int \mu_i(x)\,dx$$

where z_0 is the defuzzified output, μ_i represents a membership function, and x is the output variable.

Bisector defuzzification uses vertical lines that divide the area under the membership curve into two equal areas:

$$\int_a^z \mu_A(x)\,dx = \int_z^\beta \mu_A(x)\,dx$$

The mean of maximum (MOM) defuzzification method uses the average value of the aggregated membership function outputs.

$$z_0 = \sum_{i=1}^n \frac{\omega_i}{n}$$

The smallest of maximum defuzzification method uses the minimum value of the aggregated membership function outputs.

$$z_0 \ member \ of \ \{x \mid \mu(x) = \min \ \mu(\omega)\}$$

The largest of maximum defuzzification method uses the maximum value of the aggregated membership function outputs.

$$z_0 \ member \ of \ \{x \mid \mu(x) = \max \ \mu(\omega)\}$$

The weighted average defuzzification method calculates the weighted sum of each fuzzy set. The crisp value is set according to the weighted values and the degree of membership for fuzzy output, as determined by the following formula:

$$z_0 = \frac{\sum \mu(x)_i \, W_i}{\sum \mu(x)_i}$$

μ_i is the degree of membership in output singleton i and W_i is the fuzzy output weight value for the output singleton i.

Next, I discuss how the centroid method is implemented for this project. The following code snippet calculates the centroid defuzzification value:

```
# Calculate defuzzified result
tip = fuzz.defuzz(x_tip, aggregated, 'centroid')

# This value is needed for the plot
tip_activation = fuzz.interp_membership(x_tip, aggregated, tip)
```

This section completes the tipping fuzzy logic project. All that's left to do is load and run the following code, which is named tipping.py. Enter the following to run the program:

```
sudo python tipping.py
```

You need to close each plot after it appears to go on to the next plot.

tipping.py listing

```
import numpy as np
import skfuzzy as fuzz
import matplotlib.pyplot as plt

# Generate universe variables
#   * Quality and service on subjective ranges [0, 10]
#   * Tip has a range of [0, 25] in units of percentage points
```

```
x_qual = np.arange(0, 11, 1)
x_serv = np.arange(0, 11, 1)
x_tip  = np.arange(0, 26, 1)

# Generate fuzzy membership functions
qual_lo = fuzz.trimf(x_qual, [0, 0, 5])
qual_md = fuzz.trimf(x_qual, [0, 5, 10])
qual_hi = fuzz.trimf(x_qual, [5, 10, 10])
serv_lo = fuzz.trimf(x_serv, [0, 0, 5])
serv_md = fuzz.trimf(x_serv, [0, 5, 10])
serv_hi = fuzz.trimf(x_serv, [5, 10, 10])
tip_lo = fuzz.trimf(x_tip, [0, 0, 13])
tip_md = fuzz.trimf(x_tip, [0, 13, 25])
tip_hi = fuzz.trimf(x_tip, [13, 25, 25])

# Visualize these universes and membership functions
fig, (ax0, ax1, ax2) = plt.subplots(nrows=3, figsize=(8, 9))

ax0.plot(x_qual, qual_lo, 'b', linewidth=1.5, label='Bad')
ax0.plot(x_qual, qual_md, 'g', linewidth=1.5, label='Decent')
ax0.plot(x_qual, qual_hi, 'r', linewidth=1.5, label='Great')
ax0.set_title('Food quality')
ax0.legend()

ax1.plot(x_serv, serv_lo, 'b', linewidth=1.5, label='Poor')
ax1.plot(x_serv, serv_md, 'g', linewidth=1.5,
label='Acceptable')
ax1.plot(x_serv, serv_hi, 'r', linewidth=1.5, label='Amazing')
ax1.set_title('Service quality')
ax1.legend()

ax2.plot(x_tip, tip_lo, 'b', linewidth=1.5, label='Low')
ax2.plot(x_tip, tip_md, 'g', linewidth=1.5, label='Medium')
ax2.plot(x_tip, tip_hi, 'r', linewidth=1.5, label='High')
ax2.set_title('Tip amount')
ax2.legend()

# Turn off top/right axes
for ax in (ax0, ax1, ax2):
    ax.spines['top'].set_visible(False)
    ax.spines['right'].set_visible(False)
    ax.get_xaxis().tick_bottom()
    ax.get_yaxis().tick_left()

plt.tight_layout()
plt.show()
```

```python
# Calculate degrees of membership
# The exact values 6.5 and 9.8 do not exist on our universes
# Use fuzz.interp_membership to determine values

qual_level_lo = fuzz.interp_membership(x_qual, qual_lo, 6.5)
qual_level_md = fuzz.interp_membership(x_qual, qual_md, 6.5)
qual_level_hi = fuzz.interp_membership(x_qual, qual_hi, 6.5)

serv_level_lo = fuzz.interp_membership(x_serv, serv_lo, 9.8)
serv_level_md = fuzz.interp_membership(x_serv, serv_md, 9.8)
serv_level_hi = fuzz.interp_membership(x_serv, serv_hi, 9.8)

# Apply the rules, Rule 1 concerns bad food OR service.
# The OR operator means we take the maximum of these two.

active_rule1 = np.fmax(qual_level_lo, serv_level_lo)

# Now we apply this by clipping the top off the corresponding output
# membership function with `np.fmin`

tip_activation_lo = np.fmin(active_rule1, tip_lo)  # removed
entirely to 0

# Rule 2 is a straight if ... then construction
# if acceptable service then medium tipping. This is an AND operator
# We take the minimum for an AND operator

tip_activation_md = np.fmin(serv_level_md, tip_md)

# For rule 3 we connect high service OR high food with high tipping
active_rule3 = np.fmax(qual_level_hi, serv_level_hi)
tip_activation_hi = np.fmin(active_rule3, tip_hi)
tip0 = np.zeros_like(x_tip)

# Visualize these rule applications

fig, ax0 = plt.subplots(figsize=(8, 3))
ax0.fill_between(x_tip, tip0, tip_activation_lo, facecolor='b',
alpha=0.7)
ax0.plot(x_tip, tip_lo, 'b', linewidth=0.5, linestyle='--', )
ax0.fill_between(x_tip, tip0, tip_activation_md, facecolor='g',
alpha=0.7)
ax0.plot(x_tip, tip_md, 'g', linewidth=0.5, linestyle='--')
ax0.fill_between(x_tip, tip0, tip_activation_hi, facecolor='r',
alpha=0.7)
ax0.plot(x_tip, tip_hi, 'r', linewidth=0.5, linestyle='--')
ax0.set_title('Output membership activity')
```

```
# Turn off top/right axes

for ax in (ax0,):
    ax.spines['top'].set_visible(False)
    ax.spines['right'].set_visible(False)
    ax.get_xaxis().tick_bottom()
    ax.get_yaxis().tick_left()

plt.tight_layout()
plt.show()

# Aggregate all three output membership functions together
# This aggregation uses OR operators, hence the maximum is found

aggregated = np.fmax(tip_activation_lo, np.fmax(tip_activation_
md, tip_activation_hi))

# Calculate defuzzified result using the method of centroids
tip = fuzz.defuzz(x_tip, aggregated, 'centroid')

# display the tip percentage on the console
print tip

# Value needed for the next plot
tip_activation = fuzz.interp_membership(x_tip, aggregated, tip)

# Visualize the final results
fig, ax0 = plt.subplots(figsize=(8, 3))

ax0.plot(x_tip, tip_lo, 'b', linewidth=0.5, linestyle='--', )
ax0.plot(x_tip, tip_md, 'g', linewidth=0.5, linestyle='--')
ax0.plot(x_tip, tip_hi, 'r', linewidth=0.5, linestyle='--')
ax0.fill_between(x_tip, tip0, aggregated, facecolor='Orange',
alpha=0.7)
ax0.plot([tip, tip], [0, tip_activation], 'k', linewidth=1.5,
alpha=0.9)
ax0.set_title('Aggregated membership and result (line)')

# Turn off top/right axes

for ax in (ax0,):
    ax.spines['top'].set_visible(False)
    ax.spines['right'].set_visible(False)
    ax.get_xaxis().tick_bottom()
    ax.get_yaxis().tick_left()

plt.tight_layout()
plt.show()
```

Figure 5-11 is the first display shown on the monitor. It shows all three membership functions: food quality, service quality, and tip amount.

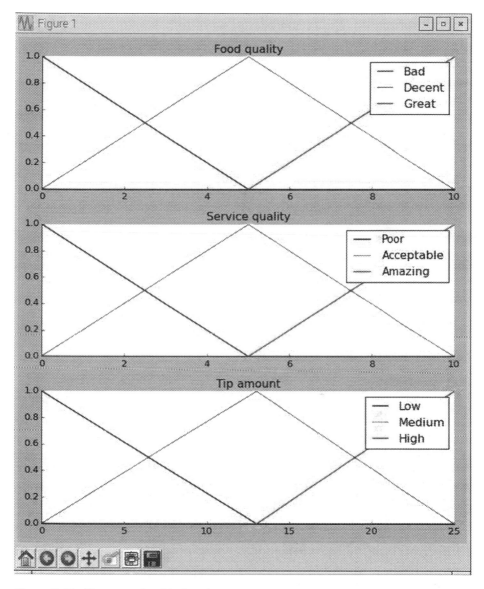

Figure 5-11. *Three membership functions*

Figure 5-12 shows the next display: the combined membership functions after all the rules are applied, and all the input and output membership are functions connected.

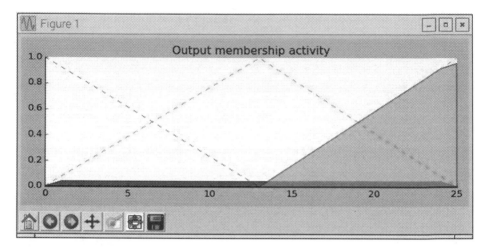

Figure 5-12. *Membership functions after rules application*

Figure 5-13 shows the next display: the post aggregation results for all the processed membership functions. In addition, there is a line indicating the crisp output for the tip percentage resulting from the defuzzification process.

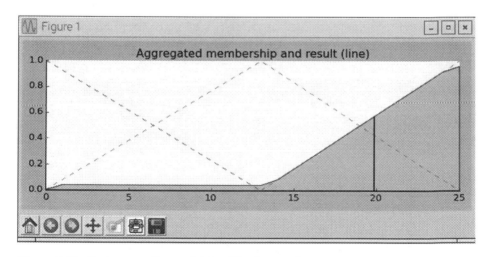

Figure 5-13. *Post aggregation and defuzzification results*

Finally, Figure 5-14 shows the text display for the tip percentage, which comes from a print statement within the program.

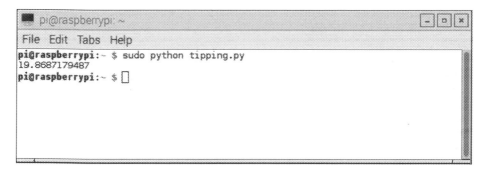

■ pi@raspberrypi: ~
```
File  Edit  Tabs  Help
pi@raspberrypi:~ $ sudo python tipping.py
19.8687179487
pi@raspberrypi:~ $ []
```

Figure 5-14. *Print statement for tip percentage*

Demo 5-2: Modifications to the tipping.py Program

In this section, I discuss modifications to the Python program to make it easier to use and significantly more portable. The main modification is to query the user about the food and service quality, rather than have static values, which was the case for the initial project. This modification is fairly easy and consists of creating two variables to hold the food and service quality levels, and two input statements to get the data into the program. The additional or modified code is as follows:

```
food_qual = raw_input('Rate the food quality, 0 to 10')
service_qual = raw_input('Rate the service quality, 0 to 10')

qual_level_lo = fuzz.interp_membership(x_qual, qual_lo,
float(food_qual))
qual_level_md = fuzz.interp_membership(x_qual, qual_md,
float(food_qual))
qual_level_hi = fuzz.interp_membership(x_qual, qual_hi,
float(food_qual))

serv_level_lo = fuzz.interp_membership(x_serv, serv_lo,
float(service_qual))
serv_level_md = fuzz.interp_membership(x_serv, serv_md,
float(service_qual))
serv_level_hi = fuzz.interp_membership(x_serv, serv_hi,
float(service_qual))
```

This modified code takes care of prompting the user to enter food and service quality ratings.

The second modification is to make the whole system completely portable, somewhat akin to the Nim game configuration discussed in the previous chapter. I would use an LCD display to show the user prompts to enter the food and the service quality ratings, and then show the resulting tip percentage. How cool would it be to have a portable fuzzy logic system that computes tip percentages to show off to your relatives and friends? The LCD display interface and software was discussed in the previous chapter. The only new required technology is a USB numeric key pad for the user to enter the quality ratings. Figure 5-15 shows a very inexpensive USB keypad that I experimented with for this modification. I am not going into all the details on how to complete this portable system, since I am reasonably confident that most of you can adapt the previous LCD discussions to this new application. Just remember, there is no longer a need for all the visualization code, which considerably reduces the size of the main program.

Figure 5-15. *Inexpensive USB numeric keypad*

This section completes the first project. It is now time to consider a more complex fuzzy logic controller project.

Demo 5-3: FLS Heating and Cooling System

I start this project assuming that you have read and understood the first project in the chapter. There should be no need to go into any detailed discussion regarding FL concepts. I simply follow the FLS algorithm in developing this project. In addition, I do not use any of the visualization code in this project because it already served its purpose in the previous project. Interested readers can easily reintroduce the code to obtain the plots to see how this system functions.

Consider a heating, ventilation, and cooling system (HVAC) that, practically speaking, is a heat pump that acts as either an air conditioner or a heater. Figure 5-16 shows a block diagram of such a system. This configuration is also known in control terminology as a *closed-loop system*.

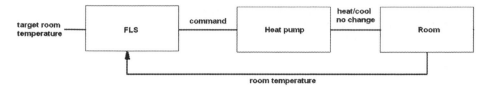

Figure 5-16. *HVAC closed-loop system*

Let's define temperature (t) as a crisp input variable to represent the room temperature that is being heated or cooled. Generally, people use the terms *hot* and *cold* as room temperature qualifiers. These terms, as well as related ones, can be developed into a set of linguistic terms, such that

```
T(t) = { cold, comfortable, hot }
```

This expression for *T(t)* represents a decomposition function for the input variable t. Each member of this linguistic decomposition set represents or is associated with a numerical temperature range. For instance, *cold* could be a range of 40°F to 60°F, while *hot* might be a range of 70°F to 90°F. Other linguistic terms could easily fill in the intervening ranges if it was decided that 20°F was an appropriate interval value.

In addition, there is another input named *target temperature*, which is set by the people who occupy the room. This is analogous to setting a room thermostat.

Figure 5-17 shows the membership functions that were created to map the crisp, non-fuzzy, room and target temperature values to the corresponding fuzzy linguistic terms. Only one set of membership functions is shown because they are common to both the room and target temperature input variables.

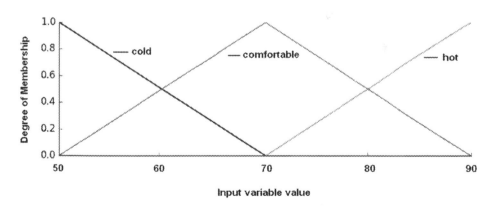

Figure 5-17. *Room and target temperature membership functions*

In this case, any given room temperature can belong to one or two groups, depending upon its values. Figure 5-18 shows that a room temperature of 65°F has a membership value of 0.5 in the *comfortable* membership function, as well as 0.5 in the

133

cold membership function. A room temperature of exactly 70°F has a membership value of 1.0 and is only in the *comfortable* membership function.

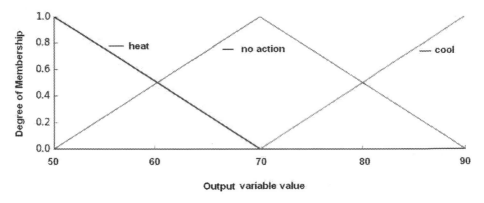

Figure 5-18. *HVAC control membership functions*

The HVAC controller also needs a set of membership functions to take based on command results. Figure 5-18 shows the set of membership functions for HVAC control. Note that it has the same shapes and output variable range as the input variables.

The following are some example rules to determine the control commands based on room and target temperatures:

- if (room temperature is *cold*) and (target temperature is *comfortable*), then the command is heat

- if (room temperature is *hot*) and (target temperature is *comfortable*), then the command is cool

- if (room temperature is *comfortable*) and (target temperature is *comfortable*), then the command is no change

The precise command actions to be taken using a preset target temperature and measured room temperature have to be determined by a human expert and codified in the rules database. Table 5-3 is a matrix detailing the precise control commands for all combinations of linguistic variables for both room and target temperatures.

Table 5-3. *Matrix of Command Actions for Room and Target Temperature Linguistic Variables*

Room Temperature	Target Temperature		
	cold	*comfortable*	*hot*
cold	no change	heat	heat
comfortable	cool	no change	heat
hot	cool	cool	no change

There are six rules required to accommodate all the combinations of the intersecting room temperature and target temperature linguistic terms that require action. The rules for no change are ignored. These are the rules:

- if room temp is *cold* and target temp is *comfortable,* then the command is heat

- if room temp is *cold* and target temp is *hot,* then the command is heat

- if room temp is *comfortable* and target temp is *cold,* then the command is cool

- if room temp is *comfortable* and target temp is *heat,* then the command is heat

- if room temp is *hot* and target temp is *cold,* then the command is cool

- if room temp is *hot* and target temp is *comfortable,* then the command is cool

Now that the set of rules have been created, it is time to discuss fuzzification.

Fuzzification

The following code segment sets up the input variable ranges and the membership functions:

```
import numpy as np
import skfuzzy as fuzz

# Generate universe variables
#   * room and target temperature range is 50 to 90
#   * same for the output control variable
x_room_temp   = np.arange(50, 91, 1)
x_target_temp = np.arange(50, 91, 1)
x_control_temp = np.arange(50, 91, 1)

# Generate fuzzy membership functions
room_temp_lo    = fuzz.trimf(x_qual, [50, 50, 70])
room_temp_md    = fuzz.trimf(x_qual, [50, 70, 90])
room_temp_hi    = fuzz.trimf(x_qual, [70, 90, 90])
target_temp_lo  = fuzz.trimf(x_serv, [50, 50, 70])
target_temp_md  = fuzz.trimf(x_serv, [50, 70, 90])
target_temp_hi  = fuzz.trimf(x_serv, [50, 90, 90])
control_temp_lo = fuzz.trimf(x_tip,  [50, 50, 70])
control_temp_md = fuzz.trimf(x_tip,  [50, 70, 90])
control_temp_hi = fuzz.trimf(x_tip,  [70, 90, 90])
```

The next step in the algorithm is to determine the fuzzified values based on values for room and target temperatures. In this project, the user is asked to input both values. In a real-word FL control system, the target temperature is manually set, while the room temperature is determined with a sensor. However, to simplify things, both inputs are manually set. The following code accepts user input and fuzzifies those inputs:

```
# Get user inputs
room_temp = raw_input('Enter room temperature 50 to 90')
target_temp = raw_input('Enter target temperature 50 to 90')

# Calculate degrees of membership
room_temp_level_lo = fuzz.interp_membership(x_room_temp,
room_temp_lo, float(room_temp))
room_temp_level_md = fuzz.interp_membership(x_room_temp,
room_temp_md, float(room_temp))
room_temp_level_hi = fuzz.interp_membership(x_room_temp,
room_temp_hi, float(room_temp))

target_temp_level_lo = fuzz.interp_membership(x_target_temp,
target_temp_lo, float(target_temp))
target_temp_level_md = fuzz.interp_membership(x_target_temp,
target_temp_md, float(target_temp))
target_temp_level_hi = fuzz.interp_membership(x_target_temp,
Target_temp_hi, float(target_temp))
```

Now on to the inference step where all the rules are applied and membership functions combined.

Inference

The following code segment applies the six rules and combines all the membership functions:

```
# Apply rule 1:  if room_temp is cold and target temp is
comfortable then command is heat
# The 'and' operator means to take the minimum by using the
'np.fmin' function
active_rule1 = np.fmin(room_temp_level_lo, target_temp_level_md)
# Combine with hi control membership function using `np.fmin`
control_activation_1 = np.fmin(active_rule1, control_temp_hi)

# Next go through all five remaining rules
#Apply rule 2: if room_temp is cold and target temp is hot then
command is heat
active_rule2 = np.fmin(room_temp_level_lo, target_temp_level_hi)
# Combine with hi control membership function using `np.fmin`
control_activation_2 = np.fmin(active_rule2, control_temp_hi)
```

```
#Apply rule 3: if room_temp is comfortable and target temp is
cold then command is cool
active_rule3 = np.fmin(room_temp_level_md, target_temp_level_lo)
# Combine with lo control membership function using `np.fmin`
control_activation_3 = np.fmin(active_rule3, control_temp_lo)
```

```
#Apply rule 4: if room_temp is comfortable and target temp is
heat then command is heat
active_rule4 = np.fmin(room_temp_level_md, target_temp_level_hi)
# Combine with hi control membership function using `np.fmin`
control_activation_4 = np.fmin(active_rule4, control_temp_hi)
```

```
#Apply rule 5: if room_temp is hot and target temp is cold then
command is cool
active_rule5 = np.fmin(room_temp_level_hi, target_temp_level_lo)
# Combine with lo control membership function using `np.fmin`
control_activation_5 = np.fmin(active_rule5, control_temp_lo)
```

```
#Apply rule 6: if room_temp is hot and target temp is
comfortable then command is cool
active_rule6 = np.fmin(room_temp_level_hi, target_temp_level_md)
# Combine with lo control membership function using `np.fmin`
control_activation_6 = np.fmin(active_rule6, control_temp_lo)
```

This section covered applying rules and combining sets. The next step is aggregation.

Aggregation

The aggregation statement is long because of the six control activation values.

```
aggregated = np.fmax(control_activation_1, control_activation_2,
                     control_activation_3, control_activation_4,
                     control_activation_5, control_activation_6)
```

It is time for the defuzzification once the aggregation is completed.

Defuzzification

The centroid method will be applied for this project as it was done for the previous project.

```
# Calculate defuzzified result using the method of centroids
control_value = fuzz.defuzz(x_control_temp, aggregated,
'centroid')
```

Now, simply display the crisp output value.

```
print control_value
```

The following is the complete listing for the hvac.py program.

```python
import numpy as np
import skfuzzy as fuzz

# Generate universe variables
#   * room and target temperature range is 50 to 90
#   * same for the output control variable
x_room_temp    = np.arange(50, 91, 1)
x_target_temp  = np.arange(50, 91, 1)
x_control_temp = np.arange(50, 91, 1)

# Generate fuzzy membership functions
room_temp_lo     = fuzz.trimf(x_room_temp,   [50, 50, 70])
room_temp_md     = fuzz.trimf(x_room_temp,   [50, 70, 90])
room_temp_hi     = fuzz.trimf(x_room_temp,   [70, 90, 90])
target_temp_lo   = fuzz.trimf(x_target_temp, [50, 50, 70])
target_temp_md   = fuzz.trimf(x_target_temp, [50, 70, 90])
target_temp_hi   = fuzz.trimf(x_target_temp, [50, 90, 90])
control_temp_lo  = fuzz.trimf(x_control_temp,[50, 50, 70])
control_temp_md  = fuzz.trimf(x_control_temp,[50, 70, 90])
control_temp_hi  = fuzz.trimf(x_control_temp,[70, 90, 90])

# Get user inputs
room_temp = raw_input('Enter room temperature 50 to 90: ')
target_temp = raw_input('Enter target temperature 50 to 90: ')

# Calculate degrees of membership
room_temp_level_lo = fuzz.interp_membership(x_room_temp,
room_temp_lo, float(room_temp))
room_temp_level_md = fuzz.interp_membership(x_room_temp,
room_temp_md, float(room_temp))
room_temp_level_hi = fuzz.interp_membership(x_room_temp,
room_temp_hi, float(room_temp))

target_temp_level_lo = fuzz.interp_membership(x_target_temp,
target_temp_lo, float(target_temp))
target_temp_level_md = fuzz.interp_membership(x_target_temp,
target_temp_md, float(target_temp))
target_temp_level_hi = fuzz.interp_membership(x_target_temp,
target_temp_hi, float(target_temp))

# Apply all six rules
# rule 1:  if room_temp is cold and target temp is comfortable
then command is heat
active_rule1 = np.fmin(room_temp_level_lo, target_temp_level_md)
control_activation_1 = np.fmin(active_rule1, control_temp_hi)
```

```
# rule 2: if room_temp is cold and target temp is hot then
command is heat
active_rule2 = np.fmin(room_temp_level_lo, target_temp_level_hi)
control_activation_2 = np.fmin(active_rule2, control_temp_hi)

# rule 3: if room_temp is comfortable and target temp is cold
then command is cool
active_rule3 = np.fmin(room_temp_level_md, target_temp_level_lo)
control_activation_3 = np.fmin(active_rule3, control_temp_lo)

# rule 4: if room_temp is comfortable and target temp is heat
then command is heat
active_rule4 = np.fmin(room_temp_level_md, target_temp_level_hi)
control_activation_4 = np.fmin(active_rule4, control_temp_hi)

# rule 5: if room_temp is hot and target temp is cold then
command is cool
active_rule5 = np.fmin(room_temp_level_hi, target_temp_level_lo)
control_activation_5 = np.fmin(active_rule5, control_temp_lo)

# rule 6: if room_temp is hot and target temp is comfortable then
command is cool
active_rule6 = np.fmin(room_temp_level_hi, target_temp_level_md)
control_activation_6 = np.fmin(active_rule6, control_temp_lo)

# Aggregate all six output membership functions together
# Combine outputs to ease the complexity as fmax() only as two
args
c1 = np.fmax(control_activation1, control_activation2)
c2 = np.fmax(control_activation3, control_activation4)
c3 = np.fmax(control_activation5, control_activation6)
c4 = np.fmax(c2,c3)
aggregated = np.fmax(c1, c4)

# Calculate defuzzified result using the method of centroids
control_value = fuzz.defuzz(x_control_temp, aggregated,
'centroid')

# Display the crisp output value
print control_value
```

Testing the Control Program

Tables 5-4 through 5-8 show the results of testing the control program throughout a representative range of room and target temperature inputs.

Table 5-4. *Target Set at 50*

Room Temperature	Target Temperature	Command Output
51*	51*	70.00
60	50	57.78
70	50	56.67
80	50	57.78
90	50	56.67

Table 5-5. *Target Set at 60*

Room Temperature	Target Temperature	Command Output
50	60	82.22
60	60	70.00
70	60	66.40
80	60	66.40
90	60	57.78

Table 5-6. *Target Set at 70*

Room Temperature	Target Temperature	Command Output
50	70	83.33
60	70	82.22
70	70	82.22
80	70	70.00
90	70	56.67

Table 5-7. *Target Set at 80*

Room Temperature	Target Temperature	Command Output
50	80	83.33
60	80	82.22
70	80	83.33
80	80	70.00
90	80	57.78

Table 5-8. *Target Set at 90*

Room Temperature	Target Temperature	Command Output
50	90	83.33
60	90	82.22
70	90	83.33
80	90	82.22
89*	89*	70.00

■ **Note**   The temperatures with an asterisk (*) were slightly shifted because the defuzzification method throws an error when the temperatures match and are at the extremes of the variable range.

I carefully studied the results and derived these conclusions from the test data:

- A command value of approximately 65 to 75 means no change

- A command value of approximately 82 to 83 means that heating is required

- A command value of approximately 56 to 65 means that cooling is required

The "no change" range was approximately ±4 around the target temperature. This is actually not too bad of a finding since it prevents the system from unnecessary operation while still achieving the majority "opinion" for the desired room temperature.

Demo 5-4: Modifications to the HVAC Program

For this demo, I made a simple modification to the control program: one of three LEDs lights up, based on whether heating, cooling, or no change is determined from user input. The following code is appended to the prior listing, except the additional import and configuration statements should be placed at the start of the program, just as I did with previous programs that used LEDs. I provide comments that indicate the GPIO pins used in this modification. They are the same ones that were used in the prs.py game, so use the LED interconnection diagram shown in that project.

```
# Include the following at the beginning of the hvac.py program
import RPi.GPIO as GPIO
import time

# Setup GPIO pins
# Set the BCM mode
GPIO.setmode(GPIO.BCM)
```

```
# Outputs
GPIO.setup( 4, GPIO.OUT) # heat command
GPIO.setup(17, GPIO.OUT) # cool command
GPIO.setup(27, GPIO.OUT) # no change command

# Ensure all LEDs are off to start
GPIO.output( 4, GPIO.LOW)
GPIO.output(17, GPIO.LOW)
GPIO.output(27, GPIO.LOW)

# The following should be appended to the existing code
if control_value > 65 and control_value < 75: # no change
    GPIO.output(27, GPIO.HIGH)
    time.sleep(5)
    GPIO.output(27, GPIO.LOW)
elif control_value > 82 and control_value < 84: # heat
    GPIO.output(4, GPIO.HIGH)
    time.sleep(5)
    GPIO.output(4, GPIO.LOW)
elif control_value > 56 and control_value < 68: # cool
    GPIO.output(17, GPIO.HIGH)
    time.sleep(5)
    GPIO.output(17, GPIO.LOW)
else:
    print 'strange value calculated'
# This next statement used in debugging phase
print 'Thats all folks'
```

hvac_led.py—the complete program with the LED modifications—is available on this book's website. Figure 5-19 shows the Raspberry Pi physical setup with the three control LEDs connected to a solderless breadboard.

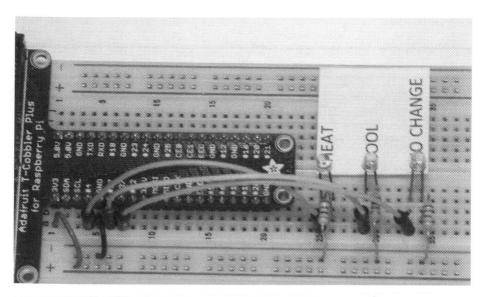

Figure 5-19. *Physical setup*

Summary

This chapter focused on fuzzy logic, which is a very clever approach to handling non-precise values that are present in almost every human situation. My approach was to use several practical projects to bring fuzzy logic into an understandable framework from where you could develop your own FL projects.

This chapter had very detailed demonstrations, including a seven-step algorithm for developing a fuzzy logic system (FLS).

The first demonstration showed how to compute a tip based on food quality and service quality. The seven-step algorithm resulted in a program that quickly computed a tip percentage based on user ratings. I even suggested a way to make the project completely portable.

The second demonstration was somewhat more technical than the first. It involved creating a heating and cooling FL control system. This system type is commercially available in HVAC products. In fact, one manufacturer advertises that its system incorporates fuzzy logic. Admittedly, this chapter's project is a scaled-down version of a commercial HVAC system, but it nonetheless incorporates all the important parts of an FLS.

CHAPTER 6

■ ■ ■

Machine Learning

This chapter starts an exploration into the broad topic of machine learning, which I introduced in Chapter 2. Machine learning is a hot topic in current industry and academia. Companies such as Google, Amazon, and Facebook have invested many millions of dollars in machine learning to improve their products and services. I begin with some fairly simple demonstrations on the Raspberry Pi to examine how a computer can "learn" in a primitive or naive sense. First, I would like to acknowledge that I drew much inspiration and knowledge for this chapter from Bert van Dam's book *Artificial Intelligence: 23 Projects to Bring Your Microcontroller to Life* (Elektor Electronics Publishing, 2009). Although van Dam did not use a Raspberry Pi as a microcontroller, the concepts and techniques he applied are completely valid and especially appreciated.

Parts List

For the first demonstration, you need the parts listed in Table 6-1.

Table 6-1. *Parts List*

Description	Quantity	Remarks
Pi Cobbler	1	40-pin version, either T or DIP form factor acceptable
solderless breadboard	1	300 insertion points with power supply strips
solderless breadboard	1	300 insertion points
jumper wires	1 package	
LED	2	green and yellow LEDs, if possible
2.2kΩ resistor	6	1/4 watt
220Ω resistor	2	1/4 watt
10Ω resistor	2	1/2 watt
push button	1	tactile
MCP3008	1	8-channel ADC chip DIP

© Donald J. Norris 2017
D. J. Norris, *Beginning Artificial Intelligence with the Raspberry Pi*,
DOI 10.1007/978-1-4842-2743-5_6

There is a robot demonstration discussed in this chapter that you can build by following the instructions in the appendix. It is also feasible to simply read the robot discussion and gain an appreciation of the concepts.

Demo 6-1: Color Selection

In this demonstration, you teach the computer your preferred color, which is either green or yellow. First, the Raspberry Pi must be set up according to the Fritzing diagram shown in Figure 6-1.

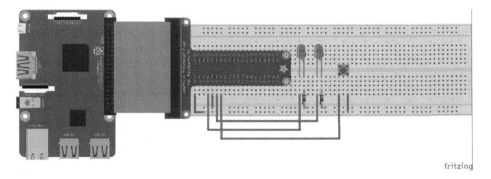

Figure 6-1. *Fritzing diagram*

■ **Caution** Ensure that you connect one side of the push button switch to 3.3 V and not 5 V because you will destroy the GPIO pin if you inadvertently connect it to the higher voltage.

Next, I explain how the color selection algorithm works.

Algorithm

Consider the horizontal bar shown in Figure 6-2. It has a total numerical scale of 0 to 255. The left half of the bar has a scale of 0 to 127, which represents the green LED activation. The right half has a scale of 128 to 255, which represents the yellow LED activation.

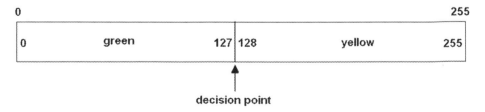

Figure 6-2. *LED activation bar*

Let's create an integer random-number generator that produces a number between 0 and 255, inclusively. This is easily done with the following function, which I have used in previous Python programs:

```
decision = randint(0,255)
```

randint() is the random integer generator method from the Python random library. The variable decision is a value between 0 and 255. If it is between 0 and 127, the green LED is lit; otherwise, the value is between 128 and 255, in which case the yellow LED is lit. Now, if the decision point remains unchanged, there is a 50/50 chance (or probability, over the long run) that the green LED lights up in each program repetition; there is an equal chance that the yellow LED will light. But that is not the goal of this program. The goal is to "teach" the program to select your favorite color. This goal can eventually be reached by moving the decision point so that it favors the favorite color selection. Let's decide that green is the favorite color. Therefore, the decision point changes each time the green LED lights up because the user pressed the push button. This button press creates an interrupt with a callback function that increments the decision point value. Eventually, the decision point will be increased to such a value that just about every random number generated will fall within the green LED portion of the bar, as shown in Figure 6-3.

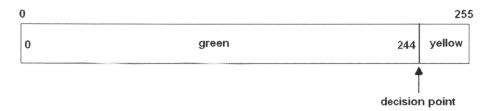

Figure 6-3. *Adjusted number bar*

The following program, named color_selection.py, implements the algorithm:

```
!/usr/bin/python
# import statements
import random
import time
import RPi.GPIO as GPIO

# initialize global variable for decision point
global dp
dp = 127

# Setup GPIO pins
# Set the BCM mode
GPIO.setmode(GPIO.BCM)
```

```
# Outputs
GPIO.setup( 4, GPIO.OUT)
GPIO.setup(17, GPIO.OUT)

# Input
GPIO.setup(27, GPIO.IN, pull_up_down = GPIO.PUD_DOWN)

# Setup the callback function
def changeDecisionPt(channel):
    global dp
    dp = dp + 1
    if dp == 255: # do not increase dp beyond 255
        dp =255

# Add event detection and callback assignment
GPIO.add_event_detect(27, GPIO.RISING, callback=changeDecisionPt)

while True:
    rn = random.randint(0,255)
    # useful to check on the dp value
    print 'dp = ', dp
    if rn <= dp:
        GPIO.output(4, GPIO.HIGH)
        time.sleep(2)
        GPIO.output(4, GPIO.LOW)
    else:
        GPIO.output(17, GPIO.HIGH)
        time.sleep(2)
        GPIO.output(17, GPIO.LOW)
```

▓ **Note**   Press CTRL+C to exit the program.

When the program began, it was easy to see that the LEDs were on and off about equal amounts of time. However, as I continually pressed the push button, it rapidly became apparent that the green LED stayed lit for a longer time, until the dp value equaled 255 and the yellow LED never lit. The program thus "learned" that my favorite color was green.

But did the computer actually learn anything? This is more of a philosophical question than a technical one. It is the type of question that has continually bothered AI researchers and enthusiasts. I could easily restart the program, and the computer would reset the decision point and "forgot" the previous program execution. Likewise, I could change the program such that the dp value is stored externally in a separate data file that would load each time the program is run, thus remembering the favorite color selection. I will sidetrack the question of what computer learning actually means and focus on AI practicalities, as was the path taken by Dr. McCarthy, who I mentioned in Chapter 1.

The next section extends the concepts discussed in this simple demonstration.

Roulette Wheel Algorithm

Figure 6-4 shows a very simplified roulette wheel with four equal sectors (A through D), which represent events in a problem domain that compose the complete circle.

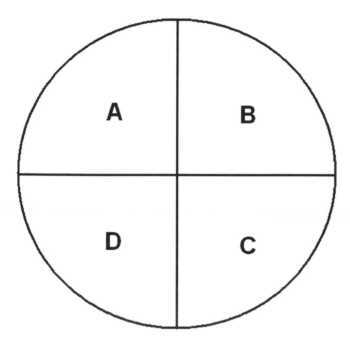

Figure 6-4. *Simple roulette wheel*

There is an average 0.25 probability that any segment will be selected on a given spin of the wheel. An equation to compute this event probability is directly related to the area of each segment. It can be expressed as follows:

$$p_A = \frac{Area_A}{Area_A + Area_B + Area_C + Area_D}$$

A particular issue with using an equation such as this is that even though only p_A may be needed, the representative areas B, C, and D must also be calculated to derive a valid probability for event A. From a computational point of view, it is very advantageous to focus on p_A and not be concerned with the other event probabilities. All you really need to know is that a p_A exists for the particular event A, and that it can be modified to accommodate a dynamic situation. In AI terminology, A, B, C, and D are known as *fitness*. In addition, the initial assumption is that all fitness ranges are equal, given that there is no apparent evidence to change this obvious choice.

It is somewhat easier to discuss fitness using a horizontal bar, as with the first example in this chapter. Figure 6-5 shows the fitness variables set in a horizontal bar, with 25 arbitrary values assigned to each one. Also shown on the bar are the results of three random draws, whose percentage values can range from 0 to 100. My selection of the individual fitness ranges makes it a one-to-one conversion with the draw percentages.

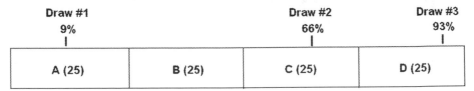

Figure 6-5. *Four fitness variables with three random draws*

The matching fitness for each draw is shown in Table 6-2.

Table 6-2. *Initial Fitness Selection*

Draw Number	Draw Percentage	Numerical Value	Fitness Selected
1	9	9	A
2	60	60	C
3	93	93	D

However, let's say that the initial assumption was wrong and that the four fitness ranges were not equal, but are as shown in Figure 6-6. The same draw percentages from Figure 6-5 are also shown.

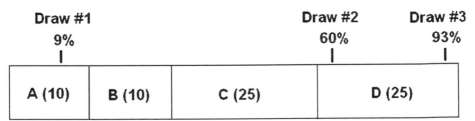

Figure 6-6. *True fitness ranges*

This new information changes the fitness choices, as displayed in Table 6-3.

Table 6-3. *Modified Fitness Selection*

Draw Number	Draw Percentage	Numerical Value	Fitness Selected
1	9	6.3	A
2	60	42	D
3	93	65.1	D

The now reduced A and B fitness ranges leads to the draw #2 fitness choice, which changes from C to D. This scenario is precisely the same activity that happened in the color selection example, where every button press changed the decision point, which in-turn changed the fitness ranges for the two color selections.

Modifying the fitness range and the consequent selection of a strategy are the fundamental bases for the roulette wheel algorithm. As you will shortly learn, this algorithm is very useful in implementing a learning behavior for an autonomous vehicle, such as a small mobile robot. The roulette algorithm is used in medicine in the study of chromosome survival statistics, for example.

Demo 6-2: Autonomous Robot

Meet Alfie, a name I picked for my small mobile and autonomous robot. Alfie is pictured in Figure 6-7.

Figure 6-7. *Alfie*

I mentioned that the build instructions for Alfie are in the appendix. Feel free to read the following section without concern about all the tedious technical details involved in building the robot. However, you are certainly able to replicate this demonstration after you build and program Alfie.

The robot's main task is to avoid all obstacles in its path. The path the robot takes is randomly generated in 2-second increments. Sometimes the path is straight ahead, whereas other times it is a circling motion to the left or right. Technically, the robot is not really avoiding obstacles because that would imply a predetermined path. It is avoiding all containment surfaces, actually, which are any nearby walls and doors.

The robot has an ultrasonic sensor that is beaming or "looking" forward. The objective is that if the ultrasonic sensor detects an obstacle, the robot must take immediate action to avoid it. The following are the only actions that the robot can take:

- drive forward

- turn left

- turn right

There is no option for simply stopping. The robot must continue to move, even though it may not be the best option in a particular situation.

Autonomous Algorithm

Let's start implementing the roulette wheel algorithm by arbitrarily assigning a fitness value of 20 to each of the actions. This initial value can be changed if it is found to be ineffective in the algorithm. Next, a random choice or draw is made. This draw is done every 2 seconds to prevent the robot from settling into a static behavior and not "learning" anything. I use the same 256 numerical range that was in the color selection example. The equation for a fitness selection is as follows:

$$draw = \left(randomInt * \left(A + B + C \right) \right) / 255$$

randomInt ranges from 0 to 255.

The horizontal bar display for this setup is shown in Figure 6-8.

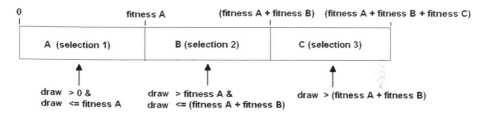

Figure 6-8. *Robot roulette wheel fitness configuration*

The fitness regions are continually updated and modified based on the robot's activities and whether it has encountered an obstacle. Typically, if an obstacle is encountered, the fitness for the particular activity is decremented by one, thus slightly reducing its overall probability of being chosen in a draw. You can imagine that, over a long enough time span, all the activity finesses is reduced to 0. At that point, the robot is commanded to stop, essentially giving up in its quest to avoid obstacles.

The following code segment contains the initialization statements for all the component modules and the selection logic for the roulette wheel algorithm:

```
import RPi.GPIO as GPIO
import time
GPIO.setmode(GPIO.BCM)

GPIO.setup(18, GPIO.OUT)
GPIO.setup(19, GPIO.OUT)

pwmL = GPIO.PWM(18,20) # pin 18 is left wheel pwm
pwmR = GPIO.PWM(19,20) # pin 19 is right wheel pwm

# must 'start' the motors with 0 rotation speeds
pwmL.start(2.8)
pwmR.start(2.8)

# ultrasonic sensor pins
TRIG = 23 # an output
ECHO = 24 # an input

# set the output pin
GPIO.setup(TRIG, GPIO.OUT)

# set the input pin
GPIO.setup(ECHO, GPIO.IN)

# initialize sensor
GPIO.output(TRIG, GPIO.LOW)
time.sleep(1)

if fitA + fitB + fitC == 0:
    select = 0
    robotAction(select)
elif draw >= 0 and draw <= fitA:
    select = 1
    robotAction(select)
elif draw > fitA and draw <= (fitA + fitB):
    select = 2
    robotAction(select)
elif draw > (fitA + fitB):
    select = 3
    robotAction(select)
```

The robotAction(select) method commands the robot to do one of the actions, or to stop in the extreme case where all the finesses have been reduced to 0. The selected robotAction is effective for only 2 seconds, until another draw is generated and an action is randomly selected. It could be the same as the one that just completed or one of the other two actions. The selection probabilities change as obstacles are encountered.

The following code implements the `robotAction` method:

```
def robotAction(select):
    if select == 0:
        # stop immediately
        exit()
    elif select == 1:
        pwmL.ChangeDutyCycle(3.6)
        pwmR.ChangeDutyCycle(2.2)
    elif select == 2:
        pwmL.ChangeDutyCycle(3.6)
        pwmR.ChangeDutyCycle(2.8)
    elif select == 3:
        pwmL.ChangeDutyCycle(2.8)
        pwmR.ChangeDutyCycle(2.2)
```

The robot program utilizes a polling routine to indicate when the robot is within 10 inches or 25.4 cm of an obstacle. This routine causes the robot to momentarily stop and then back up for 2 seconds, at which point a new draw is generated. In addition, the fitness that was in effect when the obstacle was detected is decremented by one unit. This activity is all set in an infinite loop, such that the robot continues to roam or reaches a quiescent state where it just rotates in place. All the fitness levels could also be reduced to 0, stopping it permanently.

The operation and wiring of the ultrasonic sensor is covered in the appendix, but now it is important to realize that when the ultrasonic sensor's distance output values reach 10 inches or 25.4 cm, the polling routine will jump to the backup action and decrement the current active fitness sector.

The following code segment lists the distance calculation routine for the ultrasonic sensor:

```
# forever loop to continually generate distance measurements
while True:
    # generate a 10 usec trigger pulse
    GPIO.output(TRIG, GPIO.HIGH)
    time.sleep(0.000010)
    GPIO.output(TRIG, GPIO.LOW)

    # following code detects the time duration for the echo pulse
    while GPIO.input(ECHO) == 0:
        pulse_start = time.time()
    while GPIO.input(ECHO) == 1:
        pulse_end = time.time()
    pulse_duration = pulse_end - pulse_start

    # distance calculation
    distance = pulse_duration * 17150
```

```
# round distance to two decimal points
distance = round(distance, 2)

# for debug
print 'distance = ', dist, ' cm'

# check for 25.4 cm distance or less
if distance < 25.40:
    backup()
```

The backup() method is only called if the detected distance falls below 10 inches or 25.4 cm. In this routine, the robot is commanded to move backward from whatever position it is in when the ultrasonic sensor polling routine triggers the method. The backup method also decrements the active fitness controlling the robot when the backup event is initiated. The following is the backup method listing:

```
def backup():
    global fitA, fitB, fitC, pwmL, pwmR
    if select == 1:
        fitA = fitA - 1
        if fitA < 0:
            fitA = 0
    elif select == 2:
        fitB = fitB - 1
        if fitB < 0:
            fitB = 0
    else:
        fitC = fitC -1
        if fitC < 0:
            fitC = 0

    # now, drive the robot in reverse for 2 secs.
    pwmL.ChangeDutyCycle(2.2)
    pwmR.ChangeDutyCycle(3.6)
    time.sleep(2) # unconditional time interval
```

I have now covered all the principal modules that make up the autonomous control program. The following listing combines all the modules into a comprehensive program. I also incorporated a time routine in the main loop that ensures that each of the robot actions selected by the draw is activated for 2 seconds. The ultrasonic sensor is also running while the robot actions are being performed. The only exception is when an obstacle is detected; this causes the robot to immediately stop what it is doing and back up for an unconditional 2 seconds. This program is named robotRoulette.py.

```
import RPi.GPIO as GPIO
import time
from random import randint
```

```
global pwmL, pwmR, fitA, fitB, fitC

# initial fitness values for each of the 3 activities
fitA = 20
fitB = 20
fitC = 20

# use the BCM pin numbers
GPIO.setmode(GPIO.BCM)

# setup the motor control pins
GPIO.setup(18, GPIO.OUT)
GPIO.setup(19, GPIO.OUT)

pwmL = GPIO.PWM(18,20) # pin 18 is left wheel pwm
pwmR = GPIO.PWM(19,20) # pin 19 is right wheel pwm

# must 'start' the motors with 0 rotation speeds
pwmL.start(2.8)
pwmR.start(2.8)

# ultrasonic sensor pins
TRIG = 23 # an output
ECHO = 24 # an input

# set the output pin
GPIO.setup(TRIG, GPIO.OUT)

# set the input pin
GPIO.setup(ECHO, GPIO.IN)

# initialize sensor
GPIO.output(TRIG, GPIO.LOW)
time.sleep(1)

# robotAction module
def robotAction(select):
    global pwmL, pwmR
    if select == 0:
        # stop immediately
        exit()
    elif select == 1:
        pwmL.ChangeDutyCycle(3.6)
        pwmR.ChangeDutyCycle(2.2)
    elif select == 2:
        pwmL.ChangeDutyCycle(2.2)
        pwmR.ChangeDutyCycle(2.8)
    elif select == 3:
```

```python
        pwmL.ChangeDutyCycle(2.8)
        pwmR.ChangeDutyCycle(2.2)

# backup module
def backup(select):
    global fitA, fitB, fitC, pwmL, pwmR
    if select == 1:
        fitA = fitA - 1
        if fitA < 0:
            fitA = 0
    elif select == 2:
        fitB = fitB - 1
        if fitB < 0:
            fitB = 0
    else:
        fitC = fitC -1
        if fitC < 0:
            fitC = 0

    # now, drive the robot in reverse for 2 secs.
    pwmL.ChangeDutyCycle(2.2)
    pwmR.ChangeDutyCycle(3.6)
    time.sleep(2) # unconditional time interval

clockFlag = False

# forever loop
while True:
    if clockFlag == False:
        start = time.time()

        randomInt = randint(0, 255)
        draw = (randomInt*(fitA + fitB + fitC))/255

        if fitA + fitB + fitC == 0:
            select = 0
            robotAction(select)
        elif draw >= 0 and draw <= fitA:
            select = 1
            robotAction(select)
        elif draw > fitA and draw <= (fitA + fitB):
            select = 2
            robotAction(select)
        elif draw > (fitA + fitB):
            select = 3
            robotAction(select)

        clockFlag = True
```

```
current = time.time()

# check to see if 2 seconds (2000ms) have elapsed
if (current - start)*1000 > 2000:
    # this triggers a new draw at loop start
    clockFlag = False

# generate a 10 µsec trigger pulse
GPIO.output(TRIG, GPIO.HIGH)
time.sleep(0.000010)
GPIO.output(TRIG, GPIO.LOW)

# following code detects the time duration for the echo pulse
while GPIO.input(ECHO) == 0:
    pulse_start = time.time()

while GPIO.input(ECHO) == 1:
    pulse_end = time.time()

pulse_duration = pulse_end - pulse_start

# distance calculation
distance = pulse_duration * 17150

# round distance to two decimal points
distance = round(distance, 2)

# check for 25.4 cm distance or less
if distance < 25.40:
    backup()
```

Test Run

I placed the robot in an L-shaped hallway in my home, where it was completely enclosed by walls and doors. The robot was powered by an external cell phone battery. I was able to SSH into the Raspberry Pi through my home Wi-Fi network. I started the program by entering the following command:

```
sudo python robotRoulette.py
```

The robot immediately responded by making a turn, moving straight ahead, or backing up as it neared a wall or a door. It appeared that the robot essentially confined itself to an approximate 3 × 3 ft area, but there were occasional excursions. This behavior lasted for about 6 minutes when it began to move only in a back-and-forth motion, which probably meant the turning fitness sectors were reduced to 0, or near 0. After 7 minutes, the robot shut down as the program exited when all the fitness values finally equaled 0.

This test demonstrated that the robot did change its operational behavior based on dynamically changing fitness values. I will leave it up to you to call it learning or not.

What would you need to do if you wanted to add some additional learning to the robot car? That is the subject for the next section.

Additional Learning

It is critical to understand the basic requirements for learning if you want to add learning behaviors to the robot car. Just consider how the robot car changed its behavior in the previous example. First, the actions that the car is allowed to take were defined. They are pretty straightforward so there is really no learning involved at this point. Next, the fitness sectors were created and a randomized method of selecting a particular sector was implemented to actuate a consequent action. Again, no learning was involved. Finally, a sensor was incorporated into the scheme so that the sensor output could affect the fitness values, and ultimately, the robot's behavior. That is where the learning kicks in. Thus learning, at least in this case, requires a sensor and a technique to modify the fitness values based on the sensor output. If you reflect on this for a moment, you recognize that this is the way humans also learn. It could be by reading a book where the eyes are the sensors, or listening to music where the ears are the primary sensors. It could even be the fingers of a small child touching a hot radiator.

It is therefore likely that we will either need a new sensor or somehow modify the existing one to implement additional learning. I elected to consider energy management to be the new learning behavior. Specifically, favoring those actions that minimize energy consumption to enhance the robot car's learning potential.

Directly measuring energy consumption is difficult, but measuring energy used per unit of time is quite easy. Of course, energy used over a time period is simply power, which is easily computed using Ohm's law:

$$P = I^2 R$$

or the equivalent:

$$P = \frac{E^2}{R}$$

A small resistor needs to be inserted into the motor power supply so that the current through it or the voltage drop across it can be measured. I elected to measure the voltage drop because it is compatible with the analog-to-digital converter chip that used with the Raspberry Pi to obtain sensor readings. The resistor value has to be quite small so as to not drop the motor supply voltage to the point that it would interfere with the required motor operation.

To determine the resistor value, I placed a VOM in series with the positive motor power supply lead and measured the average current while both motors were operating in the forward direction. The average current draw was about 190 ma. A series 5Ω resistor has about a 1 V drop with this current, while dissipating 0.2 W of power. The single volt drop should not have much of an impact on motor operation, considering that the maximum full-scale voltage output from the motor power supply is 7.5 V. The robot motors are nominally rated at 6 V, but can accept somewhat higher voltages without any harm. Higher voltages simply cause the motors to rotate faster.

The voltage drop across the resistor is measured using a MCP3008 multi-channel analog-to-digital converter (ADC). The setup and installation of this ADC chip is thoroughly covered in the robot build appendix. Two ADC channels are used because the differential voltage across the resistor is required to determine the current. Figure 6-9 is a schematic of the ADC connection with the current sense resistor.

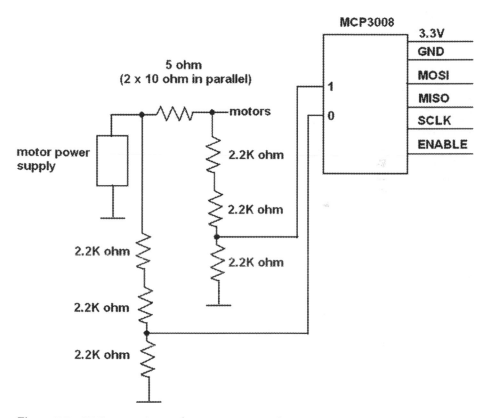

Figure 6-9. *ADC connection to the current sense resistor*

The following code is a test program that proves that the ADC is connected and functioning properly. It is a slight modification of the simpletest.py program sourced from the Adafruit Learn website:

```
# Import SPI library (for hardware SPI) and MCP3008 library.
import Adafruit_GPIO.SPI as SPI
import Adafruit_MCP3008
```

```
# Hardware SPI configuration:
SPI_PORT   = 0
SPI_DEVICE = 0
mcp = Adafruit_MCP3008.MCP3008(spi=SPI.SpiDev(SPI_PORT,
SPI_DEVICE))

print('Reading MCP3008 values, press Ctrl-C to quit...')
# Print nice channel column headers.
print('| {0:>4} | {1:>4} | {2:>4} | {3:>4} | {4:>4} | {5:>4} |
{6:>4} | {7:>4} |'.format(*range(8)))
print('-' * 57)
# Main program loop.
while True:
    # Read all the ADC channel values in a list.
    values = [0]*8
    for i in range(8):
        # The read_adc function will get the value of the
        specified channel (0-7).
        values[i] = mcp.read_adc(i)
    # Print the ADC values.
    print('| {0:>4} | {1:>4} | {2:>4} | {3:>4} | {4:>4} |
{5:>4} | {6:>4} | {7:>4} |'.format(*values))
    # Pause for half a second.
    time.sleep(0.5)
```

Figure 6-10 is a screenshot of the program output after it ran for about 30 seconds.

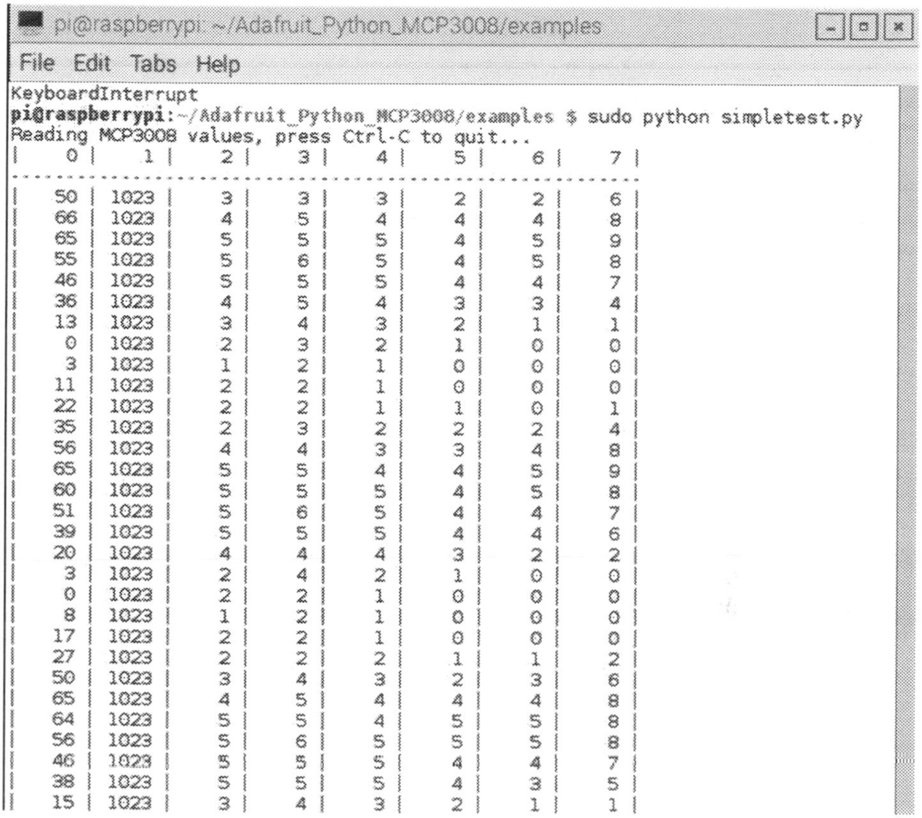

```
■ pi@raspberrypi: ~/Adafruit_Python_MCP3008/examples          [-][□][×]
File  Edit  Tabs  Help
KeyboardInterrupt
pi@raspberrypi:~/Adafruit_Python_MCP3008/examples $ sudo python simpletest.py
Reading MCP3008 values, press Ctrl-C to quit...
|    0 |    1 |   2 |   3 |   4 |   5 |   6 |   7 |
- - - - - - - - - - - - - - - - - - - - - - - - - -
|   50 | 1023 |   3 |   3 |   3 |   2 |   2 |   6 |
|   66 | 1023 |   4 |   5 |   4 |   4 |   4 |   8 |
|   65 | 1023 |   5 |   5 |   5 |   4 |   5 |   9 |
|   55 | 1023 |   5 |   6 |   5 |   4 |   5 |   8 |
|   46 | 1023 |   5 |   5 |   5 |   4 |   4 |   7 |
|   36 | 1023 |   4 |   5 |   4 |   3 |   3 |   4 |
|   13 | 1023 |   3 |   4 |   3 |   2 |   1 |   1 |
|    0 | 1023 |   2 |   3 |   2 |   1 |   0 |   0 |
|    3 | 1023 |   1 |   2 |   1 |   0 |   0 |   0 |
|   11 | 1023 |   2 |   2 |   1 |   0 |   0 |   0 |
|   22 | 1023 |   2 |   2 |   1 |   1 |   0 |   1 |
|   35 | 1023 |   2 |   3 |   2 |   2 |   2 |   4 |
|   56 | 1023 |   4 |   4 |   3 |   3 |   4 |   8 |
|   65 | 1023 |   5 |   5 |   4 |   4 |   5 |   9 |
|   60 | 1023 |   5 |   5 |   5 |   4 |   5 |   8 |
|   51 | 1023 |   5 |   6 |   5 |   4 |   4 |   7 |
|   39 | 1023 |   5 |   5 |   5 |   4 |   4 |   6 |
|   20 | 1023 |   4 |   4 |   4 |   3 |   2 |   2 |
|    3 | 1023 |   2 |   4 |   2 |   1 |   0 |   0 |
|    0 | 1023 |   2 |   2 |   1 |   0 |   0 |   0 |
|    8 | 1023 |   1 |   2 |   1 |   0 |   0 |   0 |
|   17 | 1023 |   2 |   2 |   1 |   0 |   0 |   0 |
|   27 | 1023 |   2 |   2 |   2 |   1 |   1 |   2 |
|   50 | 1023 |   3 |   4 |   3 |   2 |   3 |   6 |
|   65 | 1023 |   4 |   5 |   4 |   4 |   4 |   8 |
|   64 | 1023 |   5 |   5 |   4 |   5 |   5 |   8 |
|   56 | 1023 |   5 |   6 |   5 |   5 |   5 |   8 |
|   46 | 1023 |   5 |   5 |   5 |   4 |   4 |   7 |
|   38 | 1023 |   5 |   5 |   5 |   4 |   3 |   5 |
|   15 | 1023 |   3 |   4 |   3 |   2 |   1 |   1 |
```

Figure 6-10. *Test program output*

Notice that channel 1 shows a consistent value of 1023 because it was tied to the 3.3 V supply. V_{ref} is also tied to the 3.3 V supply, causing the maximum value to be 1023. This maximum value is a direct result of there being 10 bits in the conversion process. Also of interest is that channel 0 shows varying values, ranging from 0 to 66, while not connected to anything or basically floating. Channels 2 through 7 are also floating, but only display values from 0 to 9. It is my guess that there exists a high-impedance cross-coupling between channels 0 and 1, which is influencing the channel 0 reading. This coupling should not matter when channel 0 is actually connected to the sense resistor.

The actual total power computation requires the difference of two ADC readings from channels 0 and 1. Channel 0 is also the input motor supply voltage. I chose to use the absolute count difference across the resistor because there is almost an exact ratio of 1 count per millivolt thanks to the 1 V resistor drop and 1023 maximum ADC range. Both inputs use a voltage divider network that reduces the input voltage by two-thirds to keep them within the 3.3 V input range for the ADC chip. Theses voltage reductions are compensated for in the power calculation,

The total power dissipated includes the resistor power and the motor power. This value (expressed in watts) is computed as follows:

Let $diff = count0 - count1$

This is also the resistor's voltage drop.

The current is therefore $I = diff / 5$

Voltage drop across the motors: $E_L = 3*count0 - diff$

$$P = \frac{E_{resistor}^2}{R_{resistor}} + E_L * I = \frac{diff^2}{5} + (3*count0 - diff)*\frac{diff}{5}$$
$$= \frac{diff^2}{5} + \frac{3*count0*diff}{5} - \frac{diff^2}{5} = \frac{3*count0*diff}{5}$$

The next step is to consider how to integrate the power measurement and the energy consumption minimization approach into the existing robotRoulette program.

Demo 6-3: Adaptive Learning with an Energy Consumption Consideration

Minimizing energy consumption should be considered as a background activity for the robot car, instead of a primary activity such as driving forward or turning. The reason for this distinction is that all primary activities use energy, but some use less than others. Since all activities are involved with energy consumption, it makes no sense to create a separate fitness category for it. Instead, it is more logical to reward those activities that use less energy and to penalize activities that use more energy. The rewards and penalties take the form of slight adjustments to the respective activity fitness values. I arbitrarily decided that 0.5 points are added or subtracted to the fitness values depending upon whether the measured power level is above or below a preset milliwatt threshold value. This adjustment is included in the robotAction module. No other changes were made to the existing code except for inserting a new module that computes the power level. The new power module and modified robotAction modules are listed next.

```
global mcp, pwrThreshold
pwrThreshold = 1000 # initial threshold value of 1000 mW

def calcPower:
    global mcp
    count0 = mcp.read_adc(0)
    count1 = mcp.read_adc(1)
    diff = count0 - count1
    power = (3*count0*diff)/5
    return power

# modified robotAction module
```

```
def robotAction(select):
    global pwmL, pwmR, pwrThreshold, fitA, fitB, fitC
    if select == 0:
        # stop immediately
        exit()
    elif select == 1:
        pwmL.ChangeDutyCycle(3.6)
        pwmR.ChangeDutyCycle(2.2)
        if power() > pwrThreshold:
            fitA = fitA - 0.5
        else:
            fitA = fitA + 0.5
    elif select == 2:
        pwmL.ChangeDutyCycle(2.2)
        pwmR.ChangeDutyCycle(2.8)
        if power() > pwrThreshold:
            fitB = fitB - 0.5
        else:
            fitB = fitB + 0.5
    elif select == 3:
        pwmL.ChangeDutyCycle(2.8)
        pwmR.ChangeDutyCycle(2.2)
        if power() > pwrThreshold:
            fitC = fitC - 0.5
        else:
            fitC = fitC + 0.5
```

My expectation was that, on average, the energy consumption in the turning activities would be less than in driving forward. The reason is because only one motor is powered during a turn but two motors are powered while driving forward. This naturally leads to a gradual increase in both the fitB and fitC values, while the fitA value is reduced. Of course, the fitness adjustments related to obstacle detection are still taking place. My weighting of 0.5 fitness points for energy consumption makes that learning factor only 50 percent as effective as the obstacle-learning factor. I expected that the robot would eventually reach a quiescent state where it only turns in circles.

I renamed the main program to rre.py (short for robotRoulette_energy) after incorporating the modifications and the initializations needed to support the modifications. The complete listing follows.

```
import RPi.GPIO as GPIO
import time
from random import randint
# next two libraries must be installed IAW appendix instructions
import Adafruit_GPIO.SPI as SPI
import Adafruit_MCP3008

global pwmL, pwmR, fitA, fitB, fitC, pwrThreshold, mcp
```

```
# Hardware SPI configuration:
SPI_PORT   = 0
SPI_DEVICE = 0
mcp = Adafruit_MCP3008.MCP3008(spi=SPI.SpiDev(SPI_PORT,
SPI_DEVICE))

# initial fitness values for each of the 3 activities
fitA = 20
fitB = 20
fitC = 20

#initial pwrThreshold
pwrThreshold = 1000 # units of milliwatts

# use the BCM pin numbers
GPIO.setmode(GPIO.BCM)

# setup the motor control pins
GPIO.setup(18, GPIO.OUT)
GPIO.setup(19, GPIO.OUT)

pwmL = GPIO.PWM(18,20) # pin 18 is left wheel pwm
pwmR = GPIO.PWM(19,20) # pin 19 is right wheel pwm

# must 'start' the motors with 0 rotation speeds
pwmL.start(2.8)
pwmR.start(2.8)

# ultrasonic sensor pins
TRIG = 23 # an output
ECHO = 24 # an input

# set the output pin
GPIO.setup(TRIG, GPIO.OUT)

# set the input pin
GPIO.setup(ECHO, GPIO.IN)

# initialize sensor
GPIO.output(TRIG, GPIO.LOW)
time.sleep(1)

# modified robotAction module
def robotAction(select):
    global pwmL, pwmR, pwrThreshold, fitA, fitB, fitC
    if select == 0:
        # stop immediately
        exit()
    elif select == 1:
        pwmL.ChangeDutyCycle(3.6)
```

```
        pwmR.ChangeDutyCycle(2.2)
        if calcPower() > pwrThreshold:
            fitA = fitA - 0.5
        else:
            fitA = fitA + 0.5
    elif select == 2:
        pwmL.ChangeDutyCycle(2.2)
        pwmR.ChangeDutyCycle(2.8)
        if calcPower() > pwrThreshold:
            fitB = fitB - 0.5
        else:
            fitB = fitB + 0.5
    elif select == 3:
        pwmL.ChangeDutyCycle(2.8)
        pwmR.ChangeDutyCycle(2.2)
        if calcPower() > pwrThreshold:
            fitC = fitC - 0.5
        else:
            fitC = fitC + 0.5

# backup module
def backup(select):
    global fitA, fitB, fitC, pwmL, pwmR
    if select == 1:
        fitA = fitA - 1
        if fitA < 0:
            fitA = 0
    elif select == 2:
        fitB = fitB - 1
        if fitB < 0:
            fitB = 0
    else:
        fitC = fitC -1
        if fitC < 0:
            fitC = 0

    # now, drive the robot in reverse for 2 secs.
    pwmL.ChangeDutyCycle(2.2)
    pwmR.ChangeDutyCycle(3.6)
    time.sleep(2) # unconditional time interval

# power calculation module
def calcPower:
    global mcp
    count0 = mcp.read_adc(0)
    count1 = mcp.read_adc(1)
    count2 = mcp.read_adc(2)
    diff = count0 - count1
```

167

```
    power = (3*count0*diff)/5
    return power

clockFlag = False

# forever loop
while True:
    if clockFlag == False:
        start = time.time()

        randomInt = randint(0, 255)
        draw = (randomInt*(fitA + fitB + fitC))/255

        if fitA + fitB + fitC == 0:
            select = 0
            robotAction(select)
        elif draw >= 0 and draw <= fitA:
            select = 1
            robotAction(select)
        elif draw > fitA and draw <= (fitA + fitB):
            select = 2
            robotAction(select)
        elif draw > (fitA + fitB):
            select = 3
            robotAction(select)

        clockFlag = True

    current = time.time()

    # check to see if 2 seconds (2000ms) have elapsed
    if (current - start)*1000 > 2000:
        # this triggers a new draw at loop start
        clockFlag = False

    # generate a 10 µsec trigger pulse
    GPIO.output(TRIG, GPIO.HIGH)
    time.sleep(0.000010)
    GPIO.output(TRIG, GPIO.LOW)

    # following code detects the time duration for the echo pulse
    while GPIO.input(ECHO) == 0:
        pulse_start = time.time()

    while GPIO.input(ECHO) == 1:
        pulse_end = time.time()

    pulse_duration = pulse_end - pulse_start
```

```
# distance calculation
distance = pulse_duration * 17150

# round distance to two decimal points
distance = round(distance, 2)

# check for 25.4 cm distance or less
if distance < 25.40:
    backup()
```

Test Run

I placed the robot in the same hallway as the previous test run. I initiated another SSH session and started the program by the entering the following command:

```
sudo python rre.py
```

The robot immediately responded, as it did previously, by making a turn, moving straight ahead, or backing up as it neared a wall or door. The motions were fairly well mixed. After approximately 5 minutes, the vast majority of motions were the turning actions, with only an occasional straight-ahead action. The backups only happened if the robot came too close to a wall while turning. It certainly became apparent to me that the robot had "learned" that turning motions were indeed the best way to conserve energy.

This project concludes this chapter's focus on machine learning. The next chapter takes machine leaning to a much deeper level.

Summary

This chapter is the first of several that explore the highly interesting topic of machine learning. The first Raspberry Pi demonstration involved the user pressing a push button whenever the favored LED randomly lit. Before long, the computer "learned" the favorite color and consistently lit that particular LED. The concept of fitness was introduced in this project.

I next discussed the roulette wheel algorithm, which was a prelude to the next demonstration of an autonomous robot car that incorporated learning behaviors. Alfie, the robot car, performed a few selected actions or behaviors, which eventually became either reinforced or diminished, depending on whether the car encountered an obstacle while performing the action. Eventually, the car reached a quiescent state where it could not perform any actions and it simply shut down.

The final demonstration illustrated how to add another behavior to the robot car. This new behavior focused on energy conservation. The car rapidly learned to favor those actions that consumed less energy than the ones that consumed more than the preset threshold.

CHAPTER 7

■ ■ ■

Machine Learning: Artificial Neural Networks

This chapter continues with the exploration of machine learning and focuses on the artificial neural network (ANN). I would like to reacknowledge that several of the demonstrations were inspired by Bert van Dam.

Parts List

For Demo 7-1, you need the Alfie robot car and additional parts, which are detailed in Table 7-1.

Table 7-1. *Parts Lists*

Description	Quantity	Remarks
Pi Cobbler	1	40-pin version, either T or DIP form factor acceptable
solderless breadboard	1	700 insertion points with 2 power supply strips
jumper wires	1 package	
ultrasonic sensors	2	type HC-SR04
4.9kΩ resistor	2	1/4 watt
10kΩ resistor	6	1/4 watt
MCP3008	1	8-channel ADC chip
photo cell	1	Any of the CdS variety

Let's start by delving into one of the simplest of all ANNs: a Hopfield network.

© Donald J. Norris 2017
D. J. Norris, *Beginning Artificial Intelligence with the Raspberry Pi*,
DOI 10.1007/978-1-4842-2743-5_7

Hopfield Network

Hopfield networks were popularized by John Hopfield in 1982, when he described an ANN that implemented an associative memory model closely resembling a human's memory functions. The Hopfield network gained a bit of fame when it was discussed in Howard S. Smith's book *I, robot,* (Robot Binaries, 2008) & Press; (not to be confused with Isaac Asimov's *I, Robot* (Grosset & Dunlap, 1950), which was the basis for the 2004 Will Smith movie of the same name).

I need to describe the artificial neuron used in a Hopfield network before I describe the network itself. Figure 7-1 is a model of this artificial neuron.

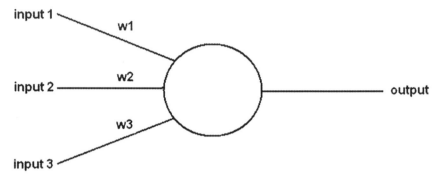

Figure 7-1. *Neuron model*

While only three inputs are shown in Figure 7-1, many more exist in complex networks. There is only one output, no matter how many inputs enter the neuron. The neuron is in a state that is consistent or maintained until it is updated. The state of a neuron is binary, with a value of 1 or –1 (at least for the Hopfield networks used in this book). An update is done by going through the following three steps.

1. The value of each input is determined and a weighted sum is calculated.

2. The neuron output is set to 1 if the weighted sum input is equal to or greater than 0; otherwise, it is set to –1.

3. The neuron retains the output value until it is updated again.

There are two methods for updating neurons, which I describe next. It is not critical for you to understand the update methods because that is done in the mathematics of the network initialization and real-time operations.

> Asynchronous: Specific neurons are selected and immediately updated. This can be done in a preselected order or randomly.

> Synchronous: All weighted input sums are calculated without outdating the neurons. Once completed, all neurons are updated.

Now that I have introduced the basic artificial neuron, it is time to discuss the Hopfield network. This network is normally described as a recurrent network where output values are fed back to the input in an undirected manner. These feedback loops have an important impact on the learning capacity of the network. The following listing provides some of the important Hopfield network properties.

- Consists of a set of N neurons, or *nodes*, as I refer to them from this point on

- Symmetric weights for all node interconnections

- No node is directly connected back to itself (i.e., no self-loops are permitted)

- No specialized input or output nodes

- Each node only has a binary or two-state output

- A firing node activates all nodes connected to it with a positive weight

- All inputs are simultaneously applied to all nodes and then feedback

- The network takes a finite number of iterations to reach an equilibrium or constant state

Figure 7-2 is a diagram of the six-node Hopfield network that I use in the next series of demonstrations.

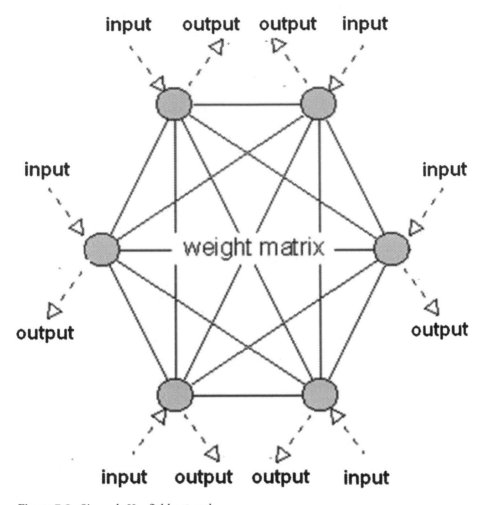

Figure 7-2. *Six-node Hopfield network*

At the beginning of this section, I mentioned that a Hopfield network was based upon an associative memory model. It is definitely helpful to explore the associative memory model and learn how it works. Examine Figure 7-3. I am positive that you recognize it as the letter S.

Figure 7-3. *Letter S*

You recognize it because the shape of the S letter is ingrained in your memory since childhood. There is not much to understand regarding this memory recall, because all of the patterns of letters and numbers are very much embedded in our memories. However, look at Figure 7-4 and try to determine what it is.

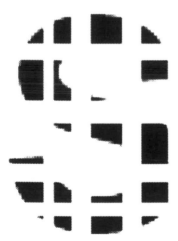

Figure 7-4. *Distorted letter*

I am pretty sure that most readers recognize the same letter S, even though over 50 percent of the letter body has been erased. Your brain and inherent memories have essentially filled in the dots to form in your mind that it is indeed the S letter. In all likelihood, you didn't recognize the distorted figure as a letter but instead "associated" the jumble of dots and black spots with the letter S. This concept of association between what is stored in machine memory and the reality of what is presented is an important point in the following demonstration.

Just as you had to learn to recognize the letter S, machines also have to be taught to recognize things. The Hopfield network example that follows only uses +1 and -1 as input symbols. What these symbols represent in the real world is largely irrelevant to this discussion. Let's begin with a six-input sample set of data consisting of the values 1, -1, -1, -1, 1, and 1. However, to be mathematically precise, I express this input data set as the following vector:

$$\begin{Bmatrix} 1 \\ -1 \\ -1 \\ -1 \\ 1 \\ 1 \end{Bmatrix}$$

This vector has to be converted into a 6×6 matrix to represent all the node interconnections that result from a six-node Hopfield network. This is easily done by multiplying the input data vector by itself.

$$\begin{Bmatrix} 1 \\ -1 \\ -1 \\ -1 \\ 1 \\ 1 \end{Bmatrix} * \begin{Bmatrix} 1 \\ -1 \\ -1 \\ -1 \\ 1 \\ 1 \end{Bmatrix} = \begin{Bmatrix} 1 & -1 & -1 & -1 & 1 & 1 \\ -1 & 1 & 1 & 1 & -1 & -1 \\ -1 & 1 & 1 & 1 & -1 & -1 \\ -1 & 1 & 1 & 1 & -1 & -1 \\ 1 & -1 & -1 & -1 & 1 & 1 \\ 1 & -1 & -1 & -1 & 1 & 1 \end{Bmatrix}$$

Table 7-2 shows the complete vector multiplication of the information.

Table 7-2. *Vector Multiplication*

	1	**-1**	**-1**	**-1**	**1**	**1**
1	1	-1	-1	-1	1	1
-1	-1	1	1	1	-1	-1
-1	-1	1	1	1	-1	-1
-1	-1	1	1	1	-1	-1
1	1	-1	-1	-1	1	1
1	1	-1	-1	-1	1	1

Fortunately, the Python numpy library provides excellent matrix operations for all future calculations, which completely automates all of these tedious and error-prone manual calculations.

Now, let's suppose that there is another set of input data represented by the following vector:

$$\begin{Bmatrix} 1 \\ -1 \\ 1 \\ -1 \\ 1 \\ -1 \end{Bmatrix}$$

Multiplying this new vector by itself yields this:

$$\begin{Bmatrix} 1 \\ -1 \\ 1 \\ -1 \\ 1 \\ -1 \end{Bmatrix} * \begin{Bmatrix} 1 \\ -1 \\ 1 \\ -1 \\ 1 \\ -1 \end{Bmatrix} = \begin{Bmatrix} 1 & -1 & 1 & -1 & 1 & -1 \\ -1 & 1 & -1 & 1 & -1 & 1 \\ 1 & -1 & 1 & -1 & 1 & -1 \\ -1 & 1 & -1 & 1 & -1 & 1 \\ 1 & -1 & 1 & -1 & 1 & -1 \\ -1 & 1 & -1 & 1 & -1 & 1 \end{Bmatrix}$$

The next step is to add the two 6×6 matrices together. This yields a single 6×6 matrix that "remembers" both sets of input data vectors. Let's call this final matrix the *weighting matrix* to conform with the matrix shown in Figure 7-1.

$$\begin{Bmatrix} 1 & -1 & -1 & -1 & 1 & 1 & 1 \\ -1 & 1 & 1 & 1 & -1 & -1 & -1 \\ -1 & 1 & 1 & 1 & -1 & -1 & -1 \\ -1 & 1 & 1 & 1 & -1 & -1 & -1 \\ 1 & -1 & -1 & -1 & 1 & 1 & 1 \\ 1 & -1 & -1 & -1 & 1 & 1 & 1 \end{Bmatrix} + \begin{Bmatrix} 1 & -1 & 1 & -1 & 1 & -1 \\ -1 & 1 & -1 & 1 & -1 & 1 \\ 1 & -1 & 1 & -1 & 1 & -1 \\ -1 & 1 & -1 & 1 & -1 & 1 \\ 1 & -1 & 1 & -1 & 1 & -1 \\ -1 & 1 & -1 & 1 & -1 & 1 \end{Bmatrix} = \begin{Bmatrix} 2 & -2 & 0 & -2 & 2 & 0 \\ -2 & 2 & 0 & 2 & -2 & 0 \\ 0 & 0 & 2 & 0 & 0 & -2 \\ -2 & 2 & 0 & 2 & -2 & 0 \\ 2 & -2 & 0 & -2 & 2 & 0 \\ 0 & 0 & -2 & 0 & 0 & 2 \end{Bmatrix}$$

Given that the input matrices only contain ±1, the summed matrix can only contain ±2 or 0, which it does.

To prove that the weighting matrix actually "remembers" the input data set vectors, I multiply the first vector by the weighting matrix and see what results.

$$\begin{Bmatrix} 1 \\ -1 \\ -1 \\ -1 \\ 1 \\ 1 \end{Bmatrix} * \begin{bmatrix} 2 & -2 & 0 & -2 & 2 & 0 \\ -2 & 2 & 0 & 2 & -2 & 0 \\ 0 & 0 & 2 & 0 & 0 & -2 \\ -2 & 2 & 0 & 2 & -2 & 0 \\ 2 & -2 & 0 & -2 & 2 & 0 \\ 0 & 0 & -2 & 0 & 0 & 2 \end{bmatrix} = \begin{Bmatrix} 8 \\ -8 \\ -4 \\ -8 \\ 8 \\ 4 \end{Bmatrix}$$

The preceding matrix multiplication process consists of six separate steps where the vector values are multiplied by every row in the weighting matrix row, and the resulting partial products are summed. For instance, the vector times the first row in the weighting matrix yields the following:

$$(1 * 2) + (-1 * -2)(-1 * 0) + (-1 * -2) + (1 * 2) + (1 * 0) = 8$$

This resulting vector must next be normalized to match the format of the input data, which only consists of a 1 or –1. The normalization rule is quite simple:

All values 0 or greater are changed to 1, while all values less than 0 are changed to –1.

It should be noted that the exact normalization of the 0 value is not an exact science. In some networks, normalizing it to 1 provides better results, while in other networks, normalizing it to –1 is preferable. For this network, I determined the former was more appropriate and yielded accurate results.

Applying this rule to the vector resultant yields the following:

$$\begin{Bmatrix} 8 \\ -8 \\ -4 \\ -8 \\ 8 \\ 4 \end{Bmatrix} \text{ apply rule } \begin{Bmatrix} 1 \\ -1 \\ -1 \\ -1 \\ 1 \\ 1 \end{Bmatrix}$$

You can now readily see that the normalized resultant vector is exactly the same as the original input data vector. You can do the preceding operations to the second input data vector, and it returns that one as well, thus proving the weighting matrix "remembers" the initial data stored in it.

At this point, you are likely thinking that these operations are interesting, but what is their practical value? How can this Hopfield network be put to any use? To answer these legitimate questions, consider the following scenario.

Let's say that the input vector represents some real-world thing, perhaps generated by one or more sensors, and the resulting vector is corrupted or distorted due to noise or a similar disturbance, much like how Figure 7-4 resembles Figure 7-3. Suppose the new input data vector is as follows, where the 0s represent no data:

$$\begin{Bmatrix} 0 \\ 0 \\ 0 \\ -1 \\ 1 \\ 1 \end{Bmatrix}$$

Next, multiply this new vector by the weighting matrix and see what happens:

$$\begin{Bmatrix} 0 \\ 0 \\ 0 \\ -1 \\ 1 \\ 1 \end{Bmatrix} * \begin{bmatrix} 2 & -2 & 0 & -2 & 2 & 0 \\ -2 & 2 & 0 & 2 & -2 & 0 \\ 0 & 0 & 2 & 0 & 0 & -2 \\ -2 & 2 & 0 & 2 & -2 & 0 \\ 2 & -2 & 0 & -2 & 2 & 0 \\ 0 & 0 & -2 & 0 & 0 & 2 \end{bmatrix} = \begin{Bmatrix} 4 \\ -4 \\ -2 \\ -4 \\ 4 \\ 2 \end{Bmatrix} \text{ normalized } = \begin{Bmatrix} 1 \\ -1 \\ -1 \\ -1 \\ 1 \\ 1 \end{Bmatrix}$$

The final, normalized resultant vector is exactly equal to the original input vector. The Hopfield network associated the corrupted input vector with what was stored within its structure and returned the vector that most closely resembled the distorted input version. This situation is very much akin to how you recognized the badly distorted letter from the original.

The next demonstration should help further define this association process.

Demo 7-1: Numerical Figure Recognition Demonstration

Figure 7-5 shows a unique way to represent the decimal numbers 0 to 9 using only six straight line segments. There is no name for this scheme because I completely made it up.

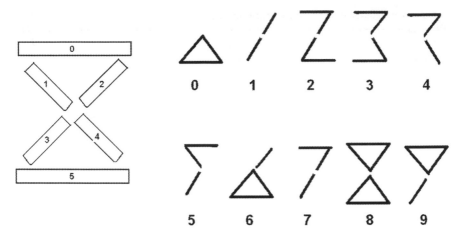

Figure 7-5. *Six-segment numerical scheme*

I am pretty confident that you can easily recognize the majority of the segmented numbers in Figure 7-5 without a problem. The numbers 4 and 5 were the hardest due to the limitation on the number of available segments.

Suppose that an input data vector is created for each of these numbers, where a 1 is used for a displayed segment and a –1 is used for a non-displayed segment. For instance, the numbers 0 and 1 would be represented by these vectors:

$$0 \approx \begin{Bmatrix} -1 \\ -1 \\ -1 \\ 1 \\ 1 \\ 1 \end{Bmatrix} \qquad 1 \approx \begin{Bmatrix} -1 \\ -1 \\ 1 \\ 1 \\ -1 \\ -1 \end{Bmatrix}$$

Next, a Hopfield network would need to be created using all ten input data vectors that are shown in Table 7-3.

Table 7-3. *Input Data Vectors for the Numerical Scheme*

Number	0	1	2	3	4	5
0	−1	−1	−1	1	1	1
1	−1	−1	1	1	−1	−1
2	1	−1	1	1	−1	1
3	1	1	−1	1	−1	1
4	1	−1	1	−1	1	−1
5	1	1	−1	−1	1	1
6	−1	−1	1	1	1	1
7	1	−1	1	1	−1	−1
8	1	1	1	1	1	1
9	1	1	1	1	−1	−1

There is a lot of manual computation that I avoided by using the Python numpy matrix library that I mentioned earlier. In the ensuing discussion, I use the phrase dot product vector to describe the result of a matrix multiplication. I have included the following sidebar to describe dot and cross products and explain how they are applied to matrices.

DOT AND CROSS PRODUCTS

A dot product is also known as a *scalar product*, which is the result of multiplying two matrices or arrays together. The only requirement for a successful operation is that the number of rows in one matrix or array must match the number of columns in the other matrix or array. The following simple Python example should suffice to show how this works:

```
>>> import numpy as np
>>> x = np.array(((2,3), (3,5)))
>>> y = np,array(((1,2), (5,-1)))
>>> np.dot(x,y)
matrix([17,1],
        [28,1])
>>>
```

The same result may be obtained by converting the arrays into matrices and using the multiplication operator (∗).

```
>>> np.mat(x) ∗ np.mat(y)
matrix([17,1],
        [28,1])
>>>
```

For the previous example, Python automatically invoked the dot product operation when the interpreter determined that two matrices were to be multiplied.

A second type of matrix-like multiplication involves the cross product. A cross product is defined as *a binary operation on two vectors in three-dimensional space. The resultant vector is orthogonal to the two input vectors.*

This next example should clarify the definition. Suppose that there are two unit vectors created, as follows:

```
>>> y = np.array([0,1,0])
>>> z = np.array([0,0,1])
>>>
```

Figure 7-6 shows these two vectors plotted in 3D space.

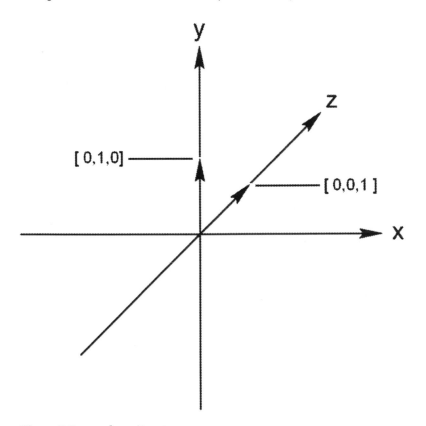

Figure 7-6. *y and z unit vectors*

The following expression computes the cross product vector for y and z.

```
>>> np.cross(y, z)
array([-1,0,0]
>>>
```

This new vector is orthogonal to y and z, and hence, must lie on the x axis, as shown in Figure 7-7.

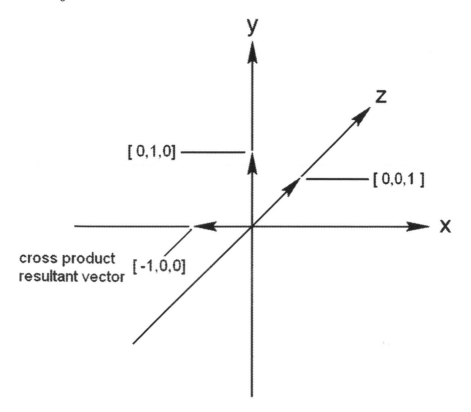

Figure 7-7. *Cross product resultant vector*

The order of the arguments in the numpy cross function is important. If you were to reverse the order, the following would result:

```
>>> np.cross(z, y)
array([1,0,0]
>>>
```

It is the same unit magnitude vector but in the opposite direction. I did not plot this one since it is pretty simple to visualize. I do not use the cross product in any of the demonstrations, but I have included it for your information.

Figure 7-8 shows the beginning and ending of a Python interactive session where I created the Hopfield weighting matrix based on all 10 input data vectors.

```
>>> import numpy as np
>>> num0 = np.array([-1,-1,-1,1,1,1])[:,None]
>>> num0sq = num0*num0.T
>>> num0sq
array([[ 1,  1,  1, -1, -1, -1],
       [ 1,  1,  1, -1, -1, -1],
       [ 1,  1,  1, -1, -1, -1],
       [-1, -1, -1,  1,  1,  1],
       [-1, -1, -1,  1,  1,  1],
       [-1, -1, -1,  1,  1,  1]])
>>> num1 = np.array([-1,-1,1,1,-1,-1])[:,None]
>>> num1sq = num1*num1.T
>>> num1sq
array([[ 1,  1, -1, -1,  1,  1],
       [ 1,  1, -1, -1,  1,  1],
       [-1, -1,  1,  1, -1, -1],
       [-1, -1,  1,  1, -1, -1],
       [ 1,  1, -1, -1,  1,  1],
       [ 1,  1, -1, -1,  1,  1]])
>>> wtg = num0sq + num1sq
>>> wtg
array([[ 2,  2,  0, -2,  0,  0],
       [ 2,  2,  0, -2,  0,  0],
       [ 0,  0,  2,  0, -2, -2],
       [-2, -2,  0,  2,  0,  0],
       [ 0,  0, -2,  0,  2,  2],
       [ 0,  0, -2,  0,  2,  2]])
>>> num2 = np.array([1,-1,1,1,-1,1])[:,None]
>>> num2sq = num2*num2.T
>>> wtg = wtg + num2sq
>>> num3 = np.array([1,1,-1,1,-1,1])[:,None]
>>> num3sq = num3*num3.T
>>> wtg = wtg + num3sq
```

♦
♦
♦

```
>>> num8 = np.array([1,1,1,1,1,1])[:,None]
>>> num8sq = num8*num8.T
>>> wtg = wtg + num8sq
>>> num9 = np.array([1,1,1,1,-1,-1])[:,None]
>>> num9sq= num9*num9.T
>>> wtg = wtg + num9sq
>>> wtg
array([[10,  4,  2,  0, -2,  0],
       [ 4, 10, -4, -2,  0,  2],
       [ 2, -4, 10,  4, -2, -4],
       [ 0, -2,  4, 10, -4,  2],
       [-2,  0, -2, -4, 10,  4],
       [ 0,  2, -4,  2,  4, 10]])
>>> ▊
```

Figure 7-8. Python session for creating the Hopfield weighting matrix

The following is the final weighting matrix:

```
array([[10,   4,   2,   0,  -2,   0],
       [ 4,  10,  -4,  -2,   0,   2],
       [ 2,  -4,  10,   4,  -2,  -4],
       [ 0,  -2,   4,  10,  -4,   2],
       [-2,   0,  -2,  -4,  10,   4],
       [ 0,   2,  -4,   2,   4,  10]])
```

I shall use this matrix and a slightly distorted number from the contrived numerical scheme and see if the Hopfield network can figure it out. Figure 7-9 shows the number 8 missing two segments.

Figure 7-9. *Distorted figure 8*

The following is the corresponding input data vector for this distorted figure:

$$\begin{Bmatrix} 1 \\ 0 \\ 0 \\ 1 \\ 1 \\ 1 \end{Bmatrix}$$

All that is needed to test the network is to multiply the distorted input vector by the weighting matrix and normalize the resulting dot product vector. Figure 7-10 shows the interactive session where the vector is multiplied by the weighting matrix and the resultant dot product vector is displayed.

```
>>> wtg = np.array([[10,4,2,0,-2,0],
... [4,10,-4,-2,0,2],
... [2,-4,10,4,-2,-4],
... [0,-2,4,10,-4,2],
... [-2,0,-2,-4,10,4],
... [0,2,-4,2,4,10]])
>>> num = np.array([1,0,0,1,1,1])[:,None]
>>> ans = np.dot(num.T,wtg)
>>> ans.T
array([[ 8],
       [ 4],
       [ 0],
       [ 8],
       [ 8],
       [16]])
>>> █
```

Figure 7-10. *Interactive Python session to compute the distorted figure*

The following shows the normalized vector. It exactly matches the figure 8 input data vector.

$$\begin{Bmatrix} 8 \\ 4 \\ 0 \\ 8 \\ 8 \\ 16 \end{Bmatrix} normalized = \begin{Bmatrix} 1 \\ 1 \\ 1 \\ 1 \\ 1 \\ 1 \end{Bmatrix}$$

This test shows once again that a Hopfield network really does store data that can readily help identify an unknown or distorted input data set given that it is part of the network. I did a brief and limited review of articles concerning the Hopfield network and character or pattern recognition, and I found that such networks typically have over a 90% success rate in recognizing proper characters from distorted or convoluted input vectors. Of course, it all depends on the amount and quality of the input data and the number of nodes created in the network. In my very simple and limited demonstration, I would be very surprised if the success rate was much over 70%, which is still impressive given its limitations and constraints.

The next demonstration considerably changes what I have done so far using a purely computation approach. It uses a more realistic application of ANN.

Demo 7-2: Autonomous Robot Car Using ANN

This demonstration uses Alfie, the robot car introduced in the previous chapter. In Alfie's last project, it was programmed to avoid all walls and doors as much as possible and also to conserve as much energy as it could while driving about. This project is significantly different in that the robot car approaches obstacles and tries to navigate around them. I dropped the energy conservation scheme because it was not important for this ANN demonstration. Alfie is equipped with another ultrasonic sensor, however, which should assist in its efforts to detect and avoid obstacles. A Hopfield network is implemented to help the robot remember past actions, which should promote the selection of better actions and behaviors in its journey through the environment.

A five-element input data vector is used with this network. The following are the elements making up the input vector:

- left sensor

- right sensor

- both sensors

- left motor

- right motor

These elements are all that is needed for the initial demonstration but more elements can easily be increased as desired. These five elements imply that a 5×5 Hopfield network should be used to support the robot car control system. The nominal values of 1 and –1 are used, as I did in the previous example. What needs to be done is associate what a 1 or –1 means to each of the elements. Let's start with the sensors. It seems very appropriate to have a 1 indicate that a sensor has not detected an object; or in the case of "both sensors," that each sensor reports an obstacle ahead. Note that I have not yet defined a threshold distance for the ultrasonic sensors. That comes a bit later. The motor elements are also fairly easy to define. A 1 indicates that a motor is running, and a –1 shows that it is stopped. Note here, too, that the motors are either running or are not running; there is no intermediate power settings. So what would the following input vector mean?

$$\begin{Bmatrix} 1 \\ 1 \\ 1 \\ 1 \\ 1 \end{Bmatrix}$$

All 1s for the sensors mean that no obstacles have been detected, and all 1s for the motors mean that the car is driving straight ahead. That is a pretty simple and unambiguous rule, which would be suitable if it not for the fact that the car is supposed to learn and not simply follow a set of stored rules. What is needed is a way for the car to learn what is a good rule or behavior, and what is not a very good rule. This approach implies that the car must try different things and determine which are good and should be remembered, and which are not good and should not be retained. Of course, what is good or not so good is fairly arbitrary, so there must be a way to assess those behaviors to keep and store, and those to be discarded.

Trying different things really means randomly activating the motors such that new paths can be tried to see if obstacles are encountered. The only motion that is prohibited is backing up, because there is no sensor facing in that direction and no way for a valid input data vector to be generated. The following are the only motions that are allowed:

- turn left

- turn right

- go straight

- stop

The stop option was not permitted in the last robot demonstration because of the nature of the experiment. This time, it is absolutely permitted. In fact, it is entirely possible that the robot eventually learns that the optimum behavior is to stop and not move at all. The way that turns are done is also a bit different from the last demonstration. In the previous test, the wheel on the side to turn stopped and other wheel kept rotating. The robot essentially pivoted on the stopped wheel. This time, the wheel on the side to turn is commanded to rotate in the opposite direction while the other wheel stops. This action allows the robot to turn within its own radius. This is generally known as making a *zero-radius turn*. Not quite accurate, but you get the idea that the actual turn radius is very small.

The next part of the robot learning process is more difficult: distinguishing good behavior or actions from not too good behavior. Fortunately, most of us had parents and teachers that were around as we were growing up to help with this important task. Unfortunately for the robot, there is no one around to help it with this critical task. It must do this on its own. We can help the robot by programming it to accept actions that "improve" its overall progress. The obvious tasks to accept are those actions that do not include detecting an obstacle. This approach is very much akin to the way the fitness values were adjusted in the previous robot demonstration. Whenever a wall or door was encountered, the fitness value in play at that time was slightly decreased. This time, there are no fitness values, just input data vectors that will either be stored or not be stored. To store the vector, all that matters is that the robot "believes" that the situation has improved. The next time the robot encounters a situation with the same vector, it recalls what was stored and repeats the action. This approach likely causes the robot to operate in a manner totally alien to what you expected, but that is fine because it is "learning" on its own terms. This is what it means for the robot car to be really autonomous. Besides, observing an unpredictable robot can be amusing, provided it does not chase your cat or tip over your expensive vase.

Another important question to answer is how the robot will recognize a new situation. Let's assume that the robot sensors have not detected anything and that we have no idea about operating motors. This is very similar to the distorted input vector that I discussed in the beginning of the Hopfield network discussion. In this case, the input data vector would be as follows:

$$\begin{Bmatrix} 1 \\ 1 \\ 1 \\ 0 \\ 0 \end{Bmatrix}$$

You may remember that you need to multiply the distorted input vector by the weighting matrix. So, we must create the weighting matrix, which in this case is

$$
\begin{Bmatrix} 1 \\ 1 \\ 1 \\ 1 \\ 1 \end{Bmatrix} * \begin{Bmatrix} 1 \\ 1 \\ 1 \\ 1 \\ 1 \end{Bmatrix} = \begin{Bmatrix} 11111 \\ 11111 \\ 11111 \\ 11111 \\ 11111 \end{Bmatrix}
$$

The new vector times the weighting matrix is therefore

$$
\begin{Bmatrix} 1 \\ 1 \\ 1 \\ 0 \\ 0 \end{Bmatrix} * \begin{Bmatrix} 11111 \\ 11111 \\ 11111 \\ 11111 \\ 11111 \end{Bmatrix} = \begin{Bmatrix} 3 \\ 3 \\ 3 \\ 3 \\ 3 \end{Bmatrix} \text{ normalized} = \begin{Bmatrix} 1 \\ 1 \\ 1 \\ 1 \\ 1 \end{Bmatrix}
$$

This vector result should not surprise you at this point in the discussion. The network has associated this unknown vector with what it knows about a vector that also contains sensor data that no objects have been detected, such as

$$
\begin{Bmatrix} 1 \\ 1 \\ 1 \\ 1 \\ 1 \end{Bmatrix}
$$

The stored action is to turn on the two motors and drive straight forward. This result leads to the following conclusion:

If the known data are correct then you should assume that the unknown data are also correct.

While this conclusion looks good and is somewhat profound, it may also lead to an erroneous action if the stored vector itself is in error. Having an erroneous stored vector is quite similar to having a false memory. That is any memory that you believe to be factual and accurate, but in reality, it is not representative of the true experience. As we age, most people tend to substitute false memories for real ones, which prompts one to think of the "good old days" that were in all likelihood not that good.

Most of this discussion has been a prelude to the software discussion that starts next.

Demo 7-3: Python Control Script for the Obstacle-Avoiding Robot Car

The robot car control program named annRobot.py uses a similar structure that was developed for the robotRoulette.py program. The motor control and ultrasonic sensor modules are identical. The random action selection code has been modified and there are several new matrix computation modules that are needed to support the Hopfield network. The new program (shown here) is quite long, with heavy annotations preceding the new sections or modules. I opted for this approach instead of presenting each new section or module, discussing it, and having a final comprehensive listing at the end. Please refer back to previous discussions or the robot build appendix for information concerning the modules already presented, such as the random draw or motor control.

```python
import RPi.GPIO as GPIO
import time
from random import randint
import numpy as np

global pwmL, pwmR

threshold = 25.4

# use the BCM pin numbers
GPIO.setmode(GPIO.BCM)

# setup the motor control pins
GPIO.setup(18, GPIO.OUT)
GPIO.setup(19, GPIO.OUT)

pwmL = GPIO.PWM(18,20) # pin 18 is left wheel pwm
pwmR = GPIO.PWM(19,20) # pin 19 is right wheel pwm

# must 'start' the motors with 0 rotation speeds
pwmL.start(2.8)
pwmR.start(2.8)

# ultrasonic sensor pins
TRIG1 = 23 # an output
ECHO1 = 24 # an input
TRIG2 = 25 # an output
ECHO2 = 27 # an input

# set the output pins
GPIO.setup(TRIG1, GPIO.OUT)
GPIO.setup(TRIG2, GPIO.OUT)
```

```
# set the input pins
GPIO.setup(ECHO1, GPIO.IN)
GPIO.setup(ECHO2, GPIO.IN)

# initialize sensors
GPIO.output(TRIG1, GPIO.LOW)
GPIO.output(TRIG2, GPIO.LOW)
time.sleep(1)

# Create an initial weighting matrix named wtg
# based on all 1's in the input data vector
vInput = np.array([1,1,1,1,1])[:,None] # actually a [1,0] matrix
wtg = vInput.T*vInput # matrix multiplication yields a 5 x 5 matrix
                      # vInput.T is the transpose form (i.e. column)
                      # The square of new and successful input data
                      # vectors  be added to wtg matrix.

# robotAction module
def robotAction(select):
    global pwmL, pwmR
    if select == 0: # drive straight
        pwmL.ChangeDutyCycle(3.6)
        pwmR.ChangeDutyCycle(2.2)
    elif select == 1: # turn left
        pwmL.ChangeDutyCycle(2.2)
        pwmR.ChangeDutyCycle(2.8)
    elif select == 2: # turn right
        pwmL.ChangeDutyCycle(2.8)
        pwmR.ChangeDutyCycle(3.6)
    elif select == 3: # stop
        pwmL.ChangeDutyCycle(2.8)
        pwmR.ChangeDutyCycle(2.8)
# flag used to trigger a new draw
clockFlag = False

# forever loop
while True:

    if clockFlag == False:
        start = time.time()
        draw = randint(0,3) # generate a random draw
        if draw == 0:   # drive forward
            select = 0
            robotAction(select)
```

```
        elif draw == 1: # turn left
            select = 1
            robotAction(select)
        elif draw == 2: # turn right
            select = 2
            robotAction(select)
        elif draw == 3: # stop
            select = 3
            robotAction(select)
        clockFlag = True
        numHits = 0

    # sensor 1 reading
    GPIO.output(TRIG1, GPIO.HIGH)
    time.sleep(0.000010)
    GPIO.output(TRIG1, GPIO.LOW)

    # following code detects the time duration for the echo pulse
    while GPIO.input(ECHO1) == 0:
        pulse_start = time.time()

    while GPIO.input(ECHO1) == 1:
        pulse_end = time.time()

    pulse_duration = pulse_end - pulse_start

    # distance calculation
    distance1 = pulse_duration * 17150

    # round distance to two decimal points
    distance1 = round(distance1, 2)

    # check for distance and set v1 as appropriate
    if distance1 < threshold:
        # set v1 to -1 to signal obstacle detected
        v1 = -1
        numHits = numHits + 1
    else:
        v1 = 1 # no obstacle detected
    time.sleep(0.1) # ensure that sensor 1 is quiet

    # sensor 2 reading
    GPIO.output(TRIG2, GPIO.HIGH)
    time.sleep(0.000010)
    GPIO.output(TRIG2, GPIO.LOW)
```

```python
# following code detects the time duration for the echo pulse
while GPIO.input(ECHO2) == 0:
    pulse_start = time.time()

while GPIO.input(ECHO2) == 1:
    pulse_end = time.time()

pulse_duration = pulse_end - pulse_start

# distance calculation
distance2 = pulse_duration * 17150

# round distance to two decimal points
distance2 = round(distance2, 2)

# check for distance and set v2 as appropriate
if distance2 < threshold:
    # set v2 to -1 to signal obstacle detected
    v2 = -1
    numHits = numHits + 1
else:
    v2 = 1 # no obstacle detected

time.sleep(0.1) # ensure that sensor 2 is quiet

# check if both sensors detected an obstacle
if  v1 == -1 and v2 == -1:
    v3 = -1 # set v3 to a -1
    numHits = numHits + 1
else:
    v3 = 1   # set v3 to a 1 indicating that both sensors
             # have not detected an obstacle

# Create a new input data vector reflecting the new situation
vInput = np.array([v1, v2, v3, 0, 0])[:,None]

# Dot product between the vector transpose and the wtg matrix
testVector = np.dot(vInput.T,wtg)
testVector = np.array(testVector).tolist()

# normalize testVector
tv = np.array([0,0,0,0,0])[:,None]
for i in range(0,4):
    if testVector[0][i] >= 0:
        tv[i][0] = 1
    else:
        tv[i][0] = -1
```

```python
# check for a solution
if(tv[0][0] != v1 or tv[1][0] != v2 or tv[2][0] != v3):
    print 'No solution found'

    # generate a random solution
    if randint(0,64) > 31:
        v4 = 1
    else:
        v4 = -1
    if randint(0,64) > 31:
        v5 = 1
    else:
        v5 = -1

    # select an action based on the random draws for v3 and v4
    if v4 ==1 and v5 == 1:
        select = 0
        robotAction(select)
    elif v4 == 1 and v5 == -1:
        select = 1
        robotAction(select)
    elif v4 == -1 and v5 == 1:
        select = 2
        robotAction(select)
    elif v4 == -1 and v5 == -1:
        select =3
        robotAction(select)

    earlyNumHits =  numHits
    numHits = 0 # reset to check if new solution is better

    # check if the new solution, if any, is better
    if  numHits < earlyNumHits or numHits == 0:
        # create the solution vector
        vInput = np.array([v1, v2, v3, v4, v5])[:,None]
        # multiply by itself
        VInputSq = vInput.T*vInput
        # Add it to the wtg matrix
        wtg = wtg + VInputSq
        # The wtg matrix now has the new solution stored in it

current = time.time()

# check to see if two seconds have elapsed
if (current - start)*1000 > 2000:
    #this triggers a new draw at loop start
    clockFlag = False
```

Test Run

The robot was powered by an external cell battery pack that enabled it to operate completely untethered. I initiated an SSH remote session, as shown in Figure 7-11, to start the annRobot program.

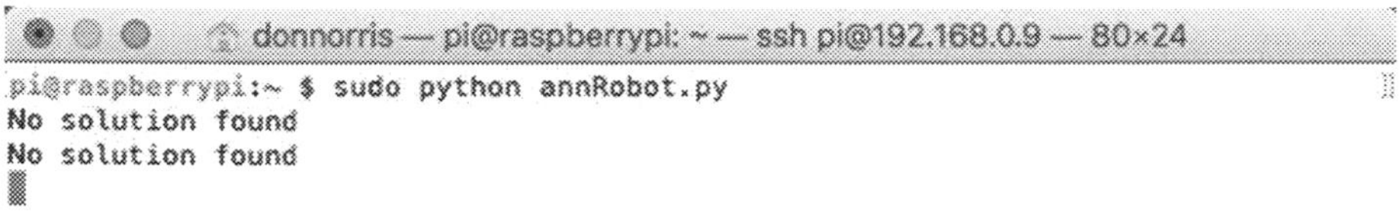

```
● ● ●      ⬆ donnorris — pi@raspberrypi: ~ — ssh pi@192.168.0.9 — 80×24
pi@raspberrypi:~ $ sudo python annRobot.py
No solution found
No solution found
▊
```

Figure 7-11. *SSH session*

The robot's moves began as turns predominantly, with an occasional straight drive. There were two solution "not found" messages shown within the first minute of operation as the robot encountered either the obstacle I placed in the playing field or a wall. I judged the overall motion as somewhat chaotic, which was expected. After about 4 to 5 minutes, the robot settled into mainly circular motions, and very occasionally moved in a straight line. Apparently, it learned that this was the best plan to avoid obstacles. It never stopped, even though that was one of the options.

The next demonstration is a modification of this one. It adds a goal-seeking behavior.

Demo 7-4: Light-Seeking Robot

The autonomous robot in Demo 7-3 was merely trying to avoid obstacles as it traveled about in its environment. This new adventure gives the robot more of a purpose by trying to travel to an objective, which will be a bright light. I will use a new light sensor in addition to the two ultrasonic sensors used in the previous project. A Hopfield network will help guide the robot to its destination. This means that an initial input data vector must be created with appropriate element definitions. The following vector defines this network:

- v1 - Light sensor measurement (t_0)
- v2 - Light sensor measurement (t_1)
- v3 - Ultrasonic senor 1
- v4 - Ultrasonic sensor 2
- v5 - Left motor
- v6 - Right motor

I use 1 and –1 for the vector values representing the states for each vector element, as shown in Table 7-4.

Table 7-4. *Input Data Vector State Definitions*

Vector Elements	Value	State Description
v1, v2	1	Change to a higher light intensity
v1, v2	–1	Same or change to a lower light intensity
v3, v4	1	No object detected
v3, v4	–1	Object detected
v5, v6	1	Motor on
v5, v6	–1	Motor off

Table 7-5 specifies all the relevant vector states that the robot will likely encounter. There are 10 states shown out of a maximum 36 combinations. I could have included all the states but it would have needlessly complicated the calculations without any realistic benefit. It is always possible to go back and add combinations if they are later deemed to be beneficial.

Table 7-5. *Relevant Vector States*

Vector Element	1	2	3	4	5	6	7	8	9	10
v1	1	–1	1	–1	1	–1	1	1	1	1
v2	–1	1	–1	1	–1	1	1	1	1	1
v3	–1	–1	1	1	–1	–1	–1	–1	1	1
v4	–1	–1	–1	–1	1	1	–1	1	–1	1
v5	1	–1	1	1	–1	–1	1	–1	1	–1
v6	1	1	–1	–1	1	1	1	1	–1	–1

This is an example of a non-useful or "irrelevant" vector:

$$\begin{Bmatrix} -1 \\ -1 \\ 1 \\ 1 \\ -1 \\ -1 \end{Bmatrix}$$

This vector means that the light intensity is unchanged, no obstacles have been detected, and both motors are off. This vector conveys no useful information to help propel the robot to its final destination; therefore, it should not be incorporated into the final weighting matrix.

The next series of steps squares each vector shown in Table 7-5 and adds them all together. All the steps are shown in Figure 7-12.

```
Last login: Tue Feb 21 14:11:25 on ttys000
Dons-MacBook-Pro:~ donnorris$ sudo python
Password:
Python 2.7.9 (v2.7.9:648dcafa7e5f, Dec 10 2014, 10:10:46)
[GCC 4.2.1 (Apple Inc. build 5666) (dot 3)] on darwin
Type "help", "copyright", "credits" or "license" for more information.
>>> import numpy as np
>>> vector1 = np.array([1,-1,-1,-1,1,1])[:,None]
>>> vector1sq = vector1.T*vector1
>>> vector1sq
array([[ 1, -1, -1, -1,  1,  1],
       [-1,  1,  1,  1, -1, -1],
       [-1,  1,  1,  1, -1, -1],
       [-1,  1,  1,  1, -1, -1],
       [ 1, -1, -1, -1,  1,  1],
       [ 1, -1, -1, -1,  1,  1]])
>>> wtg = vector1sq
>>> vector2 = np.array([-1,1,-1,-1,-1,1])[:,None]
>>> vector2sq = vector2.T*vector2
>>> wtg = wtg + vector2sq
>>> vector3 = np.array([1,-1,1,-1,1,-1])[:,None]
>>> vector3sq = vector3.T*vector3
>>> wtg = wtg + vector3sq
>>> vector4 = np.array([-1,1,1,-1,1,-1])[:,None]
>>> vector4sq = vector4.T*vector4
>>> wtg = wtg + vector4sq
>>> vector5 = np.array([1,-1,-1,1,-1,1])[:,None]
>>> vector5sq = vector5.T*vector5
>>> wtg = wtg + vector5sq
>>> vector6 = np.array([-1,1,-1,1,-1,1])[:,None]
>>> vector6sq = vector6.T*vector6
>>> wtg = wtg + vector6sq
>>> vector7 = np.array([1,1,-1,-1,1,1])[:,None]
>>> vector7sq = vector7.T*vector7
>>> wtg = wtg + vector7sq
>>> vector8 = np.array([1,1,-1,1,-1,1])[:,None]
>>> vector8sq = vector8.T*vector8
>>> wtg = wtg + vector8sq
>>> vector9 = np.array([1,1,1,-1,1,-1])[:,None]
>>> vector9sq = vector9.T*vector9
>>> wtg = wtg + vector9sq
>>> vector10 = np.array([1,1,1,1,-1,-1])[:,None]
>>> vector10sq = vector10.T*vector10
>>> wtg = wtg + vector10sq
>>> wtg
array([[ 10, -2,  0,  0,  2,  0],
       [ -2, 10,  0,  0, -2,  0],
       [  0,  0, 10, -2,  4, -10],
       [  0,  0, -2, 10, -8,  2],
       [  2, -2,  4, -8, 10, -4],
       [  0,  0, -10, 2, -4, 10]])
>>> ▓
```

Figure 7-12. *Calculations to create the weighting matrix*

The final weighting matrix, named wtg, is as follows:

```
>>> wtg
array([[ 10,  -2,   0,   0,   2,   0],
       [ -2,  10,   0,   0,  -2,   0],
       [  0,   0,  10,  -2,   4, -10],
       [  0,   0,  -2,  10,  -8,   2],
       [  2,  -2,   4,  -8,  10,  -4],
       [  0,   0, -10,   2,  -4,  10]])
```

The Unknowns

One of the real issues with autonomous robot operations is that they encounter situations that you simply cannot plan for. This issue of dealing with unknowns is the primary reason why the Hopfield network is superior to having a series of built-in rules or pre-programmed routines to deal with different situations. To illustrate, say that the robot is running normally and suddenly runs into an obstacle that completely block its path. For unknown reasons, the obstacle avoidance didn't work and the robot is struggling with the obstacle. There could have been an opening in the floor in which the drive wheels dropped into, thus stopping the forward motion, yet no obstacles were detected.

The ideal solution is to stop the motors before they overheat and/or completely exhaust the motor power supply. Let's discuss the Hopfield network solution. The following input data vector describes this situation:

$$\begin{Bmatrix} -1 \\ -1 \\ 1 \\ 1 \\ 0 \\ 0 \end{Bmatrix}$$

This vector describes the situation where the light intensity is unchanged and no obstacles are reported. The motors, while likely still running, are not part of the known input vector, and consequently, are assigned a 0 value. This vector is multiplied by the wtg matrix, with this final resultant vector:

$$\begin{Bmatrix} -8 \\ -8 \\ 8 \\ 8 \\ -4 \\ -8 \end{Bmatrix} \text{ normalized } = \begin{Bmatrix} -1 \\ -1 \\ 1 \\ 1 \\ -1 \\ -1 \end{Bmatrix}$$

The motor values in the final, normalized resultant vector are both –1, which means that they should be turned off. This is exactly the correct solution for this unlikely and unknown scenario. Properly handling the unknowns is precisely why the Hopfield network is superior to typical robotic control routines.

The next section explains how the final weighting matrix for Demo 7-4 was developed and how it is related to the broader concept of brain mapping.

Brain Mapping

There is a remarkable similarity between a Hopfield network and the human brain. Certain areas in the human brain are responsible for specific behaviors, such as vision, speech, and movement. In a loosely related manner, certain regions or sets of weighting matrix elements can be related to specific behaviors, functions, or sensory input that a weighting matrix encodes for the robot. Figure 7-13 shows these regions mapped on to the weighting matrix.

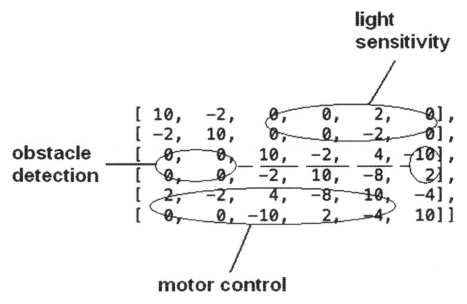

Figure 7-13. *Weighting matrix with an overlay of functions and sensory inputs*

This overlay is interesting, but what is the practical use for segmenting the weighting matrix in this manner? The answer lies in computational efficiency. In this demonstration, I focus on the motor control functions, which are directly related to the light-seeking objective. This approach only involves the motor control vectors v5 and v6 and has just eight element multiplications and sums, compared to processing the complete 36-element matrix.

In addition, it is entirely possible to target and change specific matrix values to amplify or diminish either sensory effects or motor control activations. The overlays provide much needed information if you attempt this process. The resulting matrix would likely become unstable and perhaps not even reach an equilibrium, as I discussed previously. In any case, it is easy to reconstitute the entire weighing matrix by simply running the program.

The use of a partial Hopfield network is analogous to what can happen to the human brain that experiences a stroke. Certain areas of the brain are destroyed, yet over time, patients are able to regain some lost functions through therapy and rehabilitation, because portions of the brain network are still viable and able to perform these functions, even though the brain is not as entirely "enabled" as it was prior to the stroke.

The light-intensity sensor used on the modified robot car is discussed before I discuss the control program.

Light Intensity Sensor

I used a photocell to measure light intensity. Figure 7-14 shows a typical photocell, which is technically known as a *cadmium sulphide (CdS) photoresistor.*

Figure 7-14. *Photo cell*

A photocell is also known as a *light dependent resistor* (LDR) because the resistance to the current flow through it is directly dependent on the intensity of the light striking its active surface. A voltage must also be applied to the photocell and an external resistor to generate a current flow and the subsequent voltage drop across the photocell. Figure 7-15 is the schematic of the photocell circuit installed on the robot car.

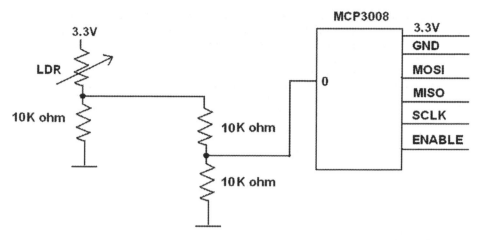

Figure 7-15. *Photo cell schematic*

The voltage measured by the MCP3008 ADC is the drop across the 10K ohm series resistor, which is halved by another voltage divider so as to not exceed the 3.3V maximum input voltage limit for the ADC. The maximum voltage expected from the photocell circuit is approximately 2.2V when the photocell is fully illuminated. The absolute voltage measured by the ADC is not important because only relative voltage comparisons are needed to tell if the robot is approaching or moving away from the light source. It is only necessary to ensure that all measured voltages are situated somewhat near the ADC mid-range to avoid saturation or cut-off.

I use the same MCP3008 circuit that was used in the Chapter 6 project on energy conservation. In this case, instead of the motor power, the ADC measures a voltage related to the light intensity illuminating the photocell. As a reminder, the MCP3008 uses the SPI bus to communicate with the RasPi. This bus must be enabled when the RasPi boots, which can be accomplished using the raspi-config application discussed in Chapter 1.

Figure 7-16 shows a photograph of the complete robot car used in the following demonstration.

Figure 7-16. *Complete light seeker robot car*

If you look carefully at the left-hand portion of the solderless breadboard, you can barely see the photocell plugged into the board. This was not an optimal placement, as I explain in the test run discussion.

This completes the hardware discussion. It's now time to discuss the software.

Python Control Script for the Goal-Seeking Robot Car

I named this control program lightSeeker.py to reflect the nature of the robot car's behavior. It uses a good portion of the annRobot.py code with the addition of the MCP3008 interface code, as well as a new module to process the light sensor. I have deleted all the random draw code from this script since this robot's primary objective is to seek out the light source, and not to avoid obstacles. I discuss the code change implications when light seeking and obstacle avoidance are both needed, after this demonstration.

The following code contains liberal comments to help you understand what is happening in the various segments and modules.

```python
import RPi.GPIO as GPIO
import time
from random import randint
import numpy as np
# next two libraries must be installed IAW appendix
instructions
import Adafruit_GPIO.SPI as SPI
import Adafruit_MCP3008

global pwmL, pwmR, mcp
lightOld = 0
hysteresis = 2

# Hardware SPI configuration:
SPI_PORT   = 0
SPI_DEVICE = 0
mcp = Adafruit_MCP3008.MCP3008(spi=SPI.SpiDev(SPI_PORT,
SPI_DEVICE))

threshold = 25.4

# use the BCM pin numbers
GPIO.setmode(GPIO.BCM)

# setup the motor control pins
GPIO.setup(18, GPIO.OUT)
GPIO.setup(19, GPIO.OUT)

pwmL = GPIO.PWM(18,20) # pin 18 is left wheel pwm
pwmR = GPIO.PWM(19,20) # pin 19 is right wheel pwm

# must 'start' the motors with 0 rotation speeds
pwmL.start(2.8)
pwmR.start(2.8)

# ultrasonic sensor pins
TRIG1 = 23 # an output
ECHO1 = 24 # an input
TRIG2 = 25 # an output
ECHO2 = 27 # an input

# set the output pins
GPIO.setup(TRIG1, GPIO.OUT)
GPIO.setup(TRIG2, GPIO.OUT)
```

```python
# set the input pins
GPIO.setup(ECHO1, GPIO.IN)
GPIO.setup(ECHO2, GPIO.IN)

# initialize sensors
GPIO.output(TRIG1, GPIO.LOW)
GPIO.output(TRIG2, GPIO.LOW)
time.sleep(1)

# The following matrix elements are all that are needed
# (and a bit more) to implement the motor control function.
# Read the brain mapping section to see why this is true.
m25 =    2
m26 =   -2
m27 =    4
m28 =   -8
m29 =   10
m30 =   -4
m31 =    0
m32 =    0
m33 = -10
m34 =    2
m35 =   -4
m36 =   10

# robotAction module
def robotAction(select):
    global pwmL, pwmR
    if select == 0: # drive straight
        pwmL.ChangeDutyCycle(3.6)
        pwmR.ChangeDutyCycle(2.2)
    elif select == 1: # turn left
        pwmL.ChangeDutyCycle(2.4)
        pwmR.ChangeDutyCycle(2.8)
    elif select == 2: # turn right
        pwmL.ChangeDutyCycle(2.8)
        pwmR.ChangeDutyCycle(3.4)
    elif select == 3: # stop
        pwmL.ChangeDutyCycle(2.8)
        pwmR.ChangeDutyCycle(2.8)

# forever loop
while True:
    # light sensor readings

    # acquire new reading
    lightNew = mcp.read_adc(0)
```

```python
v7 = 0
# debug
print 'lightNew = ',lightNew, ' lightOld = ',lightOld

# determine if moving toward or away from light source
if lightNew  > (lightOld+hysteresis):
    # moving toward the light source
    v1 = 1
    v2 = -1
elif lightNew < (lightOld-hysteresis):
    # moving away from light source
    v1 = -1
    v2 = 1
else:
    # must be stationary
    v1 = 1
    v2 = 1
    v7 = 1
# save sensor reading
lightOld = lightNew
# sensor 1 reading
GPIO.output(TRIG1, GPIO.HIGH)
time.sleep(0.000010)
GPIO.output(TRIG1, GPIO.LOW)

# following code detects the time duration for the echo pulse
while GPIO.input(ECHO1) == 0:
    pulse_start = time.timc()

while GPIO.input(ECHO1) == 1:
    pulse_end = time.time()

pulse_duration = pulse_end - pulse_start

# distance calculation
distance1 = pulse_duration * 17150

# round distance to two decimal points
distance1 = round(distance1, 2)

# check for distance and set v3 as appropriate
if distance1 < threshold:
    # set v3 to -1 to signal obstacle detected
    v3 = -1
else:
    v3 = 1 # no obstacle detected
time.sleep(0.1) # ensure that sensor 1 is quiet
```

```python
# sensor 2 reading
GPIO.output(TRIG2, GPIO.HIGH)
time.sleep(0.000010)
GPIO.output(TRIG2, GPIO.LOW)

# following code detects the time duration for the echo pulse
while GPIO.input(ECHO2) == 0:
    pulse_start = time.time()

while GPIO.input(ECHO2) == 1:
    pulse_end = time.time()

pulse_duration = pulse_end - pulse_start

# distance calculation
distance2 = pulse_duration * 17150

# round distance to two decimal points
distance2 = round(distance2, 2)

# check for distance and set v4 as appropriate
if distance2 < threshold:
    # set v4 to -1 to signal obstacle detected
    v4 = -1
else:
    v4 = 1 # no obstacle detected
time.sleep(0.1) # ensure that sensor 2 is quiet

# calculate v5 and v6
v5 = m25*v1 + m26*v2 + m27*v3 + m28*v4 # not using m29 and m30
v6 = m31*v1 + m32*v2 + m33*v3 + m34*v4 # not using m35 and m36

# normalize v5 and v6
if v5 >= 0:
    v5 = 1
else:
    v5 = -1
if v6 >  0:
    v6 = 1
else:
    v6 = -1

# motor control actions based on the new computed vector elements
if v7 == 1:
    # stop, light is unchanged
    select = 3
    robotAction(select)
```

```
        # debug
        print 'stopped'
        exit()
    elif v5 == 1 and v6 == -1:
        # drive straight ahead
        select = 0
        robotAction(select)
        # debug
        print 'driving straight ahead'
    elif v5 == -1 and v6 == -1:
        # randomly select turning left or right
        turnRnd = randint(0,1)
        if turnRnd == 0:
            # turn left
            select = 1
            robotAction(select)
            # debug
            print 'turning left'
        else:
            # turn right
            select = 2
            robotAction(select)
            # debug
            print 'turning right'

    # pause for a 2 seconds
    time.sleep(2)
(End list)
```

Test Run

I conducted the test run in the same inner hallway that I ran all the earlier demonstrations. There are no windows in the hallway and all the adjoining doors were closed. I placed a bright fluorescent, adjustable desktop lamp on the floor to serve as the light source. The robot car was placed about four feet away from the lamp and pointed in the direction of the lamp. I initiated the test run using an SSH session from my MacBook Pro laptop. Figure 7-17 shows the entire SSH session, which only lasted about 10 seconds, with the robot facing a wall about two feet away from the lamp.

```
●  ●  ●          ▓ .ssh — pi@raspberrypi: ~ — ssh pi@192.168.0.2 — 80×62
pi@raspberrypi:~ $ sudo python lightSeeker.py
lightSeeker.py:24: RuntimeWarning: This channel is already in use, continuing an
yway.  Use GPIO.setwarnings(False) to disable warnings.
  GPIO.setup(18, GPIO.OUT)
lightSeeker.py:25: RuntimeWarning: This channel is already in use, continuing an
yway.  Use GPIO.setwarnings(False) to disable warnings.
  GPIO.setup(19, GPIO.OUT)
lightSeeker.py:41: RuntimeWarning: This channel is already in use, continuing an
yway.  Use GPIO.setwarnings(False) to disable warnings.
  GPIO.setup(TRIG1, GPIO.OUT)
lightSeeker.py:42: RuntimeWarning: This channel is already in use, continuing an
yway.  Use GPIO.setwarnings(False) to disable warnings.
  GPIO.setup(TRIG2, GPIO.OUT)
lightNew =  255  lightOld =   0
driving straight ahead
lightNew =  208  lightOld =  255
turning left
lightNew =  204  lightOld =  208
turning right
lightNew =  193  lightOld =  204
turning left
lightNew =  192  lightOld =  193
stopped
pi@raspberrypi:~ $ ▓
```

Figure 7-17. SSH session

I didn't consider the hallway walls, which are painted in a very reflective white color; thus, the light sensor immediately detected this and the robot drove to the wall. When it contacted the wall, the light intensity obviously did not change, which robot sensed, and it immediately stopped—as it was programmed to do. That action showed me that the program was functioning properly, but there was a problem with the way the light sensor detected ambient light rather than the light source. Shielding the light sensor would not help much because it would still likely detect the reflected light from the walls vs. the light source itself. This is because there was more reflected light present in the environment than directly emanating from the light source. The only solution to this dilemma was to paint the hallway walls black, which my wife would not agree to, or to conduct the test in an area without any ambient light except for the light source. I did the latter in my garage in the evening. The space was large enough such that any light reflected off the walls was greatly diminished with respect to the intense light coming from the lamp. The robot drove directly to the lamp and then stopped as it was expected to do. This action confirmed that the program was functioning as expected.

In the next session, I discuss the issues presented if obstacle avoidance and light seeking are attempted at the same time.

Obstacle Avoidance and Light Seeking

Simultaneous obstacle avoidance and light seeking is a difficult problem to solve. As you probably realized, I did not place any obstacles in the path of the robot while trying out the light-seeking function. At first glance, these two functions seem to be direct opposites because the obstacle avoidance script causes the robot to take random actions to clear obstacles, while the light-seeking function tends to drive the robot closer to the light source. I admit that I placed a random selection regarding left or right turns in the light seeker script, but the intent was to arrange the robot to take a straight drive to the light source. So how do you resolve these conflicting priorities?

One approach is to simply suspend the light-seeking function if an obstacle is detected. It makes no sense to try to drive straight to the light source if an obstacle is blocking the path. In this case, let the robot take its random actions per the Hopfield network commands, and try to somehow clear the obstacles. Once cleared, resume the light seeking. This may not be the most efficient way to seek light, but it would probably be successful.

Another approach is to generate an additional set of vectors that instruct the robot to take a desired action based on light sensor measurements and ultrasonic measurements. These additional vectors definitely increase the size of the weighting matrix to account for all the sensor value combinations. For example, there would have to be a new vector element for a light to change from high to low and an obstacle reported on the right. Another case might be that the light remains constant but both sensors report an obstacle directly in front of the robot. This would cause the robot to stop using the pure light-seeking script, but that is not what you want in this case. I think you get the idea of the rapid growth in complexity that would be involved if this approach were taken. Just remember, the Hopfield network is not magic; it needs to have the desired vectors stored in it to achieve good results.

It turns out that the Hopfield network is probably not the best solution for this scenario of obstacle avoidance and goal seeking. There are other AI solutions to consider; for example, a *subsumption architecture*, where priorities are assigned to different behaviors, which is discussed in Chapter 11. The obstacle avoidance behavior would be assigned a higher priority than the light-seeking behavior and the robot would clear any obstacles before continuing its light-seeking behavior.

Summary

This was the second chapter in a series that explores machine learning. In this chapter, I focused on the Hopfield network, which is one of the simplest forms of an artificial neural network (ANN). The discussion started with an explanation of the artificial neuron model used in a Hopfield network. I then proceeded to create an example network using numerical matrices to represent the network.

The key attribute for a Hopfield network is that it acts as an associative memory, similar to the way a human brain functions. The network memory consists of a weighting matrix made up of data vectors that represent sensory inputs and motor control actions.

The first demonstration used the same robot car introduced in the last chapter. The demonstration's purpose was to show how the car navigates through an area containing obstacles. I showed how a Python program script could create and update a Hopfield network that "learned" the appropriate ways to detect and avoid obstacles. numpy library matrix functions were used in the script to simplify the calculations and improve program efficiency.

The second demonstration took a different approach by using a partial Hopfield network weighting matrix to control the robot in a goal-seeking experiment. The goal was to travel to a light source, using a photocell as the primary sensor. The ultrasonic sensors were activated but not required because no obstacles were placed in the path of the robot. I successfully demonstrated that even a partial Hopfield network can control a robot in this situation.

CHAPTER 8

■ ■ ■

Machine Learning: Deep Learning

This is the third chapter in the series on machine learning. The focus is on generalized artificial neural networks (ANNs). Covering this topic requires an extensive background discussion containing a fair amount of math, so be forewarned. The Python implementation on the Raspberry Pi also takes a good deal of discussion. I try my best to keep it all interesting and to the point.

Let's start with a brief review of some fundamentals, and then move on to some calculations for a larger three-layer, nine-node ANN using Python and matrix algorithms imported from the numpy library. You'll also look at some propagation examples, which is followed by a discussion on gradient descent (GD).

Two demonstrations are provided later in this chapter. The first one shows you how to create an untrained ANN. The second demonstration shows you how to train an ANN to generate useful results. Several practical ANN demonstrations using the techniques presented in this chapter are shown in Chapter 9. There is simply too much ANN content to present in a single chapter.

When you complete this chapter, you will have gained a good amount of theoretical and practical knowledge on how to create a useful ANN.

Generalized ANN

At this point in the book, I have covered quite a bit on the subject of ANN, but there is still a considerable amount to discuss. What should be clear to you at this stage in the book is that an ANN is a mathematical representation or model of the many neurons and their interconnections in a human brain. ANN basics were discussed in Chapter 2. I introduced you to a specialized ANN in Chapter 7 that was well suited for a fairly simple robotic application. However, the field of ANNs is quite broad and there is still much to cover.

© Donald J. Norris 2017
D. J. Norris, *Beginning Artificial Intelligence with the Raspberry Pi*,
DOI 10.1007/978-1-4842-2743-5_8

In this chapter's title, I used the phrase *deep learning*, which I also briefly mentioned in Chapter 2. Deep learning is commonly used by AI practitioners to refer to multilayer ANNs, which are able to learn by having repeated training data sets applied to them. Figure 8-1 shows a three-layer ANN.

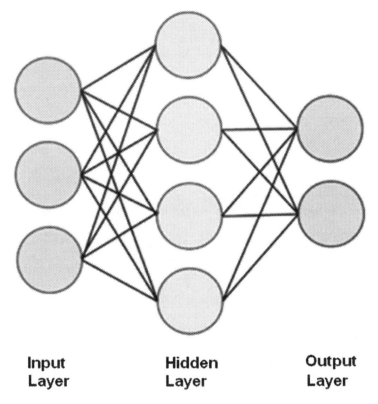

**Input
Layer**   **Hidden
Layer**   **Output
Layer**

Figure 8-1. *Three-layer ANN*

The following explains the layers shown in Figure 8-1.

- Input: Inputs are applied to this layer.

- Hidden: All layers that are not classified as input or output are hidden.

- Output: Outputs appear at this layer.

All the neurons or nodes are interconnected to each other, layer by layer. This means that the input layer connects to all the nodes in the first hidden layer. Likewise, all the nodes in the last hidden layer connect to the output nodes.

I have also referred to this network configuration as a generalized ANN to differentiate from the Hopfield network, which is a special case from the general. The Hopfield network only consists of a single layer where all the nodes serve as both inputs and outputs, and there are no hidden layers. From this point on when I speak of an ANN, I am referring to the generalized type with multiple layers.

There are two broad categories for ANNs:

- *FeedForward*: Data flow is unidirectional. Nodes send data from one layer to the next one.

- *Feedback*: Data is bidirectional using feedback loops.

Figure 8-2 shows models for both of these ANN types.

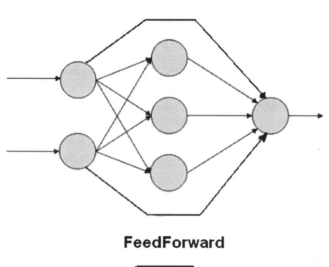

FeedForward

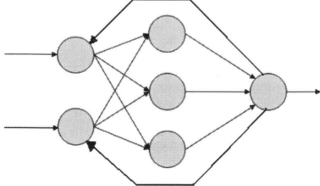

Feedback

Figure 8-2. *FeedForward and Feedback ANN models*

An input to an ANN is just a pattern of numbers that propagate through the network where each node sums the inputs and if the sum exceeds a threshold value causes the node to fire and output a number to the next connected node. The connection strength between nodes is known as the *weighting*, as I have previously described in the Hopfield network. Determining the weight values is the key element in how an ANN learns. ANN learning usually happens when many training data sets are applied to the network. These training data sets contain both input and output data. The input data creates output data, which is then compared to the true output data with error results created when the values do not agree. This error data is consequently feedback through the ANN and the weights adjusted in an incremental fashion in accordance with a pre-programmed learning algorithm. Over many training cycles, often thousands, the ANN is trained to compute the desired output for a given input. This learning technique is called *back propagation*.

Figure 8-3 shows a three-layer ANN with all the associated weights interconnecting the nodes. The weights are shown in a $w_{i,j}$ notation where i is the source node and j is the receiving or destination node. The stronger the weight the more the source node affects the destination node. Of course, the reverse is also true.

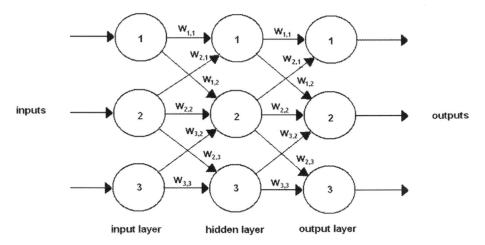

Figure 8-3. *Three-layer ANN with weights*

If you examine Figure 8-3 closely, you see that not all layer-to-layer nodes are interconnected. For instance, input layer node 1 has no connection with hidden layer node 3. This can be remedied if it is determined that the network cannot be adequately trained. Adding more node-to-node connections is quite easy to do using matrix operations, as you will see shortly. Adding more connections does no real harm because the connection weights are adjusted. The network is trained to the point where unnecessary connections are assigned a 0 weighting value, which effectively removes them from the network.

At this point, it is useful to actually follow a signal path through a simplified ANN so that that you have a good understanding of the inner workings of this type of network. I use a very simple two-layer, four-node network for this example because it more than suffices for this purpose. Figure 8-4 shows this network, which only consists of one input and one output layer. No hidden layers are necessary in this ANN.

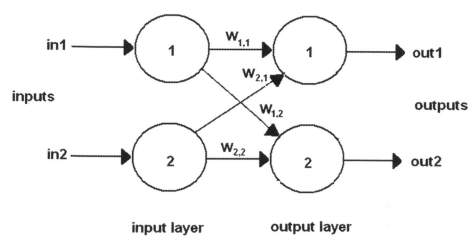

Figure 8-4. *Two-layer ANN*

Now, let's assign the following values to the inputs and weights shown in Figure 8-4, as listed in Table 8-1.

Table 8-1. *Input and Weight Values for Example ANN*

Symbol	Value
in1	0.8
in2	0.4
$w_{1,1}$	0.8
$w_{1,2}$	0.1
$w_{2,2}$	0.4
$w_{2,1}$	0.9

These values were selected randomly and do not represent nor model any physical situation. Often times, weights are randomly assigned with the intention that it is easier to promote a rapid convergence to an optimal, trained solution. With so few inputs and weights involved, I did not see it as an issue to omit a diagram with these real values. You can easily scribble out a diagram with the values if that helps you understand the following steps.

I start the calculation with node 1 in layer 2 because there are no modifications that take place between the data input and the input nodes. The input nodes exist as a convenience for network computations. There is no weighting directly applied by the input layer nodes to the data input set. Recall from Chapter 2 that the node sums all the weighted inputs from all of its interconnected nodes. In this case, node 1 in layer 2 has inputs from both nodes in layer 1. The weighted sum is therefore

$w_{1,1} * in1 + w_{2,1} * in2 = 0.8 * 0.8 + 0.9 * 0.4 = 0.64 + 0.36 = 1.00$

Let's next assume that the activation function is the standard sigmoid expression that I also described in Chapter 2. The sigmoid equation is:

$y = 1/(1 + e^{-x})$ where e = math constant 2.71828...

With x = 1.0, this equation becomes:

$y = 1/(1 + e^{-1}) = 1/(1.3679) = 0.7310$ or out1 = 0.7310

Repeating the preceding steps for the other node in layer 2 yields the following:

$w_{2,2} * in2 + w_{1,2} * in1 = 0.4*0.4 + 0.1*0.8 = 0.16 + 0.08 = 0.24$

Letting x = 0.24 yields this:

$y = 1/(1 + e^{-0.24}) = 1/(1.7866) = 0.5597$ or out2 = 0.5597

The two ANN outputs have now been determined for the specific input data set. This was a fair amount of manual calculations to perform for this extremely simple two-layer, four-node ANN. I believe you can easily see that it is nearly impossible to manually perform these calculations on much larger networks without generating errors. That is where the computer excels in performing these tedious calculations without error for large ANNs with many layers. I used numpy matrices in the last chapter when doing the Hopfield network multiplications and dot products. Similar matrix operations are applied to this network. The input vector for this example is just the two values: in1 and in2. They are expressed in a vector format as

$$\begin{Bmatrix} in1 \\ in2 \end{Bmatrix}$$

Likewise, the following is the weighting matrix:

$$\begin{Bmatrix} w_{1,1} & w_{1,2} \\ w_{2,1} & w_{2,2} \end{Bmatrix}$$

Figure 8-5 shows these matrix operations being applied in an interactive Python session. Notice that it only takes a few statements to come up with exactly the same results as was done with the manual calculations.

```
●  ●  ●                    🔒 donnorris — Python — 80×61
>>> import numpy as np
>>> wtg = np.matrix([[0.8,0.1],[0.9,0.4]])
>>> input = np.array([0.8, 0.4])[:,None]
>>> X = np.dot(input.T,wtg)
>>> X
matrix([[ 1.  ,  0.24]])
>>> Y = 1/(1 + np.exp(-X))
>>> Y
matrix([[ 0.73105858,  0.55971365]])
>>> █
```

Figure 8-5. *Interactive Python session*

The next example involves a larger ANN that is handled entirely by a Python script.

Larger ANN

This example involves a three-layer ANN that has three nodes in each layer. The ANN model is shown in Figure 8-6 with an input data set and a portion of the weighting values in an effort not to obscure the diagram.

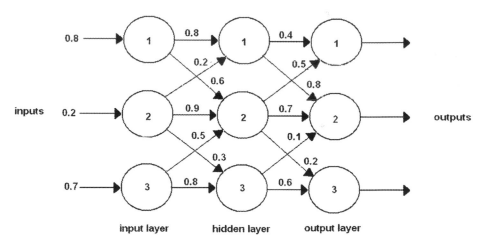

Figure 8-6. *Larger ANN*

Let's start with the input data set as that is quite simple. This is shown in a vector format as follows:

$$input = \begin{Bmatrix} 0.8 \\ 0.2 \\ 0.7 \end{Bmatrix}$$

217

There are two weighting matrices in this example. One is needed to represent the weights between the input layer (wtg$_{ih}$) and the hidden layer and the other for the weights between the hidden layer and the output layer (wtg$_{ho}$). The weights are randomly assigned as was done for the previous examples.

$$\text{wtg}_{\text{ih}} = \begin{bmatrix} w_{1,1} & w_{1,2} & w_{1,3} \\ w_{2,1} & w_{2,2} & w_{2,3} \\ w_{3,1} & w_{3,2} & w_{3,3} \end{bmatrix} = \begin{Bmatrix} 0.8 & 0.6 & 0.3 \\ 0.2 & 0.9 & 0.3 \\ 0.2 & 0.5 & 0.8 \end{Bmatrix}$$

$$\text{wtg}_{\text{ho}} = \begin{bmatrix} w_{1,1} & w_{1,2} & w_{1,3} \\ w_{2,1} & w_{2,2} & w_{2,3} \\ w_{3,1} & w_{3,2} & w_{3,3} \end{bmatrix} = \begin{Bmatrix} 0.4 & 0.8 & 0.4 \\ 0.5 & 0.7 & 0.2 \\ 0.9 & 0.1 & 0.6 \end{Bmatrix}$$

Figure 8-7 shows the matrix multiplication for the input to the hidden layer. The resultant matrix is shown as X1 in the screenshot.

```
● ● ●                          🐍 donnorris — Python — 80×18
Dons-MacBook-Pro:~ donnorris$ python
Python 2.7.9 (v2.7.9:648dcafa7e5f, Dec 10 2014, 10:10:46)
[GCC 4.2.1 (Apple Inc. build 5666) (dot 3)] on darwin
Type "help", "copyright", "credits" or "license" for more information.
>>> import numpy as np
>>> input = np.array([0.8,0.2,0.7])[:,None]
>>> wtgih = np.matrix([[0.8, 0.6, 0.3],
...                    [0.2, 0.9, 0.3],
...                    [0.2, 0.5, 0.8]])
>>> wtgih
matrix([[ 0.8,  0.6,  0.3],
        [ 0.2,  0.9,  0.3],
        [ 0.2,  0.5,  0.8]])
>>> X1 = np.dot(input.T,wtgih)
>>> X1
matrix([[ 0.82,  1.01,  0.86]])
>>> █
```

Figure 8-7. First matrix multiplication

The sigmoid activation function has to be applied next to this resultant. I called the transformed matrix O1 to indicate it was an output from the hidden layer to the real output layer. The resultant O1 matrix is:

```
matrix([[ 0.69423634,  0.73302015,  0.70266065]])
```

These are the values multiplied by the weighting matrix wtg$_{ho}$. Figure 8-8 shows this multiplication. I called the resultant matrix X2 to differentiate from the first one. The final sigmoid calculation is also shown in the screenshot, which I named O2.

```
>>> O1 = 1/(1+np.exp(-X1))
>>> O1
matrix([[ 0.69423634,  0.73302015,  0.70266065]])
>>> wtgho = np.matrix([[0.4, 0.8, 0.4],
...                     [0.5, 0.7, 0.2],
...                     [0.9, 0.1, 0.6]])
>>> wtgho
matrix([[ 0.4,  0.8,  0.4],
        [ 0.5,  0.7,  0.2],
        [ 0.9,  0.1,  0.6]])
>>> X2 = np.dot(O1,wtgho)
>>> X2
matrix([[ 1.2765992 ,  1.13876924,  0.84589496]])
>>> O2 = 1/(1 + np.exp(-X2))
>>> O2
matrix([[ 0.78187033,  0.7574536 ,  0.69970531]])
>>>
```

Figure 8-8. *Second matrix multiplication*

The matrix O2 is also the final output from the ANN, which is

```
matrix([[ 0.78187033,  0.7574536,  0.69970531]])
```

This output should reflect the input so let's compare the two and calculate the error or difference between the two. All of this is shown in Table 8-2.

Table 8-2. *Comparison of ANN Outputs with the Inputs*

Input	Output	Error
0.8	0.78187033	0.01812967
0.2	0.7574536	-0.5574536
0.7	0.69970531	0.00029469

The results are actually quite remarkable as two of the three outputs are very close to the respective input values. However, the middle value is way off, which indicates that at least some of the ANN weights must be modified. But, how do you do it?

Before I show you how that is done, please consider the situation shown in Figure 8-9.

219

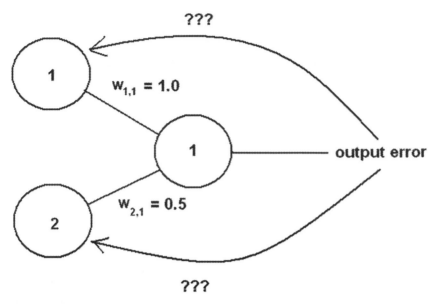

Figure 8-9. *Error allocation problem*

In Figure 8-9, two nodes are connected to one output node, which has an error value. How can the error be reflected back to the weights interconnecting the nodes? In one case, you could evenly split the error between the input nodes. However, that would not accurately represent the true error contribution from the input nodes as node 1 has twice the weight or impact as node 2. A moments thought should lead you to the correct solution that the error should be divided in direct proportion to the weighting values connecting the nodes. In the case of the two input nodes shown in Figure 8-9, node 1 should be responsible for two-thirds of the error while node 2 should have one-third of the error contribution, which is precisely the ratios of their respective weights to the sum applied to the output node.

This use of the weights in this fashion is an additional feature for the weighting matrix. Normally, weights are applied to signals propagating in a forward direction through the ANN. However, this approach uses weights with the error value, which is then propagated in a backwards direction. This is reason that error determination is also called back propagation.

Consider next what would happen if there were errors appearing at more than one output node, which is likely the case in most initial ANN startups. Figure 8-10 shows this situation.

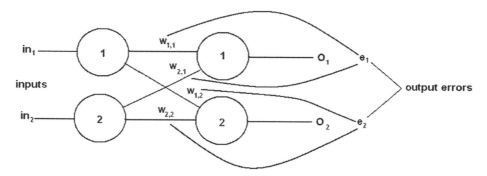

Figure 8-10. *Error allocation problem for multiple output nodes*

It turns out the process is identical for multiple nodes as it was for a single node. This is true because the output nodes are independent of one another, with no interconnecting links. If this were not true, it would be very difficult to back propagate from interlinked output nodes.

The equation to apportion the error is also very simple. It is a just a fraction based on the weights connected to the output node. For instance, to determine the correction for e_1 in Figure 8-10, the fractions applied to $w_{1,1}$ and $w_{2,1}$ are as follows:

$$w_{1,1}/(w_{1,1}+w_{2,1}) \text{ and } w_{2,1}/(w_{1,1}+w_{2,1})$$

Similarly, the following are the errors for e_2.

$$w_{1,2}/(w_{1,2}+w_{2,2}) \text{ and } w_{2,2}/(w_{1,2}+w_{2,2})$$

So far, the process to adjust the weights based on the output errors has been quite simple. The errors are easy to determine because the training data provides the correct answers. For two-layer ANNs, this is all that is needed. But how do you handle a three-layer ANN where there are most certainly errors in the hidden layer output, yet there is no training data available, which can be used to determine the error values?

Back Propagation In Three-layer ANNs

Figure 8-11 shows a three-layer, six-node ANN with two nodes per layer. I deliberately simplified this ANN so that it is relatively easy to focus on the limited back propagation required for the network.

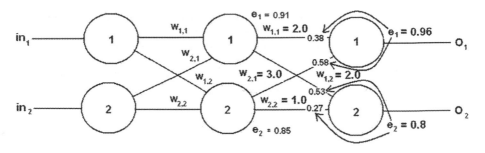

Figure 8-11. *Three-layer, six-node ANN with error values*

In Figure 8-11, you should be able to see the output error values that were arbitrarily created for this example. Individual error contributions from nodes 1 and 2 of the hidden layer are shown at the inputs to each of the output nodes. These normalized values were calculated as follows:

$$e_{1output1} * w_{1,1}/(w_{1,1} + w_{2,1}) = 0.96 * 2/(2 + 3) = 0.96 * 0.4 = 0.38$$

$$e_{1output2} * w_{2,1}/(w_{1,1} + w_{2,1}) = 0.96 * 3/(2 + 3) = 0.96 * 0.6 = 0.58$$

$$e_{2output1} * w_{1,2}/(w_{1,2} + w_{2,2}) = 0.8 * 2/(2 + 1) = 0.8 * 0.66 = 0.53$$

$$e_{2output2} * w_{2,2}/(w_{1,2} + w_{2,2}) = 0.8 * 1/(2 + 1) = 0.8 * 0.33 = 0.27$$

The total normalized error value for each hidden node is the sum of the individual error contributions to a given output node and are calculated as follows:

$$e_1 = e_{1output1} + e_{2output1} = 0.38 + 0.53 = 0.91$$

$$e_2 = e_{1output2} + e_{2output2} = 0.58 + 0.27 = 0.85$$

These values are shown next to each of the hidden nodes in Figure 8-11.

The preceding process may be continued as needed to calculate all the combined error values for any remaining hidden layers. There is no need to calculate error values for the input layer because it must be 0 for all input nodes as they simply pass the input values without any modifications.

The preceding process for calculating the hidden layer error outputs is quite tedious since it was done manually. It would be much nicer if it could be automated using matrices in a similar way that the feed forward calculations were done. The following would result if the matrices were translated on a one-to-one basis from the manual method:

$$e_{hidden} = \left\{ \begin{array}{cc} \dfrac{w_{1,1}}{w_{1,1} + w_{2,1}} & \dfrac{w_{1,2}}{w_{1,2} + w_{2,2}} \\[3mm] \dfrac{w_{2,1}}{w_{2,1} + w_{1,1}} & \dfrac{w_{2,2}}{w_{2,2} + w_{1,2}} \end{array} \right\} * \left\{ \begin{array}{c} in1 \\ in2 \end{array} \right\}$$

Unfortunately, there is no reasonable way to input the fractions that are shown in the preceding matrix. But all hope is not lost if you think about what the fractions actually do. They normalize the node's error contribution, meaning that the fraction converts to a number ranging between 0 and 1.0. The relative error contribution can also be expressed as an unnormalized number by simply using the weight numerator and dropping the denominator. The result is still acceptable because it is really only important to calculate a combined error value that is useful in the weight updates. I cover this in the next section.

Removing the denominators of all the fractions yields

$$e_{hidden} = \begin{Bmatrix} w_{1,1} & w_{1,2} \\ w_{2,1} & w_{2,2} \end{Bmatrix} * \begin{Bmatrix} in1 \\ in2 \end{Bmatrix}$$

The preceding matrix can easily be handled using numpy's matrix operations. The only catch is that the transpose of the matrix must be used in the multiplication, which again is not an issue. Figure 8-12 shows the actual matrix operations for this error backpropagation example.

```
>>> input = np.array([1.2,0.8])
>>> wtg = np.matrix([[2,2],[3,1]])
>>> wtg
matrix([[2, 2],
        [3, 1]])
>>> error = np.dot(input,wtg.T)
>>> error
matrix([[ 4. ,  4.4]])
>>>
```

Figure 8-12. *Hidden layer error matrix multiplication*

It is now time to discuss how the weighting matrix values are updated once the errors have been determined.

Updating the Weighting Matrix

Updating the weighting matrix is the heart of the ANN learning process. The quality of this matrix determines how effective the ANN is in solving its particular AI problem. However, there is a very significant problem in trying to mathematically determine a node's output given its input and weights. Consider the following equation, which is applicable to a three-layer, nine-node ANN that determines the value appearing at a particular output node:

$$O_k = \frac{1}{1+e^{-\sum_{j=1}^{3}\left(w_{j,k} \cdot \frac{1}{1+e^{-\sum_{j=1}^{3}(w_{j,k} \cdot x_i)}}\right)}}$$

O_k is the output at the k_{th} node.
$w_{j,k}$ is all the interconnecting weights between the input layer and selected output node.
x_i are the input values.

This certainly is a formidable equation even though it only deals with a relatively simple three-layer, nine-node ANN. You can probably imagine the horrendous equation that would model a six-input, five-layer ANN, which in itself is not that large of an ANN. Larger ANN equations are likely beyond human comprehension. So how is this conundrum solved?

You could try a brute-force approach, where a fast computer simply tries a series of different values for each weight. Let's say there are 1000 values to test for each weight, ranging from –1 to 1 in increments of 0.002. Negative weights are allowed in an ANN and the 0.002 increment is probably fine to determine an accurate weight. However, for our three-layer, nine-node ANN there are 18 possible weighting links. Since there are 1000 values per link, there are 18,000 possibilities to test. That means it would take approximately five hours to go through all the combinations if the computer took one second for each combination. Five hours is not that bad for a simple ANN, however, the elapsed time would grow exponentially for larger ANNs. For example, in a very practical 500-node ANN, there are about 500 million weight combinations. Testing at one second per combination would take approximately 16 years to complete. And that is only for one training set. Imagine the time taken for thousands of training sets. Obviously, there must be a better way than using the brute-force approach.

The solution for this difficult problem comes from the application of a mathematical approach named steepest descent. This approach was first created in 1847 by a French mathematics professor named Augustin Louis Cauchy. He proposed it in a treatise concerning the solution of a system of simultaneous equations. However, a period of more than 120 years elapsed before mathematicians and AI researchers applied it to ANNs. The field of ANN research rapidly developed once this technique became well known and understood.

The technique is also commonly referred to as *gradient descent*, which I start doing from this point. The underlying mathematics for gradient descent can be a bit confusing and somewhat obscure, especially when it is applied to ANNs. The following sidebar delves into the details of the gradient descent technique in order to provide those interested readers with a brief background on the subject.

EXAMINING THE GRADIENT DESCENT TECHNIQUE

Credit goes to Matt Nedrich, who wrote a great blog in early 2014 from which I have based much of this discussion. At the time, Matt was working for Atomic Objects, a software consultancy based in Ann Arbor, MI. You can view the original blog at `https://spin.atomicobject.com`.

I start by focusing on a close relative named *linear regression*. This is not the first time I have discussed linear regression. In Chapter 2, I discussed the concept of a linear predictor using mushrooms in the example. The linear predictor was a sloped line with a generalized equation form of

$$y = mx + b$$

I didn't mention it at that time, but this equation is often used a "best fit" predictor for x-y scatter plot data, which is the basis for linear regression. Consider Figure 8-13, which is also the starting gif for an automated plot sequence in Matt's blog.

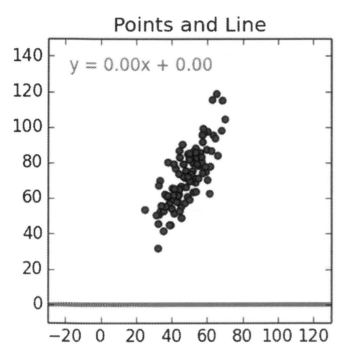

Figure 8-13. *Initial x-y scatter plot*

The linear regression technique strives to best fit a sloped line that goes through the x-y data points in such a position to minimize the total error if you were to use the sloped line alone as a y predictor for a given x. I recommend going to the blog and clicking on the gif to see the automated sequence as the line seeks a best-fit position. I can only proceed in this book with the mathematical steps that determine the sloped line's position.

There should be starting equation to kick off this linear regression technique discussion. In this case, it is the sloped line equation used in the Chapter 2 linear predictor model.

$$y = mx + b$$

where m = slope or gradient

b = y-axis intercept

225

The general approach is to use a data set of (m, b) and then determine how well that line with those parameters "fits" the x-y data points. This fit is determined by calculating y for a given x in the data set and then calculating the error using the true y in the data set. All the x's in the data set are used. This error is often referred to as the distance from the sloped line as it makes its way through data set. This error or distance is also squared to ensure that distances below the line that are negative do not cancel out the positive distances above the line. Squaring the distances also ensures that the overall error function can be differentiated.

The following is a Python method that implements this error function:

```
# y = mx + b
# m is slope, b is y-intercept
def computeErrorForLineGivenPoints(b, m, points):
    totalError = 0
    for i in range(0, len(points)):
        totalError += (points[i].y - (m * points[i].x + b)) ** 2
    return totalError / float(len(points))
```

The following is a formal error function for the code implements:

$$e_{m,b} = \frac{1}{N} \sum_{i=1}^{N} \left(y_i - \left(m * x_i + b \right) \right)^2$$

A sloped line generates the best fit when the error—as calculated by the preceding error function—is at its lowest minimum value possible for the totality of the data set. The trick now is to create some form for the error function that provides the appropriate values for *m* and *b* that produce the overall minimum. Before I go into that, it would helpful to visualize the relationships between *m, b,* and *e^m, b.* Figure 8-14 is from the blog that clearly shows the curved nature of the relationships between all the variables.

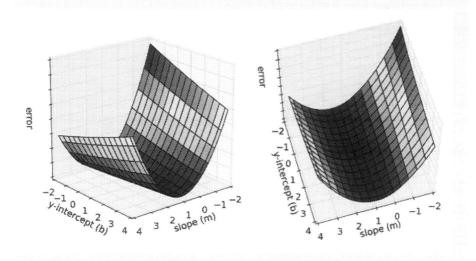

Figure 8-14. *Plots form, b and e$_{m,b}$*

It might also be helpful to imagine holding a marble high up on one of surfaces and allowing it to roll down the slope. It should just stop at the minimum point, which has an *m* and *b* associated with it as well as the minimum *e$_{m,b}$*.

Running a gradient descent search is equivalent to rolling the mythical marble down the slope. The first step in doing a gradient descent calculation is to perform two partial differentiations on the error function because it has two independent variables: *m* and *b*.

$$\frac{\partial}{\partial m} = \frac{2}{N} \sum_{i=1}^{N} -x_i \left(y_i - \left(mx_i + b \right) \right)$$

$$\frac{\partial}{\partial b} = \frac{2}{N} \sum_{i=1}^{N} -\left(y_i - \left(mx_i + b \right) \right)$$

I would like to discuss the concept of a global minimum before I describe the process of calculating the optimum *m* and *b* values. Figure 8-15 is a three-dimensional (3D) plot of an analytic continuous function with variables x and y.

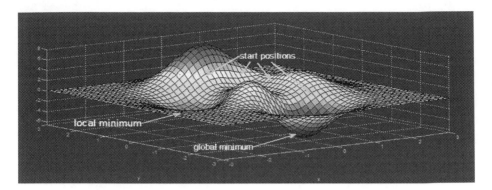

Figure 8-15. *Multiple minima 3D plot*

In this 3D plot, you can see where two minima or valleys have been identified. One is "deeper" than the other is. The deepest minimum is considered the *global minimum*, while the other is called a *local minimum*. Depending upon where you start the gradient descent, it is possible to land in a local minimum while also believing it is the global minimum. Unfortunately, computers do not have the inherent ability to look at 3D image such as Figure 8-15 and figure out where to start the gradient descent to find the true global minimum. It is therefore important to iterate over the entire ranges of the independent variables m and b, taking sufficiently small steps to locate the global minimum and rejecting all local minima. Shortly, you see that setting step size becomes an important part of the process.

All the parts necessary to start the gradient descent have now been discussed. The actual search starts by setting $m = -1$ and $b = 0$. This point may be called the origin as a simple reference. The gradient descent should begin its march downhill based on the initial error function towards the optimum solution. Each iteration should also provide an improved solution until it reaches a point where the error remains constant or starts increasing. The direction that an iteration takes is based on the two partial derivatives that were shown earlier.

The following Python code implements this gradient descent algorithm:

```python
def stepGradient(b_current, m_current, points, learningRate):
    b_gradient = 0
    m_gradient = 0
    N = float(len(points))
    for i in range(0, len(points)):
        b_gradient += -(2/N) * (points[i].y -
        ((m_current*points[i].x) + b_current))
        m_gradient += -(2/N) * points[i].x * (points[i].y -
        ((m_current * points[i].x) + b_current))
    new_b = b_current - (learningRate * b_gradient)
    new_m = m_current - (learningRate * m_gradient)
    return [new_b, new_m]
```

The learningRate variable controls the step size in the effort to locate the minimum. Too large a step size and you may miss the minimum. However, too small a step size needlessly increases the number of iterations taken before locating the minimum.

Executing the algorithm begins at the origin stated earlier. For each iteration, the *m* and *b* values are updated to yield a slightly lower error than the previous iteration. In Figure 18-16, the dot on the left plot displays the current location of the gradient descent search. The right plot displays the corresponding line of best fit for the current *m* and *b* values.

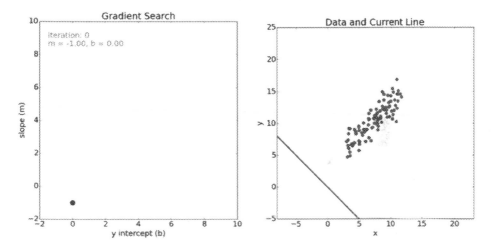

Figure 18-16. *Start of the gradient descent*

You can clearly see from the right plot that the initial guess for the line of best fit was way off. The fit vastly improves in the next iteration, as shown in Figure 18-17. The left plot now has line indicating the path taken to get there from the initial point.

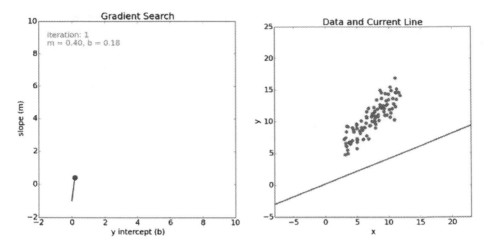

Figure 18-17. *Iteration 1 for the gradient search*

The fit continues to improve after the next iteration, as shown in Figure 18-18.

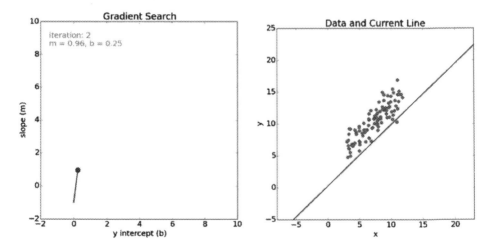

Figure 18-18. *Iteration 2 for the gradient search*

Finally, after 100 iterations, the search resolves to a very good fit, as shown in Figure 18-19.

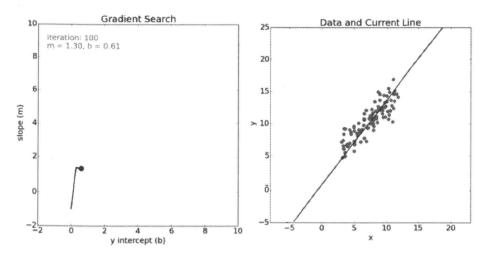

Figure 18-19. *Iteration 100 for the gradient search*

You can see from the path displayed in the left graph that the search in the last series of iterations took a slight jog downward and to the right in search of the global minimum.

Figure 18-20 is a plot of error values for the first 100 iterations in the gradient search.

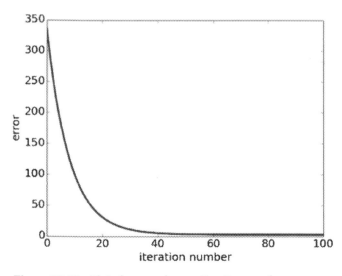

Figure 18-20. *Plot of error values vs iteration number*

It is good to check on the proper operation of the gradient search. Make sure that the error values continually decrease as the number of iterations increase. Looking at the chart it appears the error values are very close to zero after the 50th iteration. This might well indicate a broad minimum surface exists where the values of *m* and *b* would not change significantly in producing a line of best fit.

This is the final line of best fit using 100 iterations in the gradient search:

$$y = 1.3x + 0.61$$

I hope that you have gained some insight into how the gradient search technique works.

The Gradient Descent Applied to an ANN

Figure 8-21 nicely summarizes the gradient descent technique as it applies to an ANN. It must determine the global minimum by adjusting the weights $w_{i,j}$ so as to minimize the overall errors present in the ANN.

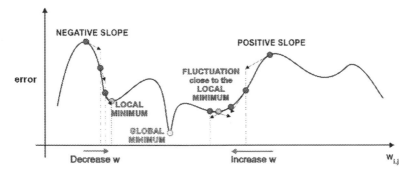

Figure 8-21. *ANN global minimum*

This adjustment becomes a function of the partial derivative of the error function with respect to a weight, $w_{j,k}$. This partial derivative is shown by these symbols: $\dfrac{\partial e}{\partial w_{j,k}}$.

This derivative is also the slope of the error function. It is the gradient descent algorithm that follows the slope down to the global minimum.

Figure 8-22 shows the three-layer, six-node ANN that is the basis network for the following discussion. Note the i, j, and k indices because they are important to follow as you go through the procedure.

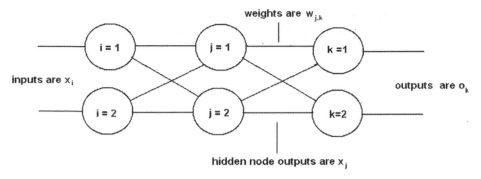

Figure 8-22. *Three-layer, six-node ANN*

There is one additional symbol required beyond those shown in Figure 8-22: the output node error, which is expressed as

$$e_k = t_k - o_k$$

t_k is the true or target value from the training set.
o_k is output resulting from the training set input x_i values.

The total error at any given node n is the preceding equation with n substituted for k. Consequently, the total error for the entire ANN is the sum of all errors for all of the individual nodes. The errors are also squared for reasons mentioned in the sidebar. This leads to the following equation for the error function:

$$e = \sum_{i=1}^{N} (t_n - o_n)^2$$

N is the total number of nodes in the ANN.

This error function is the exact one that is required to differentiate with respect to $w_{j,k}$, leading to the following form:

$$\frac{\partial e}{\partial w_{j,k}} = \frac{\partial}{\partial w_{j,k}} \sum_{i=1}^{N} (t_n - o_n)^2$$

This equation may be considerably simplified by taking note that the error at any specific node is due solely to its input connections. This means the output for the k_{th} node only depends on the $w_{j,k}$ weights on its input connections. What this realization does is to remove the summation from the error function because no other nodes contribute to the k_{th} node's output. This yields a much simpler error function:

$$\frac{\partial e}{\partial w_{j,k}} = \frac{\partial}{\partial w_{j,k}} (t_k - o_k)^2$$

The next step is to do the actual partial differentiation on the function. I simply go through the steps with minimal comments to get to the final equation without prolonging this whole derivation.

1. Chain rule applied: $\dfrac{\partial e}{\partial w_{j,k}} = \dfrac{\partial e}{\partial o_k} * \dfrac{\partial o_k}{\partial w_{j,k}}$

2. o_k is independent of $w_{j,k}$. The first partial $= -2(t_k - o_k)$

3. The output o_k has a sigmoid function applied. The second

   partial $= \dfrac{\partial o_k}{\partial w_{j,k}}$ sigmoid $\left(\sum_j w_{j,k} * o_j \right)$

4. The differential of the sigmoid is

   $\dfrac{\partial}{\partial x} \, sigmoid(x) = sigmoid(x) * (1 - sigmoid(x))$

5. Combining: $\dfrac{\partial e}{\partial w_{j,k}} = -2(t_k - o_k) *$ sigmoid $\left(\sum_j w_{j,k} * o_j \right) *$

   $\left(1 - sigmoid \left(\sum_j w_{j,k} * o_j \right) \right) * \dfrac{\partial}{\partial w_{j,k}} \left(\sum_j w_{j,k} * o_j \right)$. Note the last

   term is necessary because of the summation term in the sigmoid function. Just another application of the chain rule.

6. Simplifying:

   $\dfrac{\partial e}{\partial w_{j,k}} = -2(t_k - o_k) *$ sigmoid $\left(\sum_j w_{j,k} * o_j \right) * \left(1 - sigmoid \left(\sum_j w_{j,k} * o_j \right) \right)$

Take a breath, which I often did after a rigorous calculus session. This is the final equation that is used to adjust the weights:

$$\dfrac{\partial e}{\partial w_{j,k}} = -(t_k - o_k) * \text{sigmoid} \left(\sum_j w_{j,k} * o_j \right) * \left(1 - sigmoid \left(\sum_j w_{j,k} * o_j \right) \right) * o_j$$

You should also notice that the 2 at the beginning of the equation has been dropped. It was only a scaling factor and not important in determining the direction of the error function slope, which is the main key to the gradient descent algorithm. I do wish to congratulate my readers who have made it this far. Many folks have a very difficult time with the mathematics required to get to this stage.

It would now be very helpful to put a physical interpretation on this complex equation. The first part $(t_k - o_k)$ is just the error, which is easy to see. The sum expressions $\sum_j w_{j,k} * o_j$ inside the sigmoid functions are the inputs into the k_{th} final layer node. And the very last term o_j is the output from the j_{th} node in the hidden layer. Knowing this physical interpretation should make the creation of the other layer-to-layer error slope expressions much easier.

I state the input to hidden layer error slope equation without subjecting you to the rigorous mathematical derivation. This expression relies on the physical interpretation just presented.

$$\frac{\partial e}{\partial w_{i,j}} = -\left(e_j\right) * \text{sigmoid}\left(\sum_i w_{i,j} * o_i\right) * \left(1 - sigmoid\left(\sum_i w_{i,j} * o_i\right)\right) * o_i$$

The next step is to demonstrate how new weights are calculated using the preceding error slope expressions. It is actually quite simple as shown in the following equation:

$$new\ w_{j,k} = old\ w_{j,k} - \alpha * \frac{\partial e}{\partial w_{j,k}}$$

α= learning rate

Yes, that is exactly the same learning rate discussed in Chapter 2 where I introduced it as part of the linear predictor discussion. The learning rate is important because setting it too high may cause the gradient descent to miss the minimum, and setting it too low would cause many extra iterations and lessen the efficiency of the gradient descent algorithm.

Matrix Multiplications for Weight Change Determination

It would be very helpful to express all the preceding expressions in terms of matrices, which is the practical way real weight changes are calculated. Let the following expression represent one matrix element for the error slope expression between the hidden and the output layers:

$$\text{gd}\left(w_{j,k}\right) - \alpha * e_k * sigmoid\left(o_k\right) * \left(1 - sigmoid\left(o_k\right)\right) * o_j^T$$

o_j^T is the transpose of the hidden layer output matrix.

The following arc the matrices for the three-layer, six-node example ANN:

$$\begin{bmatrix} \text{gd}\left(w_{1,1}\right) & \text{gd}(w_{2,1}) & \text{gd}\left(w_{3,1}\right) \\ \text{gd}(w_{1,2}) & \text{gd}(w_{2,2}) & \text{gd}(w_{3,2}) \end{bmatrix} * \begin{Bmatrix} e_1 * sigmoid_1 * \left(1 - sigmoid_1\right) \\ e_2 * sigmoid_2 * \left(1 - sigmoid_2\right) \end{Bmatrix} * \begin{Bmatrix} o_1 & o_2 \end{Bmatrix}$$

o_1 and o_2 are outputs from the hidden layer.

This completes all the necessary preparatory background in order to start updating the weights.

Worked-through Example

It's important to go through a manual example before showing the Python approach, so that you truly understand the process when you run it as a Python script. Figure 8-23 is a slightly modified version of Figure 8-11, on which I have inserted arbitrary hidden node output values to have sufficient data to complete the example.

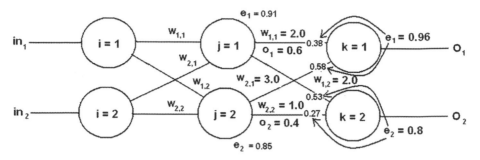

Figure 8-23. *Example ANN used for manual calculations*

Let's start by updating $w_{1,1}$, which is the weight-connecting node 1 in the hidden layer to node 1 in the output layer. Currently, it has a value of 2.0. This is the error slope equation used for these layer links:

$$\frac{\partial e}{\partial w_{j,k}} = -(t_k - o_k) * sigmoid\left(\sum_j w_{j,k} * o_j\right) * \left(1 - sigmoid\left(\sum_j w_{j,k} * o_j\right)\right) * o_j$$

Substitute the values, as shown in the following figure yields:

$$(t_k - o_k) = e_1 = 0.96$$

$$\left(\sum_j w_{j,k} * o_j\right) = (2.0 * 0.6) + (3.0 * 0.4) = 2.4$$

$$sigmoid = \frac{1}{\left(1 + e^{-2.4}\right)} = 0.9168$$

$1 - sigmoid = 0.0832$
$o_1 = 0.6$

Multiply the applicable values with the negative sign yields:

$$-0.96 * 0.9168 * 0.0832 * 0.6 = -0.04394$$

Let's assume a learning rate of 0.15, which is not too aggressive and the following is the new weight:

$$2.0 - 0.15 * (-0.04394) = 2.0 + 0.0066 = 2.0066$$

This is not a large change from the original but you must keep in mind that there is hundreds, if not thousands of iterations performed before the global minimum is reached. Small changes rapidly accumulate to some rather large changes in the weights.

The other weights in the network can be adjusted in the same manner as demonstrated.

There are some important issues regarding how well an ANN can learn, which I discuss next.

Issues with ANN Learning

You should realize that not all ANNs learn well, just as not all people learn the same way. Fortunately for ANNs, it has nothing to do with intelligence but rather for more mundane items directly related to the sigmoid activation function. Figure 8-24 is a modified version of Figure 2-12 showing the input and output ranges for the sigmoid function.

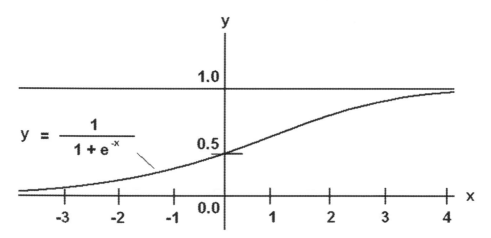

Figure 8-24. *Annotated sigmoid function*

Looking at Figure 8-24, you should see that if the x inputs are larger than 2.5, the y output has very small changes. This is because the sigmoid function asymptotically approaches 1.0 around that x value. Small changes for large input changes imply very small gradient changes happen. ANN learning becomes suppressed in this situation because the gradient descent algorithm depends upon a reasonable slope being present. Thus, ANN training sets should limit the input x values to what might be called a *pseudo-linear range* of roughly –3 to 3. Values of x outside this range causes a saturation effect for ANN learning, and no effective weight updates happen.

In a similar fashion, the sigmoid function cannot output values greater than one or less than zero. Output values in those ranges are not possible and weights must be appropriately scaled back such that the allowable output range is always maintained. In reality, the output range should be 0.01 to 0.99 because of the asymptotic nature described earlier.

Initial Weight Selection

Based on the issues just discussed, I believe you can probably realize that it is very important to select a good initial set of ANN weights so that learning can take effect without bumping into input saturation or output limit problems. The obvious choice is to constrain weight selection to the pseudo-linear range I mentioned earlier (i.e., ±3). Often, weights are further constrained to ±1 to be a bit more conservative.

There has been a "rule of thumb" developed over the years by AI researchers and mathematicians that roughly states:

The weights should be initially allocated using a normal distribution set at a mean value equal to the inverse of the square root of the number of nodes in the ANN.

For a 36-node, three-layer ANN, which I have previously used, the mean is $\frac{1}{\sqrt{36}}$ or 0.16667. Figure 8-25 shows a normal probability distribution with this mean and ±2 approximate standard deviations are also clearly indicated.

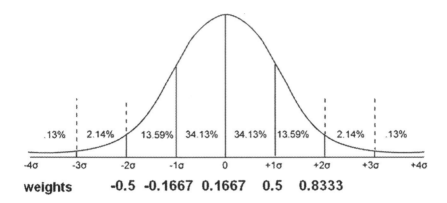

$$\text{approximate sd } (\sigma) = \frac{\text{largest value - smallest value}}{6} = \frac{1 - (1)}{6} = 0.333$$

Figure 8-25. *Normal distribution of initial weights for a 36-node ANN*

A random selection of weights in the range of approximately –0.5 to 0.8333 would nicely provide an excellent starting point for ANN learning for a 36-node network.

Finally, you should avoid setting all weights to the same value because ANN learning depends upon an unequal weight distribution. And obviously, do not set all the weights to 0 because that completely disables the ANN.

This last section completes all of my background discussion on ANN. It is finally time to generate a full-fledged ANN on the Raspberry Pi using Python.

Demo 8-1: ANN Python Scripts

This first demonstration shows you how to create an untrained ANN using Python. I start by discussing the modules that constitute the ANN. Once I have done that, all the modules put into an operative package and the script run. The first module to discuss is the one that creates and initializes the ANN.

Initialization

This module's structure depends largely on the type of ANN to be built. I am building a three-layer, nine-node ANN for this demonstration, which means there must objects representing each layer. In addition, the inputs, outputs, and weights must be created and appropriately labeled. Table 8-3 details the objects and references that are needed for this module.

Table 8-3. *Initialization Module Objects and References*

Name	Description
inode	Number of nodes in the input layer
hnode	Number of nodes in the hidden layer
onode	Number of nodes in the output layer
wtgih	Weight matrix between input and hidden layers
wtgho	Weight matrix between hidden and output layers
wij	Individual weight matrix element
input	Array for inputs
output	Array for outputs
ohidden	Array for hidden layer outputs
lr	Learning rate

The basic initialization module structure begins as follows:

```
def __init__ (self, inode, hnode, onode, lr):
    # Set local variables
    self.inode = inode
    self.hnode = hnode
    self.onode = onode
    self.lr = lr
```

You need to call the init module with the proper values for the ANN to be created. For a three-layer, nine-node network with a moderate learning rate, the values are as follows:

- inode = 3

- hnode = 3

- onode = 3

- lr = 0.25

239

The next item to discuss is how to create and initialize the key weighting matrices based on all the previous background discussions. I use a normal distribution for the weight generation with a mean of 0.1667 and a standard deviation of 0.3333. Fortunately, numpy has a very nice function that automates this process. The first matrix to create is the wtgih, whose dimensions are inode × hnode, or 3 × 3, for our example.

This next Python statement generates this matrix:

```
self.wtgih = np.random.normal(0.1667, 0.3333, self.hnodes,
              self.inodes)
```

The following is a sample output from an interactive session that was generated by the preceding statement:

```
>>>import numpy as np
>>>wtgih = np.random.normal(0.1667, 0.3333, [3, 3])
>>>wtgih
array([[ 0.44602141,  0.58021837,  0.00499487],
       [ 0.40433922, -0.31695922, -0.40410581],
       [ 0.63401073, -0.37218566,  0.14726115]])
```

The resulting matrix wtgih is well formed with excellent starting values.

At this point, the init module can be completed using the matrix generating statements shown earlier.

```
def __init__ (self, inode, hnode, onode, lr):
    # Set local variables
    self.inode = inode
    self.hnode = hnode
    self.onode = onode
    self.lr = lr

    # mean is the reciprocal of the sq root total nodes
    mean = 1/(pow((inode + hnode + onode), 0.5)

    # standard deviation (sd) is approximately 1/6 total weight range
    # total range = 2
    sd = 0.3333

    # generate both weighting matrices
    # input to hidden layer matrix
    self.wtgih = np.random.normal(mean, sd, (hnode, inode])

    # hidden to output layer matrix
    self.wtgho = np.random.normal(mean, sd, [onode, hnode])
```

At this point, I introduce a second module that allows some simple tests to run on the network created by the `init` module. This new module is named `testNet` to reflect its purpose. The takes an input data set or tuple in Python terms and returns an output set. The following process runs in the module:

1. Input data tuple converted to an array.

2. The array is multiplied by the wtgih weighting matrix. This is now the input to the hidden layer.

3. This new array is then adjusted by the sigmoid function.

4. The adjusted array from the hidden layer is multiplied by the wtgho matrix. This now the input to the output layer.

5. This new array is then adjusted by the sigmoid function yielding the final output array.

The module listing follows:

```
def testNet(self, input):
    # convert input tuple to an array
    input = np.array(input, ndmin=2).T

    # multiply input by wtgih
    hInput = np.dot(self.wtgih, input)

    # sigmoid adjustment
    hOutput = 1/(1 + np.exp(-hInput))

    # multiply hidden layer output by wtgho
    oInput = np.dot(self.wtgho, hOutput)

    # sigmoid adjustment
    oOutput = 1/(1 + np.exp(-oInput))

    return oOutput
```

Test Run

Figure 8-26 shows an interactive Python session that I ran on a Raspberry Pi 3 to test this preliminary code.

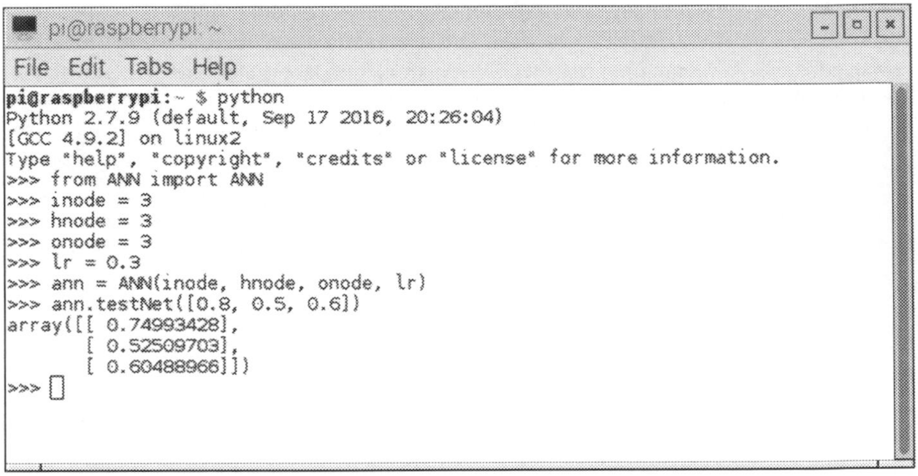

```
●  pi@raspberrypi: ~                                    [-][□][×]
File  Edit  Tabs  Help
pi@raspberrypi:~ $ python
Python 2.7.9 (default, Sep 17 2016, 20:26:04)
[GCC 4.9.2] on linux2
Type "help", "copyright", "credits" or "license" for more information.
>>> from ANN import ANN
>>> inode = 3
>>> hnode = 3
>>> onode = 3
>>> lr = 0.3
>>> ann = ANN(inode, hnode, onode, lr)
>>> ann.testNet([0.8, 0.5, 0.6])
array([[ 0.74993428],
       [ 0.52509703],
       [ 0.60488966]])
>>> []
```

Figure 8-26. *Interactive Python session*

The init and testNet modules were both part of a class named ANN, which in turn were in a file named ANN.py. I first started Python and imported the class from the file so that the interpreter would recognize the class name. I next instantiated an object named ann with all nodes set to 3 and a learning rate equal to 0.3. The learning rate is not needed yet, but it must be present or you cannot instantiate an object. The act of instantiating an object automatically causes the init module to run. It is expecting size values for all three nodes and a learning rate value.

I next ran the testNet module with the three input values. These are shown in Table 8-4 along with the respective calculated output values. I also included the manually calculated error values.

Table 8-4. *Initial Test*

Input	Output	Error	Percent error
0.8	0.74993428	–0.05006572	6.3
0.5	0.52509703	0.02509703	5.0
0.6	0.60488966	0.00488966	0.8

The errors are not too much considering this is a totally untrained ANN. The next section discusses how to train an ANN to greatly improve its accuracy.

Demo 8-2: Training an ANN

In this demonstration, I show you how to train an ANN using a third module named `trainNet`, which has been added to the ANN class definition. This module functions in a very similar fashion to the `testNet` function by calculating an output set based on an input data set. However, the `trainNet` module input data is a predetermined training set instead of an arbitrary data tuple as I just demonstrated. This new module also calculates an error set by comparing the ANN outputs with its inputs and using the differences for training the network. The outputs are calculated in exactly the same manner as was done in `testNet` module. The arguments to `trainNet` now include both an input list and a training list. The following statements create these arrays from the list arguments:

```
def trainNet(self, inputT, train):
    # This module depends on the values, arrays and matrices
    # created when the init module is run.

    # create the arrays from the list arguments
    self.inputT = np.array(inputT, ndmin=2).T
    self.train = np.array(train, ndmin=2).T
```

The error is as stated before is the difference between the training set outputs and the actual outputs. The error equation for the k_{th} output node as previously stated is:

$$e_k = t_k - o_k$$

The matrix notation for the output errors is

```
self.eOutput = self.train - self.oOutput
```

The hidden layer error array in matrix notation for this example ANN is

$$hError = \begin{Bmatrix} \begin{bmatrix} w_{1,1} & w_{1,2} & w_{1,3} \\ w_{2,1} & w_{2,2} & w_{2,3} \\ w_{3,1} & w_{3,2} & w_{3,3} \end{bmatrix}^T * \begin{Bmatrix} e_1 \\ e_2 \\ e_3^T \end{Bmatrix} \end{Bmatrix}$$

The following is the Python statement to generate this array:

```
self.hError = np.dot(self.wtgho.T, self.eOutput)
```

The following is the update equation for adjusting a link between the j_{th} and k_{th} layers, as previously shown:

$$gd(w_{j,k}) = \alpha * e_k * sigmoid(o_k) * (1 - sigmoid(o_k)) * o_j^T$$

The new $gd(w_{j,k})$ array must be added to the original because these are adjustments to the original. The preceding equations can be neatly packaged into this single Python statement:

```
self.wtgho += self.lr * np.dot((self.eOutput * self.oOutputT *
(1 - self.oOutputT)), self.hOutputT.T)
```

Writing the code for the weight updates between the input and hidden layers uses precisely the same format.

```
self.wtgih += self.lr * np.dot((self.hError * self.hOutputT *
(1 - self.hOutputT)), self.inputT.T)
```

Putting all the preceding code segments together along with the previous modules produces the ANN.py listing. Note that I have included comments regarding the functions for each segment, along with additional debug statements.

```
import numpy as np

class ANN:

    def __init__ (self, inode, hnode, onode, lr):
        # set local variables
        self.inode = inode
        self.hnode = hnode
        self.onode = onode
        self.lr = lr

        # mean is the reciprocal of the sq root of the total nodes
        mean = 1/(pow((inode + hnode + onode), 0.5))

        # standard deviation is approximately 1/6 of total range
        # range = 2
        stdev = 0.3333

        # generate both weighting matrices
        # input to hidden layer matrix
        self.wtgih = np.random.normal(mean, stdev, [hnode, inode])
        print 'wtgih'
        print self.wtgih
        print

        # hidden to output layer matrix
        self.wtgho = np.random.normal(mean, stdev, [onode, hnode])
        print 'wtgho'
        print self.wtgho
        print
```

```python
def testNet(self, input):
    # convert input tuple to an array
    input = np.array(input, ndmin=2).T

    # multiply input by wtgih
    hInput = np.dot(self.wtgih, input)

    # sigmoid adjustment
    hOutput = 1/(1 + np.exp(-hInput))

    # multiply hidden layer output by wtgho
    oInput = np.dot(self.wtgho, hOutput)

    # sigmoid adjustment
    oOutput = 1/(1 + np.exp(-oInput))

    return oOutput

def trainNet(self, inputT, train):

    # This module depends on the values, arrays and matrices
    # created when the init module is run.

    # create the arrays from the list arguments
    self.inputT = np.array(inputT, ndmin=2).T
    self.train = np.array(train, ndmin=2).T

    # multiply inputT array by wtgih
    self.hInputT = np.dot(self.wtgih, self.inputT)

    # sigmoid adjustment
    self.hOutputT = 1/(1 + np.exp(-self.hInputT))

    # multiply hidden layer output by wtgho
    self.oInputT = np.dot(self.wtgho, self.hOutputT)
    # sigmoid adjustment
    self.oOutputT = 1/(1 + np.exp(-self.oInputT))

    # calculate output errors
    self.eOutput = self.train - self.oOutputT

    # calculate hidden layer error array
    self.hError = np.dot(self.wtgho.T, self.eOutput)

    # update weight matrix wtgho
    self.wtgho += self.lr * np.dot((self.eOutput *
    self.oOutputT * (1 - self.oOutputT)), self.hOutputT.T)
```

```
# update weight matrix wtgih
self.wtgih += self.lr * np.dot((self.hError *
self.hOutputT * (1 - self.hOutputT)), self.inputT.T)
print 'updated wtgih'
print wtgih
print
print 'updated wtgho'
print wtgho
print
```

Test Run

Figure 8-27 shows an interactive Python session where I instantiated a three-layer, nine-node ANN with a learning rate equal to 0.20.

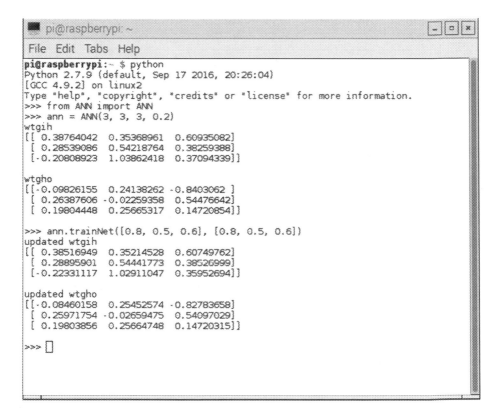

Figure 8-27. *Interactive Python session*

I have included several debug print statements in the ANN script, which allows for a direct comparison between the initial weight matrices and the updated ones. You should see there are only small changes between them, which is what was expected and desired. It is an important fact that the gradient descent works well using small increments to avoid missing the global minimum. I could only do one iteration in this session because the code was not set up for multiple iterations.

Congratulations for staying with me to this point! I covered a lot of topics concerning both ANN fundamentals and implementations. You should now be fully prepared to understand and appreciate the interesting practical ANN demonstrations presented in the next chapter.

Summary

This was the third of four chapters concerning artificial neural networks (ANNs). In this chapter, I focused on deep learning, which is really nothing more than the fundamentals and concepts behind multilayer ANNs.

After a brief review of some fundamentals, I completed a step-by-step manual calculation of a two-layer, six-node ANN. I subsequently redid the calculations using a Python script.

Next were the calculations for a larger, three-layer, nine-node ANN. Those calculations were done entirely with Python and matrix algorithms imported from the numpy library.

I discussed the errors that exist within an untrained ANN and how they are propagated. This was important to understand because it serves as the basis for the back propagation technique used to adjust weights in an effort to optimize the ANN.

Next, I went through a complete back propagation example, which illustrated how weights could be updated to reduce overall network errors. A sidebar followed wherein the gradient descent (GD) technique was introduced using a linear regression example.

A discussion involving the application of GD to an example ANN followed. The GD algorithm uses the slope of the error function in an effort to locate a global minimum, which is necessary to achieve a well-performing ANN.

I provided a complete example illustrating how to update weights using the GD algorithm. Issues with ANN learning and initial weight selection were discussed.

The chapter concluded with a thorough example of a Python script that initializes and trains any sized ANN.

CHAPTER 9

▓ ▓ ▓

Machine Learning: Practical ANN Demonstrations

This is the final chapter in the series exploring machine learning. I demonstrate two practical examples of an artificial neuron network (ANN) based on the concepts and Python implementations discussed in the previous chapters. You should review the material in at least the two previous chapters to gain the most benefit from reading and even duplicating this chapter's demonstrations.

I would like to give much credit to Tariq Rashid, whose book *Make Your Own Neural Network* (CreateSpace Independent Publishing Platform, 2016) was a source of inspiration and guidance for me in preparing this and other chapters in my book. I highly recommend Tariq's book to readers who wish to gain more insight into practical ANNs. Tariq also has a blog at `http://makeyourownneuralnetwork.blogspot.co.uk/`, which I found to be a highly useful source of information and lively discussions.

The demonstrations in this chapter are centered on recognizing handwritten numbers. They are classic ANN projects that fully demonstrate the learning capability of an ANN.

Parts List

You need additional parts for the demonstrations, which are detailed in Table 9-1.

© Donald J. Norris 2017
D. J. Norris, *Beginning Artificial Intelligence with the Raspberry Pi*,
DOI 10.1007/978-1-4842-2743-5_9

Table 9-1. *Parts Lists*

Description	Quantity	Remarks
Pi Cobbler	1	40-pin version, either T or DIP form factor acceptable
solderless breadboard	1	700 insertion points with 1 power supply strip
jumper wires	1 package	
220Ω resistor	1	1/4 watt
LED	1	
Pi Camera	1	version 2
tactile push button switch	1	with solderless connections

Demo 9-1: MNIST Data Set

I will show you how an ANN can recognize handwritten numbers. The training and test data used in this project come directly from two Mixed National Institute of Standards and Technology (MNIST) databases. These databases have been widely used for training and testing ANNs for many years and are an accepted standard for rating how accurate a particular ANN is for accomplishing a task.

The genesis for the MNIST databases comes from input images taken from handwritten numeric symbols by 500 people, half of which were US Census Bureau employees and the other half were high school students. The original black-and-white images were also normalized to fit a 20 × 20-pixel-image bounding block and further anti-aliased, which generated a one-byte grayscale value for each pixel. What this means will be made very clear to you shortly.

The MNIST data sets are quite large, consisting of 60,000 training images (104MB) and 10,000 testing images (18MB). Both data sets are freely available in a comma-separated value (CSV) format from the following websites:

> Training set:
> http://www.pjreddie.com/media/files/mnist_
> train.csv
>
> Test set:
> http://www.pjreddie.com/media/files/mnist_
> test.csv

The training set should be used to train the ANN. All the included records are labeled, meaning that the CSV data is identified with the corresponding image it is representing. The test set is used to check how well the ANN functions in recognizing test CSV data. The test data set also contains labels as an aid to verify whether the ANN successfully identified the correct number. Separating training from test data is always a good idea because the ANN could return stored patterns if the training data was also the test data. This situation would not be a good indicator of how well the ANN actually learned.

Figure 9-1 shows only the beginning of the first record contained in the training data set as displayed by a hex editor application running on my MacBook Pro.

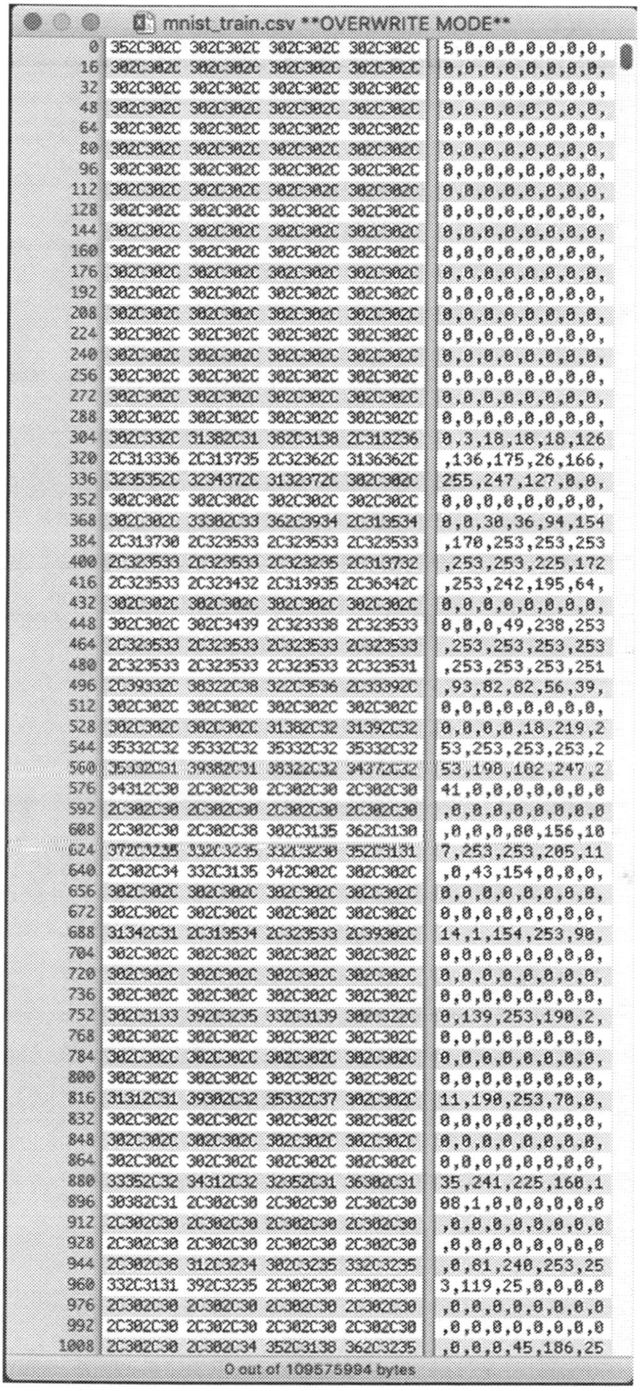

Figure 9-1. *A portion of the first record in the MNIST training data set*

There are 784 bytes composing one image because each image in the database has been resized to 28 × 28 pixels or 784 overall. Each pixel value represents the equivalent grayscale value of a pixel. One byte has a numeric range of 0 to 255, where 0 is total white and 255 is total black. Each database image therefore consists of 784 pixel values, 785 commas, and 1 byte for the label, which sums to 1570 bytes overall. While one record of this size is not too hard to handle, having more than 60,000 of them in one file tends to overload most programs, especially programs that are expected to run on a Raspberry Pi. Fortunately, there are two very small subsets of both the larger MNIST train and the test data sets, which are available at the following websites:

- Test data set

  ```
  https://raw.githubusercontent.com/makeyour
  ownneuralnetwork/makeyourownneuralnetwork/
  master/mnist_dataset/mnist_test_10.csv
  ```

- Train data set

  ```
  https://raw.githubusercontent.com/makeyour
  ownneuralnetwork/makeyourownneuralnetwork/
  master/mnist_dataset/mnist_train_100.csv
  ```

I opened both downloaded data sets using the hex editor and they appeared to be just fine. However, to use the data in a Python script, you need to use some statements to access these data sets. The following Python statements instantiate a file object named `dataFile`, read the data line by line into a list object named `dataList`, and finally close the file. These statement types are a very common way to read data files with Python:

```
dataFile = open("mnist_train_100.csv")
dataList = dataFile.readlines()
dataFile.close()
```

Figure 9-2 shows an interactive session on a Raspberry Pi where I used the preceding statements to create the `dataList` object.

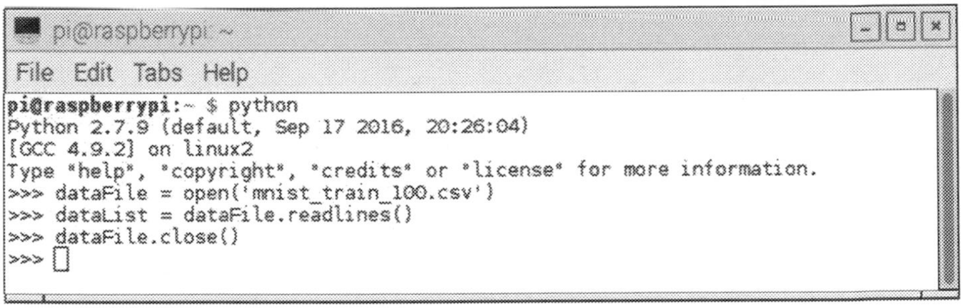

Figure 9-2. *Interactive Python session creating a dataList object*

I ran the Python session in the same directory where the MNIST data set was located. If you do not have the data set in the same directory, then you have to prepend the appropriate path to the MNIST data set name to avoid the Python error of not finding the file.

You may start examining the data once it has been read. I entered len(dataList) to find out the number of records that were put into the dataList object. The return value was 100, as expected. Figure 9-3 shows this statement along with a display of the first record, which I directed by entering dataList[0].

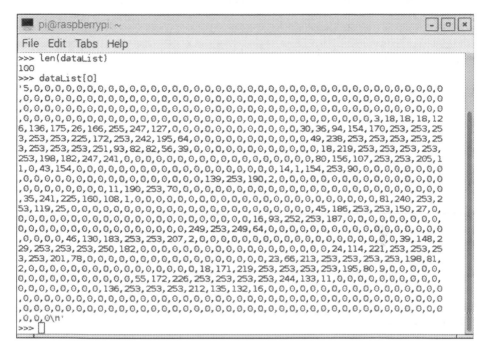

Figure 9-3. *dataList properties*

If you closely examine the datalist[0] display in the figure, you probably see that the data begins and ends with apostrophes. This indicates that the dataList[0] record is recognized as a string by the Python interpreter. It may look like numbers but it is considered just a string of ASCII characters according to Python. The character just before the ending apostrophe is \n, which is the "escaped" letter n. This indicates to Python that the first record ends and it should place a new line at that point. New line characters are delimiters for the record set, telling Python where one record ends and the next begins. All 100 records are indexed, meaning they may be individually accessed by using the appropriate index number along the list name, as I did to access the first record (i.e., dataList[0]). The indices are 0 based, ranging from 0 to 99 in this case.

Next, I show you how to image a record, instead of simply looking at sterile numbers that make little to no sense.

Imaging a MNIST Record

It is actually fairly easy to image a data record using a few Python commands. I used the Python GUI IDLE 2 to accomplish the next steps. A GUI environment is necessary to show the resultant image. You can use the Python 3 GUI if so desired, but you need to modify the following installation statements for Python 3. The matplotlib library is required to create and display the image; more specifically, the `imshow` and `show` methods contained in the pyplot package, which is part of the overall matplotlib library. Enter the following commands to install the matplotlib library:

```
sudo apt-get update
sudo apt-get install python-matplotlib
```

Once the installation is completed, you are ready to enter the next commands to read in the data from the 100-record, abbreviated data set. Enter these commands:

```
import numpy as np
import matplotlib.pyplot as plt
dataFile = open('mnist_train_100.csv')
dataList = dataFile.readlines()
dataFile.close()
```

The first two import commands are not needed for the data-read portion, but I always want to put any import statements at the start of a code block. The `dataFile` logical reference is created with the open statement and it points to the start of the 100-record file. The actual read happens with the next statement that reads in 100 separate records into a list object named `dataList`. The `readlines` method just reads one character after another until it encounters a new-line character (`\n`). At that instant, it creates a new record for the list and resumes the character-by-character reads until it encounters the end-of-file (EOF) character, which ceases the read process. The `close` method just "destroys" the `dataFile` logical reference so that the file will not be inadvertently modified.

The script is set to image a selected record once the data set is in memory. The following code accomplishes this objective:

```
record0 = dataList[0].split(',')
imageArray = np.asfarray(record0[1:]).reshape((28, 28))
plt.imshow(imageArray, cmap='Greys', interpolation='None')
plt.show()
```

The first command creates a small list object named `record0` that consists of all 785 elements in the first record that were read into the large `dataList` object. There are 785 separate list elements in the `record0` object because the `split` method created them by using the comma delimiter as an indicator for separation. The second command uses the `imshow` method to create the image to be displayed. It starts with the second list element and it is a grayscale image that is shaped into a 28 × 28–pixel array. Note the spelling of `Greys` in the `imshow` argument list. Finally, the `show` method actually displays the image in the IDLE 2 GUI.

Figure 9-4 shows all of the preceding commands running in an IDLE 2 GUI.

```
*Python 2.7.9 Shell*                                        _ □ ×

File  Edit  Shell  Debug  Options  Windows  Help

Python 2.7.9 (default, Sep 17 2016, 20:26:04)
[GCC 4.9.2] on linux2
Type "copyright", "credits" or "license()" for more information.
>>> import numpy as np
>>> import matplotlib.pyplot as plt
>>> dataFile = open('mnist_train_100.csv')
>>> dataList = dataFile.readlines()
>>> dataFile.close()
>>> record0 = dataList[0].split(',')
>>> imageArray = np.asfarray(record0[1:]).reshape((28, 28))
>>> plt.imshow(imageArray, cmap='Greys', interpolation='None')
<matplotlib.image.AxesImage object at 0x73313f90>
>>> plt.show()

                                                      Ln: 14 Col: 0
```

Figure 9-4. *IDLE 2 GUI interactive Python session*

The resulting number image is shown in Figure 9-5.

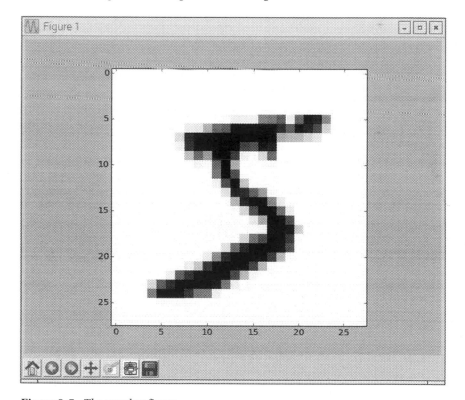

Figure 9-5. *The number figure*

As you can see, the image shows a rather casually written number 5, which is one of the many records to be used to train the ANN. Incidentally, if you go back and look at Figure 9-1, you see the number 5 as the label for the first record, which confirms the record identity.

At this point, I turn the discussion toward how to prepare the data sets so that they can be used effectively with an ANN.

Adjusting the Input and Output Data Sets

You certainly know that all MNIST data sets contain values ranging from 0 to 255, which is well beyond the range that any ANN that I have developed so far can accept. The input values should be in a preferred range of 0.01 to 1.0, which matches the sigmoid function input requirements quite nicely. The following Python statement adjusts the values range for a MNIST data set record to match the preferred range for an ANN input data set:

```
adjustedRecord0 = (np.asfarray(record0[1:]) / 255.0 * 0.99) + 0.01
```

Figure 9-6 shows an adjusted record set created in an interactive Python session. A portion of the record set is also shown in the screenshot, confirming that the new MNIST values fall within the desired input value range.

```
■ pi@raspberrypi: ~                                    [ - ][ □ ][ x ]

File  Edit  Tabs  Help

pi@raspberrypi:~ $ python
Python 2.7.9 (default, Sep 17 2016, 20:26:04)
[GCC 4.9.2] on linux2
Type "help", "copyright", "credits" or "license" for more information.
>>> import numpy as np
>>> dataFile = open('mnist_train_100.csv')
>>> dataList = dataFile.readlines()
>>> dataFile.close()
>>> record0 = dataList[0].split(',')
>>> adjustedRecord0 = (np.asfarray(record0[1:])/255.0 * 0.99) + 0.01
>>> print adjustedRecord0
[ 0.01        0.01        0.01        0.01        0.01        0.01        0.01
  0.01        0.01        0.01        0.01        0.01        0.01        0.01
  0.01        0.01        0.01        0.01        0.01        0.01        0.01
  0.01        0.01        0.01        0.01        0.01        0.01        0.01
  0.01        0.01        0.01        0.01        0.01        0.01        0.01
  0.01        0.01        0.01        0.01        0.01        0.01        0.01
  0.01        0.01        0.01        0.01        0.01        0.01        0.01
  0.01        0.01        0.01        0.01        0.01        0.01        0.01
  0.01        0.01        0.01        0.01        0.01        0.01        0.01
  0.01        0.01        0.01        0.01        0.01        0.01        0.01
  0.01        0.01        0.01        0.01        0.01        0.01        0.01
  0.01        0.01        0.01        0.01        0.01        0.01        0.01
  0.01        0.01        0.01        0.01        0.01        0.01        0.01
  0.01        0.01        0.01        0.01        0.01        0.01        0.01
  0.01        0.01        0.01        0.01        0.01        0.01        0.01
  0.01        0.01        0.01        0.01        0.01        0.01        0.01
  0.01        0.01        0.01        0.01        0.01        0.01        0.01
  0.01        0.01        0.01        0.01        0.01        0.01        0.01
  0.01        0.01        0.01        0.01        0.01        0.01        0.01
  0.01        0.01        0.01        0.01        0.01        0.01        0.01
  0.01        0.01        0.01        0.01        0.01        0.02164706
  0.07988235  0.07988235  0.07988235  0.49917647  0.538       0.68941176
  0.11094118  0.65447059  1.          0.96894118  0.50305882  0.01        0.01
  0.01        0.01        0.01        0.01        0.01        0.01        0.01
  0.01        0.01        0.01        0.12647059  0.14976471  0.37494118
  0.60788235  0.67        0.99223529  0.99223529  0.99223529  0.99223529
  0.99223529  0.88352941  0.67776471  0.99223529  0.94952941  0.76705882
  0.25847059  0.01        0.01        0.01        0.01        0.01        0.01
  0.01        0.01        0.01        0.01        0.01        0.20023529
  0.934       0.99223529  0.99223529  0.99223529  0.99223529  0.99223529
  0.99223529  0.99223529  0.99223529  0.98447059  0.37105882  0.32835294
  0.32835294  0.22741176  0.16141176  0.01        0.01        0.01        0.01
  0.01        0.01        0.01        0.01        0.01        0.01        0.01
  0.01        0.07988235  0.86023529  0.99223529  0.99223529  0.99223529
  0.99223529  0.99223529  0.77870588  0.71658824  0.96894118  0.94564706
  0.01        0.01        0.01        0.01        0.01        0.01        0.01
  0.01        0.01        0.01        0.01        0.01        0.01        0.01
  0.01        0.01        0.01        0.01        0.32058824  0.61564706
  0.42541176  0.99223529  0.99223529  0.80588235  0.05270588  0.01
  0.17694118  0.60788235  0.01        0.01        0.01        0.01        0.01
  0.01        0.01        0.01        0.01        0.01        0.01        0.01
  0.01        0.01        0.01        0.01        0.01        0.01        0.01
  0.06435294  0.01388235  0.60788235  0.99223529  0.35941176  0.01        0.01
  0.01        0.01        0.01        0.01        0.01        0.01        0.01
  0.01        0.01        0.01        0.01        0.01        0.01        0.01
```

Figure 9-6. *Adjusted MNIST data set*

The preceding discussion takes care of the input, but what should an output data set look like? The answer lies in considering the purpose that the ANN serves. Its purpose is to recognize a handwritten number whose value ranges from 0 to 9. It would make sense to have the ANN just output a high value near one of the output nodes associated with the recognized number. Thus, an ideal output array such as the following shows that a handwritten number 5 was detected by the ANN.

$$\begin{Bmatrix} 0 \\ 0 \\ 0 \\ 0 \\ 0 \\ 1 \\ 0 \\ 0 \\ 0 \\ 0 \end{Bmatrix}$$

The actual values in such an array would not be 0 or 1, but instead values near 0 for low recognition and near 1 for high recognition. It is also entirely possible to have the ANN output intermediate values on several nodes, such as 0.4 and 0.6, indicating that the ANN cannot choose a unique value, but "thinks" the input number could be one of several candidates. This is quite similar to a human unable to decide what the causally written number is, such as confusing a four for a nine.

The next code segment creates a sample train array that is needed to update the ANN weights so that it can recognize a specific number. Let's create a train array for the first record in the small MNIST training data set by using the realistic input values earlier discussed. The Python code is quite simple, as shown in the following:

```
import numpy as np
dataFile = open('mnist_train_100.csv')
dataList = dataFile.readlines()
dataFile.close()
record0 = dataList[0].split(',')
onodes = 10
train = np.zeros(onodes) + 0.01
train[int[record0[0]] = 0.99
print train
```

The preceding program segment should be very familiar to you by now, except for the last few lines. The following line creates a 10-element array with all values equal to 0.01:

```
train = np.zeros(onodes) + 0.01
```

Next, the following line takes the first element in the first record (the label) and converts it to an integer, and subsequently sets it equal to 0.99:

```
train[int([record0[0])] = 0.99
```

Figure 9-7 shows the preceding code segment run in an interactive Python session.

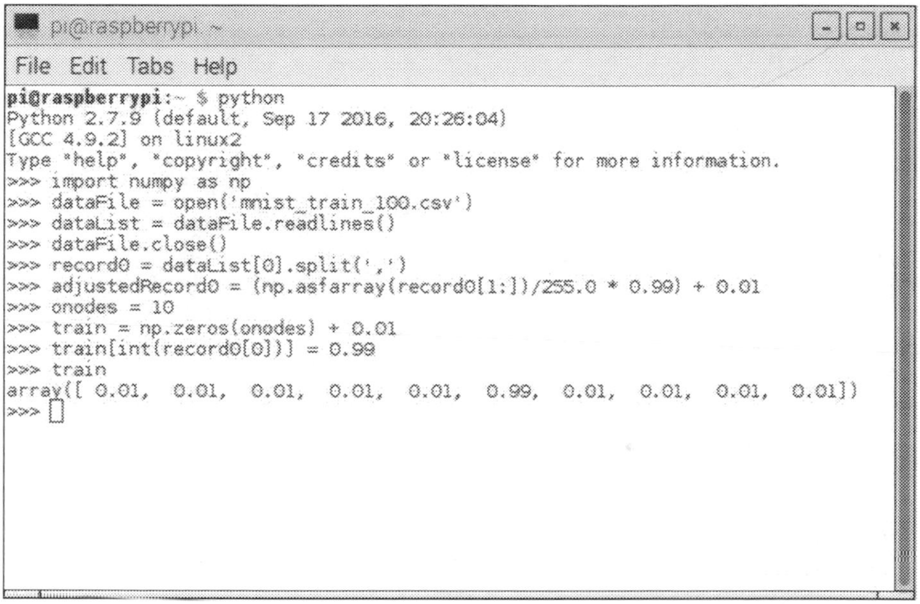

```
pi@raspberrypi:~ $ python
Python 2.7.9 (default, Sep 17 2016, 20:26:04)
[GCC 4.9.2] on linux2
Type "help", "copyright", "credits" or "license" for more information.
>>> import numpy as np
>>> dataFile = open('mnist_train_100.csv')
>>> dataList = dataFile.readlines()
>>> dataFile.close()
>>> record0 = dataList[0].split(',')
>>> adjustedRecord0 = (np.asfarray(record0[1:])/255.0 * 0.99) + 0.01
>>> onodes = 10
>>> train = np.zeros(onodes) + 0.01
>>> train[int(record0[0])] = 0.99
>>> train
array([ 0.01,  0.01,  0.01,  0.01,  0.01,  0.99,  0.01,  0.01,  0.01,  0.01])
>>> 
```

Figure 9-7. *Creating a training array interactive session*

You can clearly see the train array created where the sixth element has been set to 0.99 because the label equaled 5.

It is time to focus on how to configure this ANN now that the data set input and training sets have been developed.

Configuring the ANN for Handwritten Number Detection

The first step in this process is to decide on the basic ANN configuration. I have primarily used three-layer ANNs up to this point and I see no real reason to change that approach. The number of output nodes is determined to be 10 based on the previous discussion. What remains is to figure out the number of input and hidden nodes to create.

Figuring out the number of input nodes is relatively easy because there are 784 separate pixel values that must be examined. This means that the ANN needs 784 input nodes. That seems like a lot, but the nature of this problem dictates that is the number required to take advantage of all the data present in the problem domain.

Determining the number of nodes in the hidden layer is a more difficult issue to resolve. There is no analytic method available to determine the appropriate number. I have done a fair amount of research on this topic and have determined that most AI researchers use a variety of "rules of thumb" to determine this number. The following are among the most common:

- Use the mean of the input layer nodes (N_i) and output layer nodes (N_o).

- Take the square root of N_i times N_o.

- The number of hidden layer nodes (N_h) should be between the size of the N_i and N_o.

- Nh should be 2/3 the size of N_i plus N_o.

- Nh should be less than twice the size of the N_i.

One fact that became abundantly clear to me is that an ANN configuration often turns into a trial-and-error situation. There are two related terms that you should be familiar with and those are *under-fitting* and *over-fitting*. Under-fitting happens in an ANN when there are too few nodes present to support adequate training. The symptoms of under-fitting are that the ANN cannot be trained and/or the error is high enough to render the ANN unusable. The converse is true of over-fitting, in which there is a surplus of nodes, training is hampered by too many links, and the ANN performance suffers. When over-fitting occurs, the ANN has so much information processing capacity that the limited amount of data contained in the training set is not sufficient to train all the nodes in the hidden layer. Additionally, a large number of unneeded nodes in the hidden layer increases the time that it takes to train the network. This increased training time can make it impossible to adequately train the ANN. To achieve optimal performance, the goal is to neither under-fit nor over-fit an ANN.

Based on the preceding discussion and my research, I came to the following conclusion on setting the appropriate number of hidden layer nodes:

The number of hidden layer nodes in a three-layer ANN should be set at the square of the number of output nodes, but should not exceed the mean of the input and output layer nodes.

This conclusion might be considered a "mashup" of the various rules of thumb stated earlier. I have also noted anecdotally that there seems to be a squaring relationship that often pops up in ANN technology. This relationship was present when the mean was calculated for the initial weighting and when the error function slope was calculated. Squaring the 10 output nodes means that 100 hidden layer nodes should be set. This value seems appropriate for an initial try. It can easily be changed if the ANN performs poorly.

At this point, it is appropriate to incorporate all the preceding code segments into a Python script that also imports the ANN.py script developed in the last chapter. The following listing is named trainANN.py:

```
# trainANN.py
import numpy as np
import matplotlib.pyplot as plt
from ANN import ANN
```

```
# setup the network configuration
inode = 784
hnode = 100
onode = 10

# set the learning rate
lr = 0.2

# instantiate an ANN object named ann
ann = ANN(inode, hnode, onode, lr)

# create the training list data
dataFile = open('mnist_train_100.csv')
dataList = dataFile.readlines()
dataFile.close()

# train the ANN using all the records in the list
for record in dataList:
    recordx = record.split(',')
    inputT = (np.asfarray(recordx[1:])/255.0 * 0.99) + 0.01
    train = np.zeros(onode) + 0.01
    train[int(recordx[0])] = 0.99
    # training begins here
    ann.trainNet(inputT, train)
```

The Python code is remarkably concise for the amount of computations being carried out. Separating the ANN class definition from the test code is always a good idea because the class may be easily updated or extended without requiring modifications to the test code.

I executed the trainANN script in an interactive session and it ran without errors, but of course, nothing displayed. It now needs some test data to see how well it functions.

Test Run

The subset of MNIST test data that I downloaded is set up in the same way as the training data because it is in the same format as the training data. The following familiar Python code prepares the test data:

```
import numpy as np
testDataFile = open('mnist_test_10.csv')
testDataList = testDataFile.readlines()
testDataFile.close()
```

It would be wise to image the first test data record before tactually testing it with the ANN. Figure 9-8 shows a session with IDLE 2 that imaged the record.

Figure 9-8. *IDLE 2 GUI interactive Python session*

The number that displayed is shown in Figure 9-9.

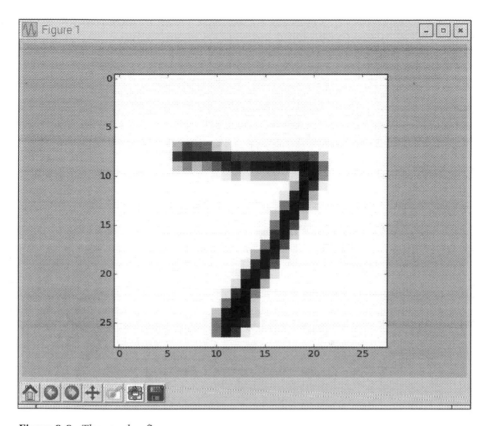

Figure 9-9. *The number figure*

The next step is to add the following code to the trainANN.py script. Technically, this script both trains and tests the ANN. You may wish to give it a new name to reflect its new function. I just kept the old name and tried to remember that it now tests the ANN. The additional Python code is in the following:

```
# create the test list data
testDataFile = open('mnist_test_10.csv')
testDataList = testDataFile.readlines()
testDataFile.close()

# iterate through all 10 test records and display output arrays
for record in testDataList:
    recordz = record.split(',')
    # determine record label
    labelz = int(recordz[0])
    # rescale and offset record values
    inputz = (np.asfarray(recordz[1:])/255.0 * 0.99) + 0.01
    outputz = ann.testNet(inputz)
    print 'output for label = ', labelz
    print outputz
```

Figure 9-10 shows the results of running the newly modified trainANN script. Ten output arrays were output but only six are shown in the screenshot due to limitations in the screen capture process.

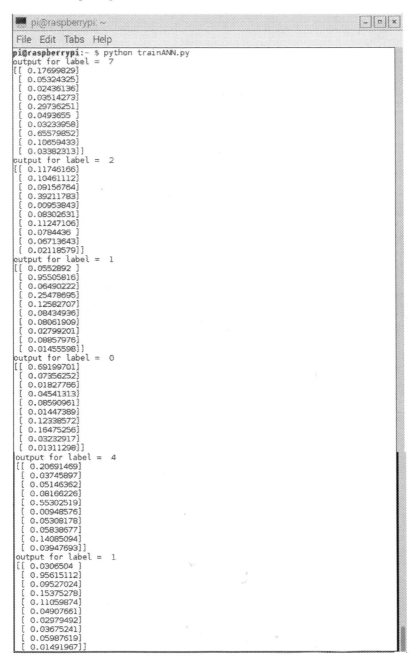

Figure 9-10. *trainANN output with test inputs*

Table 9-2 neatly summarizes the results comparing the label value with the index of the highest value in the output array.

Table 9-2. *Test Results*

Label	7	2	1	0	4	1	4	9	5	9
Index	7	3	1	0	4	1	7	6	0	7
Match	x		x	x	x	x				

The 50 percent was rather disappointing, but maybe that was to be expected because the ANN was trained with only 100 records out of more than 60,000 available for training. I did notice that the output values were fairly high for those records that matched, whereas the ones that didn't match had a uniform spread of random-like values.

I next slightly modified the code to automatically calculate the success rate, especially considering that I was going to run 10,000 test records through and I did not want to manually calculate that test run. I also deleted the display code for the output arrays. The following code implements these changes:

```
match = 0
no_match = 0
# iterate through all test records and display output arrays
for record in testDataList:
    recordz = record.split(',')
    # determine record label
    labelz = int(recordz[0])
    # rescale and offset record values
    inputz = (np.asfarray(recordz[1:])/255.0 * 0.99) + 0.01
    outputz = ann.testNet(inputz)
    max_value = np.argmax(outputz)
    if max_ value == labelz:
        match = match + 1
    else:
        no_match = no_match + 1
print 'success match rate = ', float(match)/float(match + no_match)
```

I ran the trainANN script six times and saw some interesting results, as shown in Figure 9-11.

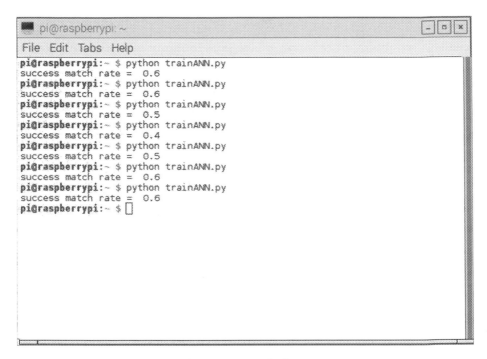

Figure 9-11. *trainANN script with success rate calculations*

The success rate varied from 0.4 to 0.6; it used the same test input data set. The only reasonable explanation is that some weight matrices were better fitted than others were. These matrices are generated using a random normal distribution, as I discussed in Chapter 8, and apparently, some are slightly better suited to produce more accurate results than others are. Let's hope that these random variations disappear when the ANN is trained using the full 60,000 training record set. To use the 60,000 record set only requires the following change to the file's open statement in the trainANN.py script:

```
dataFile = open('mnist_train.csv')
```

I made this change and reran the 10 test data records. I was pleasantly surprised that the success rate now equaled 0.90. Incidentally, the Raspberry Pi took about 5 minutes to process the full training set, which I didn't think was very long for a quad-core, 1.2GHz processor.

The next step is to run the full 10,000-record test data set. You can do that by again changing only one statement:

```
testDataFile = open('mnist_test.csv')
```

This time, the script took about 8 minutes to complete and displayed a very respectable 0.9381 success match rate.

I next wanted to see wanted to see how the match success rate varied with different learning rates. To do this, I added a new loop around both the train and test code in the trainANN.py script, where the learn rate was changed in 0.1 increments from 0.1 to 0.9. Figure 9-12 shows the results for this test.

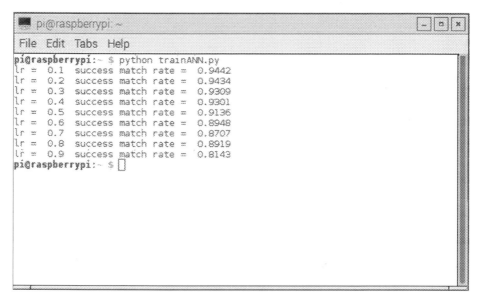

Figure 9-12. *Match success rates with different learning rates*

The maximum success match rate of 0.9442 was for a learning rate equal to 0.1. This is a very good recognition rate, comparable with many larger and more complex research-grade ANNs. I really believe that you will be pleased to have created such a well-performing ANN if you have duplicated what I have done to this point. I can say from personal experience that most college AI students have not accomplished what you have done in this chapter. You should be very happy with the background and education you have achieved to this point.

However, do not be timid about trying some additional experiments to see how the ANN performs with different parameters, including changing the number of hidden nodes. One technique that Tariq mentions in his book is the concept of epochs, where the ANN is trained multiple times using the same training data set. Each complete training cycle is termed an *epoch*. Tariq, as well as other AI researchers, have found that it is often possible to over-train an ANN, resulting in an overall poorer performance than could be expected from just running several epochs. The exact reason for this phenomenon is unknown, except that researchers do speculate that the ANN is over-fitted due to the excessive data inputs. See the previous the discussion regarding over-fitting, which explains the symptoms that appear with this type of training.

The fun and interesting aspect of ANNs is that there is a lot of variety present, with which you can experiment to try to tweak out additional performance. While 94 to 95 percent recognition accuracy is nothing to be ashamed of, it is also worthwhile to try to improve the ANN just a little more. You could also try building a convolutional ANN, which purportedly has a 98.5 percent success rate with the MNIST test data set. A blog by Dr. Adrian Rosebrock at www.pyimagesearch.com explains how this is done. It is a bit complicated, but using a great Python library named Keras, along with Adrian's custom libraries, allows a rapid and trouble-free ANN build. These are highly recommended for those of you who want to go the extra step.

In the next section, I show you a complementary project that uses a Pi Camera for handwritten number recognition.

Demo 9-2: Handwritten Number Recognition with a Pi Camera

The very first thing you must do is ensure that the Pi Camera has been enabled in the Raspberry Pi configuration. The easiest way to do this is to run the raspi-config utility by entering the following command at the command line:

```
sudo raspi-config
```

You then see the menu displayed, as shown in Figure 9-13.

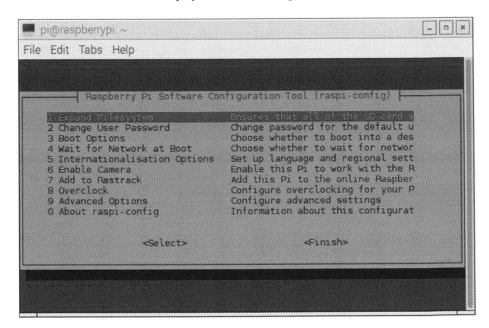

Figure 9-13. raspi-config menu

Select 6 Enable Camera. This option installs the drivers for the Pi Camera. The drivers enable the camera device and the Jessie operating system to work together.

The next step is to install the Pi Camera. The camera connects to the Raspberry Pi using a flex ribbon cable that should already be attached to the camera when purchased. The cable's free end plugs into the camera serial interface (CSI) connector, which is located on the board and directly behind the RJ-45 connector. To plug in the cable, you must first carefully pull directly up on two black plastic tabs on each side of a slim plastic bar. Be very careful because this is a flimsy piece of plastic that can easily be broken from using too much force. The plastic piece will become loose, yet is still attached to the connector body.

Next, carefully insert the flex cable into the socket with the exposed, silver-colored contacts facing **away** from the RJ-45 connector. The blue backing on the ribbon cable should face the RJ-45 connector. Ensure that the cable is firmly seated at the bottom of the connector and that the cable is perpendicular to the board and not slanted in any way in the connector. Next, gently push down on the black plastic tabs to lock the cable in place. Note that there is no clicking or other noise to indicate the plastic piece is completely seated. Just use firm but gentle pressure to lock it in place. As a caution, I have noticed that the cable can become dislodged if the camera is moved about, causing the ribbon cable to slightly shift in the connector. If this happens, you usually see that the software reports that it cannot connect with the camera any more. If you see that error, just reseat the connector. Figure 9-14 is a close-up of the camera ribbon cable connected to the CSI connector.

Figure 9-14. *Camera ribbon cable connected*

You will next need to install some Python libraries, which are required for taking pictures with Python. That task is easily accomplished by entering the following commands:

```
sudo apt-get update
sudo apt-get install python-picamera
```

You are ready to take pictures once all of the preceding is done. I will take you through a step-by-step Python interactive session to demonstrate how to image a handwritten number.

First, you need a handwritten number as the subject. I suggest using a black, fine-point Sharpie to draw a single number on a piece of white paper that is approximately 4 × 4 inches. I drew the number 9 as my subject. You can draw whatever number you want. Figure 9-15 shows my handwritten number.

Figure 9-15. *Subject handwritten number*

It may look a bit odd because the image was captured using a monochrome effect from the Pi Camera, which I explain shortly. Take my word for the fact that the paper was white and the number was very dark. The following is the Python interactive session, with comments following each command:

```
>>> import picamera
```

The picamera package contains all the modules needed to capture, save, and read images.

```
>>> camera = picamera.PiCamera()
```

This instantiates an object named `camera`, upon which the desired operations can be called.

```
>>> camera.color_effects = (128, 128)
```

This command sets up the Pi Camera to take black-and-white images, which are more technically described as *monochrome* or even "shades of gray."

```
>>> camera.capture('ninebw.jpg')
```

The image is taken or captured with this command. In this case, it is stored in the current directory with the name `ninebw.jpg`. It is in the default high-resolution format of 1920 × 1080 pixels. I recommend that the piece of paper with the number on it be placed about 5 inches in front of the camera and supported such that it is perpendicular to the camera. The Pi Camera lens has a very wide angle, so it will completely fill the sensor with the subject at such a close distance. The resulting image will be drastically reduced and resized in the processing script.

Figure 9-16 shows the Pi Camera version 2 in a clear plastic holder facing the paper with the number written on it. Incidentally, the inexpensive holder is available on Amazon.com.

Figure 9-16. *Pi Camera set up to capture image*

The complete interactive Python session that captures the number image is shown in Figure 9-17.

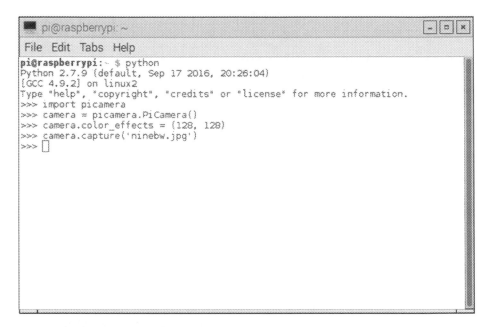

Figure 9-17. *Interactive Python session*

I modified the trainANN.py script so that it used the image Figure 9-15 as the test data input. The complete listing named trainANN_Image.py is shown next, with clarifying explanations following the listing.

```
import numpy as np
import matplotlib.pyplot as plt
from ANN import ANN
import PIL
from PIL import Image

# setup the network configuration
inode = 784
hnode = 100
onode = 10

# set the learning rate
lr = 0.1

# instantiate an ANN object named ann
ann = ANN(inode, hnode, onode, lr)
```

```python
# create the training list data
dataFile = open('mnist_train.csv')
dataList = dataFile.readlines()
dataFile.close()

# train the ANN using all the records in the list
for record in dataList:
    recordx = record.split(',')
    inputT = (np.asfarray(recordx[1:])/255.0 * 0.99) + 0.01
    train = np.zeros(onode) + 0.01
    train[int(recordx[0])] = 0.99
    # training begins here
    ann.trainNet(inputT, train)

# create the test list data from an image
img = Image.open('ninebw.jpg')
img = img.resize((28, 28), PIL.Image.ANTIALIAS)

# read pixels into list
pixels = list(img.getdata())

# convert into single values from tuples
pixels = [i[0] for i in pixels]

# save to a temp file named test.csv with comma separators
a = np.array(pixels)
a.tofile('test.csv', sep=',')

# open the temp file and read into a list
testDataFile = open('test.csv')
testDataList =  testDataFile.readlines()
testDataFile.close()

# iterate through all the list elements and submit to the ANN
for record in testDataList:
    recordx = record.split(',')
    input = (np.asfarray(recordx[0:])/255.0 * 0.99) + 0.01
    output = ann.testNet(input)

# display output
print output
```

Please note that I did not have to change the basic ANN class to incorporate these modifications into the trainANN_Image script, which is a powerful reason for separating class definitions from the functional or application code.

The next discussion just concerns the changes that were made to the original trainAN.py script to accommodate the new imaging processing function.

Modifying the trainAN.py Script

Start with the following command:

```
import PIL
from PIL import Image
```

The Python imaging library (PIL) and Image, one of its components, are required to process an image using Python.

```
img = Image.open('ninebw.jpg')
img = img.resize((28, 28), PIL.Image.ANTIALIAS)
```

These commands load the file, which is hard-coded in the script, and then proceeds to resize it to just a 28 × 28 pixels–sized image. The anti-alias argument ensures that no artifacts are created during the downsizing operation.

```
pixels = list(img.getdata())
```

This command converts the 784 pixel values into a list named pixels.

```
a = np.array(pixels)
a.tofile('test.csv', sep=',')
```

The pixels list is then converted into an array suitable to be stored as a comma-separated array in a file named test.csv. This newly created file is then processed in exactly the same manner as all the other test files in the unmodified trainANN.py script.

Figure 9-18 shows the output data array, in which you clearly see that the very last element is the highest of the entire array that corresponds to the ANN believing that it has recognize the number 9, which is the correct answer.

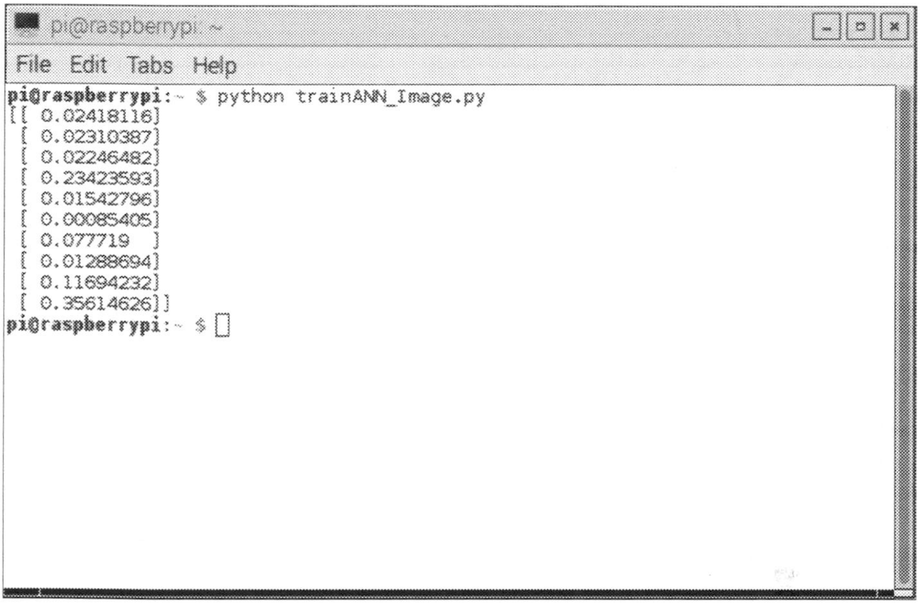

```
pi@raspberrypi: ~                                              [ - ][ □ ][ x ]
File  Edit  Tabs  Help
pi@raspberrypi:~ $ python trainANN_Image.py
[[ 0.02418116]
 [ 0.02310387]
 [ 0.02246482]
 [ 0.23423593]
 [ 0.01542796]
 [ 0.00085405]
 [ 0.077719  ]
 [ 0.01288694]
 [ 0.11694232]
 [ 0.35614626]]
pi@raspberrypi:~ $ □
```

Figure 9-18. *Output data array*

This demonstration took a considerable amount of effort to prepare and run to show that a Raspberry Pi–controlled camera coupled with a well-trained ANN can literally recognize a number written in a fashion it had never seen before.

The final portion of this demonstration describes how to automate the image-recognition process.

Automated Number Recognition with an ANN

Automating the process of imaging with an ANN is a fairly simple task. I used an interrupt-driven structure wherein the image capture and processing is initiated by pressing a push button connected to one of the Raspberry Pi GPIO pins.

The first item is the hardware setup, which consists of connecting the Pi Camera, a push button, and an LED to the Raspberry Pi using the Pi Cobbler I/O adapter. Figure 9-19 is a Fritzing diagram showing the connections for the LED and push button to the Pi Cobbler.

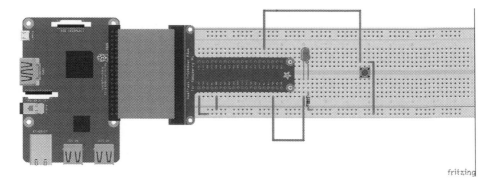

Figure 9-19. *LED and push button connections*

I saw no need for a separate schematic because the connections are clearly shown in Figure 9-19. The Pi Camera is connected as previously discussed.

There is a "forever loop" in the new script, which I named automatedImager.py, that simply flashes an LED while awaiting the interrupt signal to start the image processing. The complete script is listed next with indicating the new modifications from the trainANN_Image.py script.

```
import numpy as np
import matplotlib.pyplot as plt
from ANN import ANN
import PIL
from PIL import Image
import RPi.GPIO as GPIO
import time
import picamera

# instantiate and configure a Pi Camera object
camera = picamera.PiCamera()
camera.color_effects = (128, 128)

# setup the i/o pins 12 and 19
GPIO.setmode(GPIO.BCM)
GPIO.setup(12, GPIO.IN, pull_up_down=GPIO.PUD_DOWN)
GPIO.setup(19, GPIO.OUT)

# this is the callback function where all the processing is done
def processImage(self):
    # capture an image
    camera.capture('test.jpg')

    # create the test list data from an image
    img = Image.open('test.jpg')
    img = img.resize((28, 28), PIL.Image.ANTIALIAS)
```

```
    # read pixels into list
    pixels = list(img.getdata())

    # convert into single values from tuples
    pixels = [i[0] for i in pixels]

    # save to a temp file named test.csv with comma separators
    a = np.array(pixels)
    a.tofile('test.csv', sep=',')

    # open the temp file and read into a list
    testDataFile = open('test.csv')
    testDataList =  testDataFile.readlines()
    testDataFile.close()

    # iterate through all the list elements and submit to the ANN
    for record in testDataList:
        recordx = record.split(',')
        input = (np.asfarray(recordx[0:])/255.0 * 0.99) + 0.01
        output = ann.testNet(input)

    # display output
    print output

# event detection
GPIO.add_event_detect(12, GPIO.RISING, callback=processImage)

# setup the network configuration
inode = 784
hnode = 100
onode = 10

# set the learning rate
lr = 0.1 # optimal value

# instantiate an ANN object named ann
ann = ANN(inode, hnode, onode, lr)

# create the training list data
dataFile = open('mnist_train.csv')
dataList = dataFile.readlines()
dataFile.close()

# train the ANN using all the records in the list
for record in dataList:
    recordx = record.split(',')
```

```
    inputT = (np.asfarray(recordx[1:])/255.0 * 0.99) + 0.01
    train = np.zeros(onode) + 0.01
    train[int(recordx[0])] = 0.99
    # training begins here
    ann.trainNet(inputT, train)

while True:
    # blink an LED forever
    GPIO.output(19, GPIO.HIGH)
    time.sleep(1)
    GPIO.output(19, GPIO.LOW)
    time.sleep(1)
```

Test Run

I set up the Pi Camera in exactly the same manner as I did for the manual test run. The LED started blinking after the training finished, indicating that the system was ready for a push button press to activate the image capture and ANN analysis. The results of the ANN test run are shown in Figure 9-20.

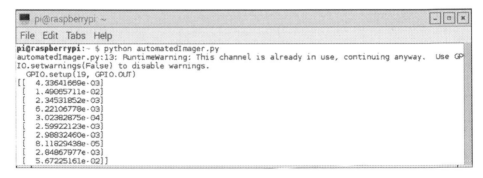

Figure 9-20. *Automated test run output*

The last array element was the highest value in the array, indicating that the ANN recognized the number as a 9, which is the correct number.

This project concludes the practical demonstrations that I wished to show you. You should consider them as a starting point for further experimentation and practice with ANNs.

Summary

Two ANN demonstrations were presented in this chapter. These demonstrations showed how a trained ANN could recognize handwritten numbers. The training data set consisted of 60,000 records from the MNIST database.

The first demonstration used 10,000 test data records from a database separate from the MNIST training database. It turned out that a three-layer ANN achieved a 94.5 percent successful recognition rate.

The second demonstration used a Pi Camera to recognize a handwritten number. A Python script converted a captured image into an input data record that successfully recognized the handwritten number.

A slightly modified version of the Python script was then demonstrated, which fully automated the image-recognition process.

CHAPTER 10

■ ■ ■

Evolutionary Computing

This chapter deals with evolutionary computing (EC). I'll start by defining EC and its scope so that you understand what is being discussed in this chapter and how it applies to AI. The following lists some of the major subtopics in the field of EC:

- Evolutionary programming

- Evolution strategies

- Genetic algorithms

- Genetic programming

- Classifier systems

This list is by no means comprehensive, as the scope of many AI topics is often subject to the viewpoints of AI practitioners, but it serves me well and more than encompasses all the items discussed in this chapter.

I'll begin with a story that should place the underlying EC concepts of evolution and mutation in a proper context.

Alife

Many years ago, there existed a large cavern in a subtropical jungle that was home to an amphibian creature, which I will simply call an *alife*. Alifes were gentle animals that made up a large colony (numbering in the tens of thousands) that lived in the cavern for a very long time. They ate lichen, moss, and other nutrients that were generously supplied by several clear water streams that flowed through the cavern. The alifes were quite prolific and bred very quickly, with generational times measured in weeks. Their colony size was also quite stable, basically set at an equilibrium point based on constant birth and death rates, and a stable food supply. All in all, the alife community seemed quite content with conditions as they were. Then a catastrophe struck.

A major earthquake shook the region, which was so strong that it collapsed the cavern roof, exposing the alifes to the outside world for the first time in eons. The alifes didn't realize what had happened, having fairly primitive brains, and just continued with their ordinary ways. However, a hawk happened to be circling nearby and dove down through the newly opened hole to investigate. There it discovered the delicious alife colony and started consuming them. Having its fill, the hawk flew back to its nest area

© Donald J. Norris 2017

D. J. Norris, *Beginning Artificial Intelligence with the Raspberry Pi*,

DOI 10.1007/978-1-4842-2743-5_10

and communicated with other hawks about what it found. Very shortly, there were vast amounts of hungry hawks devouring the alifes. Things looked pretty grim for the alifes.

Fortunately, some groups of alifes were able to shelter in rocks and holes that the hawks could not reach. But it would only be a matter of time before the colony would be exterminated. Then, something remarkable happened. A skin cell on the top of the head of a newborn alife changed or mutated so that it became sensitive to light. The alife didn't know what to do but primitive instincts directed it to avoid any light. This alife proceeded to have offspring and they too had the light-sensitive cells. Interestingly, each generation of alife became better at detecting light than the previous ones. These light-sensitive alifes quickly became somewhat adept at hiding from the hawks to the point that they were the only alifes that survived. The hawks left when it became apparent to them that the free lunch was over.

Another mutation happened with alifes, wherein a second set of light-sensitive cells developed fairly close to the first set. Over many generations, these light-sensitive cells evolved into primitive eyes. These alifes could now see, and more importantly, with two eyes they could perceive the third dimension of depth. With this new sense of depth, the alifes could venture forth and start exploring the world beyond their cavern home.

When the alifes started venturing from the cavern, they were exposed to the strong sunlight and their top skin cells started mutating, and became tougher and more protective. Their mouths also started mutating because they needed more food energy to move about in the jungle. They grew teeth and their digestive system changed to accommodate the raw meat proteins they were now consuming. Their bodies also started to grow to handle the new mass of organs and body parts. This evolution process continued for a very long time, until the present time. Today, there are alifes are among us, but we do not call them that; instead, we call them alligators.

I am sure that you recognize my story as fiction, except for the important parts of mutation and evolution that were necessary for the alifes to continue their species. The adaptation of species to survive in a hostile environment was the primary idea put forth in Charles Darwin's thesis *On the Origin of Species*.

When it occurs in nature, mutation is always at a very small scale and usually based upon some random process. This idea is carried through in evolutionary computing, where changes or mutations are also very small and have little impact on the overall process, whatever that maybe. The mutations are also created by using a compatible pseudo-random mechanism. I'll now further develop these ideas in a discussion of evolution programming (EP).

Evolutionary Programing

EP was created by Dr. Lawrence Fogel in the early 1960s. It can be viewed as an optimization strategy using randomly selected trial solutions to test against one or more objectives. Trial solutions are also known as *individual populations*. Mutations are then applied to existing individuals, which create new individuals or offspring. The mutations can have a wide effect on the resultant behavior of the new individuals. New individuals are then compared in a "tournament" to select which ones survive to form a new individual population.

EP differs from a *genetic algorithm* (GA) because it focuses on the behavioral linkages between parents and offspring; whereas a GA tries to emulate nature's genetic operations that occur in a genome, including encoding behaviors and recombinations using genetic crossovers.

EP is also very similar to *evolution strategy* (ES), even though they were developed independently of each other. The main difference is that EP uses a random process to select individuals from a population, compared to a deterministic approach used in ES. In ES, poorly performing individuals are deleted from the individual population based on well-defined metrics.

Now that I have introduced EC and discussed its fundamental components, it is time to show you a practical EC demonstration.

Demo 10-1: Manual Calculation

I begin this demonstration with some manual calculations, as I have done in other chapters. However, it would be helpful to state the purpose so that you have an idea about what the demonstration is supposed to show. The purpose is to generate a list of six integers whose values range from 0 to 100 and whose sum is 371. I can guess that most readers can easily come up with a list without any real issues.

I will take you through my reasoning to illustrate how I developed a list.

1. First, I recognized that that each number is likely more than 60 because there are only six numbers available to sum to the target value.

2. Next, I selected a number (say 71) and subtracted it from the target, which caused a new target of 300 to be created with the five numbers left.

3. I repeated these steps using other numbers until I arrived at the following list. The last number was simply the remainder after I selected the fifth integer.

   [71, 90, 65, 70, 25, 50]

This process was not randomized in any way as I reasoned my selections throughout the process. This process should be classified as *deterministic*. A traditional script or program could be written to codify it. Incidentally, I could have also created the following list because there was no stipulation that integers could not be repeated:

   [60, 60, 60, 60, 60, 71]

It is just a quirk of human nature that we usually do not think or reason in that manner.

I would consider the preceding manual calculations as fairly trivial for a human. However, it is not so trivial for a computer, and this is where the following Python demonstration comes into play.

Python Script

Credit must go to Will Larson. I am using his code from a 2009 article entitled "Genetic Algorithms: Cool Name & Damn Simple" (https://lethain.com/genetic-algorithms-cool-name-damn-simple/) from his blog, which is called *Irrational Exuberance*. I highly recommend that you take a look at it.

The problem to be solved is the same one used in the manual calculations section on determining six integers with values ranging from 0 to 100 and summing to a target value of 371.

The first item to consider in formulating a solution is how to structure it to fit into the EC paradigm. There are individuals to create who will eventually form a population. The individuals for this specific case will be six element lists consisting of integers whose values range from 0 to 100. Multiple individuals make up a population. The following code segment creates the individuals:

```
from random import randint
def individual(length, min, max):
    # generates an individual
    return [randint(min, max) for x in xrange(length)]
```

Figure 10-1 shows an interactive Python session where I generated several individuals.

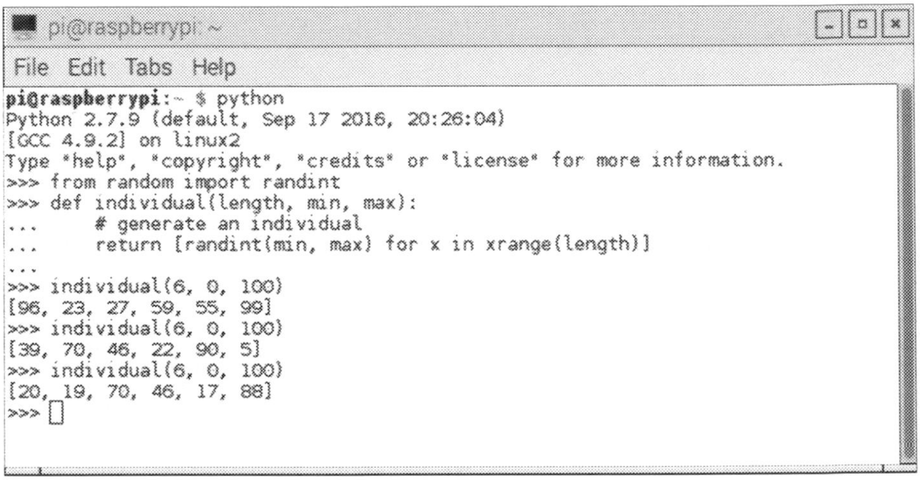

Figure 10-1. *Interactive Python session individual generation*

The individuals generated must be collected so that they form a population, which is the next part of the solution structure. The following code segment generates a population. This segment depends upon the previous code segment to have already been entered:

```
def population(count, length, min, max):
    # generate a population
    return [individual(length, min, max) for x in xrange(count)]
```

Figure 10-2 shows an interactive Python session where I generated several populations.

```
■ pi@raspberrypi: ~                                          [-][□][×]

File  Edit  Tabs  Help

pi@raspberrypi:~ $ python
Python 2.7.9 (default, Sep 17 2016, 20:26:04)
[GCC 4.9.2] on linux2
Type "help", "copyright", "credits" or "license" for more information.
>>> from random import randint
>>> def individual(length, min, max):
...     # generate an individual
...     return [randint(min, max) for x in xrange(length)]
...
>>> individual(6, 0, 100)
[96, 23, 27, 59, 55, 99]
>>> individual(6, 0, 100)
[39, 70, 46, 22, 90, 5]
>>> individual(6, 0, 100)
[20, 19, 70, 46, 17, 88]
>>>
>>> def population(count, length, min, max):
...     return [individual(length, min, max) for x in xrange(count)]
...
>>> population(3, 6, 0, 100)
[[43, 28, 95, 77, 59, 48], [32, 3, 93, 45, 49, 48], [37, 68, 64, 69, 33, 65]]
>>> population(3, 6, 0, 100)
[[90, 35, 44, 73, 40, 54], [98, 46, 47, 52, 28, 9], [79, 74, 91, 77, 58, 47]]
>>> population(3, 6, 0, 100)
[[9, 0, 90, 84, 45, 45], [93, 74, 38, 77, 91, 41], [23, 78, 24, 39, 27, 95]]
>>> []
```

Figure 10-2. *Interactive Python session population generation*

The next step in this process is to create a function that measures how well a particular individual performs in meeting the stated objective (i.e., integer lists values summing to a target value). This function is called a *fitness function*. Note that the fitness function requires the individual function to have been previously entered. The following is a code segment implementation for the fitness function:

```
from operator import add
def fitness(individual, target):
    # calculate fitness, lower the better
    sum = reduce(add, individual, 0)
    return abs(target - sum)
```

Figure 10-3 shows an interactive Python session where I tested several individuals against a constant target value.

285

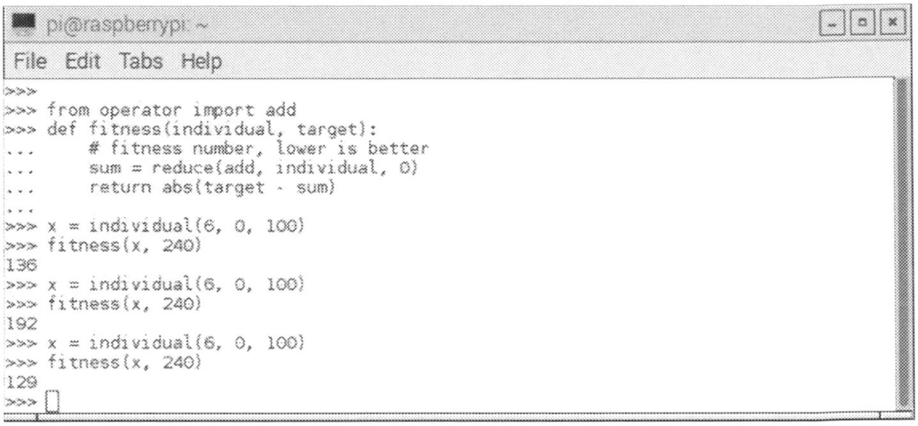

```
>>>
>>> from operator import add
>>> def fitness(individual, target):
...     # fitness number, lower is better
...     sum = reduce(add, individual, 0)
...     return abs(target - sum)
...
>>> x = individual(6, 0, 100)
>>> fitness(x, 240)
136
>>> x = individual(6, 0, 100)
>>> fitness(x, 240)
192
>>> x = individual(6, 0, 100)
>>> fitness(x, 240)
129
>>> []
```

Figure 10-3. *Interactive Python session fitness tests*

This particular fitness function is much simpler than similar fitness tests that I have demonstrated in past chapters. In this one, only the absolute value of the difference between the summed elements contained in an individual list and a target value is calculated. The best case would be a 0.0 value, which I will shortly demonstrate.

The only missing element in the structure is how to change or evolve the population to meet the objective. Only by the purest luck would an initial solution also be an optimal solution. There must be a strategy stated to properly implement an evolutionary function. The following is the strategy set forth for this structure:

- Take 20% of the top performers (elitism rate) from a prior population and include them in a new one.

- Breed approximately 75% of the new population as children.

- Take the first length/2 elements from a father and the last length/2 elements from a mother to form a child.

- It is forbidden to have a father and a mother as the same individual.

- Randomly select 5% from the population.

- Mutate 1% of the new population.

This strategy is by no means a standard one, or even a very comprehensive one, but it will suffice for this problem and it is fairly representative of those used for similar problems.

Figure 10-4 is an interactive Python session that shows how children are formed in this strategy.

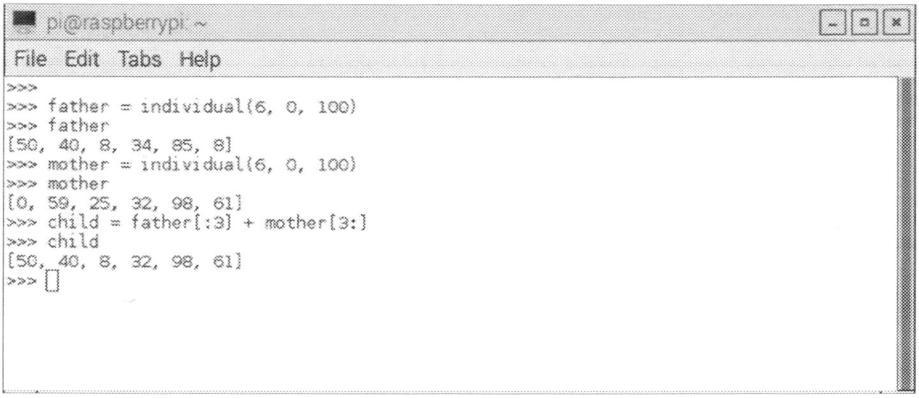

```
  pi@raspberrypi: ~                                              [-][□][×]
 File  Edit  Tabs  Help
>>>
>>> father = individual(6, 0, 100)
>>> father
[50, 40, 8, 34, 85, 8]
>>> mother = individual(6, 0, 100)
>>> mother
[0, 59, 25, 32, 98, 61]
>>> child = father[:3] + mother[3:]
>>> child
[50, 40, 8, 32, 98, 61]
>>> []
```

Figure 10-4. Forming children for a new population

The mutating part of the strategy is a bit more complex, which I show, in part, with the next code segment before trying to explain it:

```python
from random import random, randint
chance_to_mutate = 0.01
for i in population:
    if chance_to_mutate > random():
        place_to_mutate = randint(0, len(i))
        i[place_to_mutate] = randint(min(i), max(i))
...
...
```

The chance_to_mutate variable is set to 0.01, representing a 1% chance for mutation, which is very low as I noted earlier. The statement for i in population: iterates through the entire population and causes a mutation only when the random number generator is less than .01, which is not very often. The actual individual chosen to be mutated is accomplished by the place_to_mutate = randint(0, len(i)) statement, which is not likely the individual that happened to be iterated upon at the time the random number was less than .01. Finally, the actual mutation is done by this statement: i[place_to_mutate] = randint(min(i), max(i)). The integer values in the selected individual are randomly generated based upon the population's min and max values.

The whole strategy design, which includes a mix of selecting the best-performing individuals, breeding children from all portions of the population, and the occasional mutations is geared toward finding the global maximum and avoiding local maximums. This is precisely the same thought process that was going on in the gradient descent algorithm for ANNs, where the goal was to locate a global minimum and avoid local minimums. You can look at Figure 8-15 to visualize the process for locating the global maximum or highest peak instead of the deepest valley, representing the global minimum.

There is much more to the evolve function than what was shown. The remaining code is shown next in the complete script listing.

There is one more function to explain before the complete script is shown. This function is named grade and it calculates an overall fitness measure for a whole population. The Python built-in reduce function sums the fitness scores for each individual and averages the sum by the population size. The following code implements the grade function:

```
def grade(pop, target):
    'Find average fitness for a population.'
    summed = reduce(add, (fitness(x, target) for x in pop))
    return summed / (len(pop) * 1.0)
```

This last function listing concludes my discussion on all the functions that compose the Python script. The following is a complete listing of the final script, along with instructions on how to run the script within an interactive Python session. Note that I did modify the instructions to display the first generation number that met the target and the final solution itself. The population in the example is equal to 100 and each individual has six elements with values ranging between 0 and 100.

```
"""
# Example usage
>>> from genetic import *
>>> target = 371
>>> p_count = 100
>>> i_length = 6
>>> i_min = 0
>>> i_max = 100
>>> p = population(p_count, i_length, i_min, i_max)
>>> fitness_history = [grade(p, target),]
>>> fitFlag = 0
>>> for i in xrange(100):
...     p = evolve(p, target)
...     fitness_history.append(grade(p, target))
...     if grade(p, target) == 0:
...         if fitFlag == 0:
...             fitFlag = 1
...             print 'Generation = ', i
...             print p[0]
>>> for datum in fitness_history:
...     print datum
"""

from random import randint, random
from operator import add

def individual(length, min, max):
    'Create a member of the population.'
    return [ randint(min,max) for x in xrange(length) ]

def population(count, length, min, max):
    """
    Create a number of individuals (i.e. a population).
```

```
    count: the number of individuals in the population
    length: the number of values per individual
    min: the minimum possible value in an individual's list of values
    max: the maximum possible value in an individual's list of values

    """
    return [ individual(length, min, max) for x in xrange(count) ]

def fitness(individual, target):
    """
    Determine the fitness of an individual. Higher is better.

    individual: the individual to evaluate
    target: the target number individuals are aiming for
    """
    sum = reduce(add, individual, 0)
    return abs(target-sum)

def grade(pop, target):
    'Find average fitness for a population.'
    summed = reduce(add, (fitness(x, target) for x in pop))
    return summed / (len(pop) * 1.0)

def evolve(pop, target, retain=0.2, random_select=0.05,
mutate=0.01):
    graded = [ (fitness(x, target), x) for x in pop]
    graded = [ x[1] for x in sorted(graded)]
    retain_length = int(len(graded)*retain)
    parents = graded[:retain_length]
    # randomly add other individuals to
    # promote genetic diversity
    for individual in graded[retain_length:]:
        if random_select > random():
            parents.append(individual)
    # mutate some individuals
    for individual in parents:
        if mutate > random():
            pos_to_mutate = randint(0, len(individual)-1)
            # this mutation is not ideal, because it
            # restricts the range of possible values,
            # but the function is unaware of the min/max
            # values used to create the individuals,
            individual[pos_to_mutate] = randint(
                min(individual), max(individual))
    # crossover parents to create children
    parents_length = len(parents)
    desired_length = len(pop) - parents_length
    children = []
    while len(children) < desired_length:
```

```
        male = randint(0, parents_length-1)
        female = randint(0, parents_length-1)
        if male != female:
            male = parents[male]
            female = parents[female]
            half = len(male) / 2
            child = male[:half] + female[half:]
            children.append(child)
    parents.extend(children)
    return parents
```

Figure 10-5 shows an interactive session in which I entered all the statements shown in the instructions portion of the script comments.

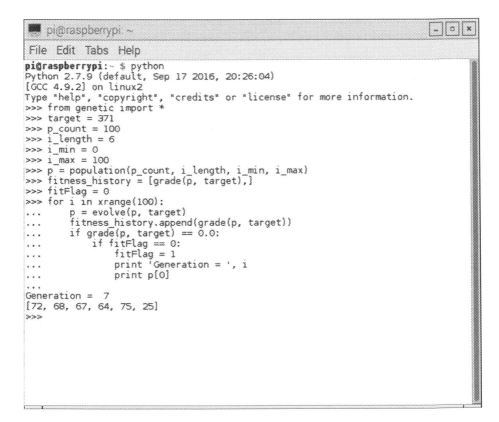

Figure 10-5. *Interactive Python session running the script*

You should be able to see in the screenshot that a solution was found after only seven generations had evolved. The solution was [72, 68, 67, 64, 75, 25], which does sum to the target value of 371. The script does not stop after the first successful solution is found, but continues to evolve and mutate, slightly degrading and then improving until it has run through its preset cycle number.

A portion of the history of the fitness numbers associated with each generation is shown in Figure 10-6.

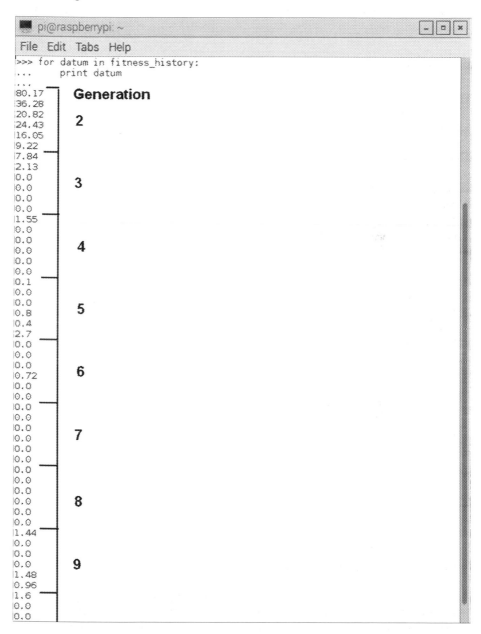

Figure 10-6. Fitness history list

In Figure 10-6, I annotated where generation 7 has a 0.0 fitness value for each of its individuals. Overall, this genetic programming approach is very efficient, especially for the relatively simple objective of determining a target sum given a list of six randomly generated integer numbers.

The next demonstration is a slight variant from Conway's Game of Life, which is a classic project incorporating genetic programming with artificial life (alife) that breed and die according to a set of conditions based on their proximity to each other, which I explain later.

Demo 10-2: Conway's Game of Life

The Game of Life, or as it is commonly known, Life, is a cellular automaton project created by British mathematician John Conway in 1970. The game starts with an initial condition, but it needs no further user input to play to its completion. This modus operandi is called a *zero-player game*, which means that the automatons—or *cells*, as I shall refer to them from now on—evolve on their own according to the following set of rules or conditions:

1. Any live cell with fewer than two live neighbors dies, as if caused by underpopulation.

2. Any live cell with two or three live neighbors lives to the next generation.

3. Any live cell with more than three live neighbors dies, as if by overpopulation.

4. Any dead cell with exactly three live neighbors becomes a live cell, as if by reproduction.

The board field, or universe, for this game is theoretically an infinite, orthogonal set of grid squares where a cell can occupy a grid in either an alive or a dead state. *Alive* is synonymous with *populated* and *dead* is synonymous with *unpopulated*. Each cell has a maximum of eight neighbors, except for the edge cells in our real-world, practical grid system, where an infinite grid is not possible.

The grid is "seeded" with an initial placement of cells, which can be randomly or deterministically placed. The cellular rules are then immediately applied, causing births and deaths to happen simultaneously. This application is known as *time tick* in game terminology. A new generation is thus formed and the rules are immediately reapplied. Ultimately, the game settles into an equilibrium state, where cells cycle between two stable cellular configurations, they roam about forever, or they all die.

From a historical perspective, Conway was very much interested in Professor John von Neumann's attempts at creating a computing machine that could replicate itself. von Neumann eventually succeeded by describing a mathematical model based on a rectangular grid governed by a very complex set of rules. The Conway game was a big simplification of von Neumann's concepts. The game was published in the October 1970 issue of *Scientific American* in Martin Gardener's "Mathematical Games" column. It instantly became a huge success and generated much interest from fellow AI researchers and enthusiastic readers.

The game can also be extended to the point that it is comparable to the universal Turing machine, first proposed by Alan Turning in the 1940s (explained in an earlier chapter).

The game has another important influence on AI in that it likely kick-started the mathematical field of study known as *cellular automata*. The game simulates the birth and death of a colony of organisms in a surprising close relationship to real-life processes occurring in nature. This game has led directly to many other similar simulation games modeling nature's own processes. These simulations have been applied in computer science, biology, physics, biochemistry, economics, mathematics, and many others.

I demonstrate Conway's Game of Life using a neat Raspberry Pi accessory board known as a Sense HAT. Figure 10-7 shows a Sense HAT board. The HAT name represents a line of accessory boards known as Hardware Attached on Top (HAT) boards, which feature a standardized format that allows them to be directly plugged into the 40-pin GPIO header and mechanically fastened to the Raspberry Pi 2 and 3 model boards.

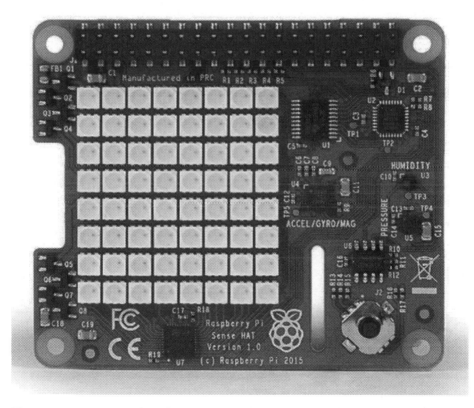

Figure 10-7. Sense HAT board

Every HAT board supports an autoconfiguration system that allows automatic GPIO and driver setup. This automatic configuration is achieved using two dedicated pins on the 40-pin GPIO header that are reserved for an I2C eeprom. This eeprom holds the board manufacturer's information, GPIO setup, and a device tree fragment, which is a description of the attached hardware, which in turn allows the Linux OS to automatically load any required drivers.

The Sense HAT board has an 8 × 8 RGB LED array, which provides a very nice grid display for all the cellular automatons. In addition, there is a powerful Python library that provides a good deal of functionality for the LED array and for a variety of onboard sensors, which include the following:

- Gyroscope

- Accelerometer

- Magnetometer

- Temperature

- Barometric pressure

- Humidity

There is also a five-way position joystick on the board to support applications that need that type of user control. I do not use any of the sensors or the joystick for the Game of Life application, just the 8 × 8 LED array.

Sense HAT Hardware Installation

First, ensure that the Raspberry Pi is completely powered down. The Sense HAT is designed to mount on top of a Raspberry Pi. It comes with a 40-pin GPIO male pin extension header that you must first plug into the female 40-pin header on the Raspberry Pi. The Sense HAT is then mounted on top of the Raspberry Pi using the 40 male pins as a guide. These pins should simply push through the 40-pin female header on the Sense board. All that's left is to attach the supplied stand-offs, which provide firm support between the Raspberry Pi and the Sense HAT. Figure 10-8 shows a mounted Sense HAT on a Raspberry Pi.

Figure 10-8. *Sense HAT mounted onto a Raspberry Pi*

There is one more item that you should know. The Raspberry Pi and Sense HAT require a power supply capable of providing 2.5A at 5V. Failing to use a sufficiently powerful power supply will likely cause strange behavior, such as the Linux OS failing to recognize the Sense HAT, which I unfortunately confirmed as a fact.

Sense HAT Software Installation

The Python library supporting the Sense HAT must be loaded prior to running any of the scripts that will run the Life game. First, ensure that the Raspberry Pi is connected to the Internet, and then enter the following commands to load the software:

```
sudo apt-get update
sudo apt-get install sense-hat
sudo reboot
```

You want to run the following test to ensure that the Sense HAT is working properly with the newly installed software. Enter the following in an interactive Python session:

```
from sense_hat import SenseHat
sense = SenseHat()
sense.show_message("Hello World!")
```

If all went well with the installation, you show see the `Hello World!` message scrolling across the LED array. If you don't see it, I would recheck that the Sense HAT is securely fastened to the Raspberry Pi and that all 40 pins go through their respective socket holes. It very well might be that you inadvertently bent one of the pins such that it is has been forced out of the way. If that's the case, just carefully straighten it and reseat all the pins.

Once the software checks out, you are ready to run a Python version of the Game of Life on this combination of Sense HAT/Raspberry Pi. I now turn the discussion to the game software.

Game of Life: Python Version

I begin this section by giving credit to Mr. Swee Meng Ng, a very talented Malaysian developer who posted much of the code I used in this project on GitHub.com. Swee goes by the username sweemeng on GitHub. He has a blog at `www.nomadiccodemonkey.com`. Take a look at it if you want an appreciation for the code development efforts that are ongoing in that part of the world.

You should first load the following Python scripts from `https://github.com/sweemeng/sweemengs-game-of-life.git` into your home directory:

- genelab.ppy
- designer.py
- gameoflife.py

genelab.py is the first script that I'll discuss. It is the main one in this application. By *main*, I mean it incorporates the starting point, initialization, generation creation, and mutation, and finally, it enforces the behavioral rules. However, this script needs two helper scripts to work properly. These helper scripts are named designer.py and gameoflife.py, which I discuss shortly. I have added my own comments to Swee Meng's scripts to help relate portions of it to concepts that have already been discussed, and hopefully, to clarify the purpose of the code segments.

```
import random
import time
# first helper
from designer import CellDesigner
from designer import GeneBank
# second helper
from gameoflife import GameOfLife
# not exactly a helper but needed for the display
from sense_hat import SenseHat

# you can customize your colors here
WHITE = [ 0, 0, 0 ]
RED = [ 120, 0, 0 ]
```

```python
# begin class definition
class Genelab(object):
    # begin initialization
    def __init__(self):
        self.survive_min = 5 # Cycle
        self.surival_record = 0
        self.designer = CellDesigner()
        self.gene_bank = GeneBank()
        self.game = GameOfLife()
        self.sense = SenseHat()

    # random starting point
    def get_start_point(self):
        x = random.randint(0, 7)
        y = random.randint(0, 7)
        return x, y

    # create a fresh generation (population)
    # or mutate an existing one
    def get_new_gen(self):
        if len(self.gene_bank.bank) == 0:
            print("creating new generation")
            self.designer.generate_genome()
        elif len(self.gene_bank.bank) == 1:
            print("Mutating first gen")
            self.designer.destroy()
            seq_x = self.gene_bank.bank[0]
            self.designer.mutate(seq_x)
        else:
            self.designer.destroy()
            coin_toss = random.choice([0, 1])
            if coin_toss:
                print("Breeding")
                seq_x = self.gene_bank.random_choice()
                seq_y = self.gene_bank.random_choice()
                self.designer.cross_breed(seq_x, seq_y)
            else:
                print("Mutating")
                seq_x = self.gene_bank.random_choice()
                self.designer.mutate(seq_x)

    # a method to start the whole game, i.e. lab.run()
    def run(self):
        self.get_new_gen()
        x, y = self.get_start_point()
        cells = self.designer.generate_cells(x, y)
        self.game.set_cells(cells)
```

```
# count is the generation number
count = 1
self.game.destroy_world()
# forever loop. Change this if you only want a finite run
while True:
    try:
        # essentially where the rules are applied
        if not self.game.everyone_alive():
            if count > self.survive_min:
                # Surivival the fittest

                self.gene_bank.add_gene(self.designer.genome)
                self.survival_record = count

            print("Everyone died, making new gen")
            print("Species survived %s cycle" % count)
            self.sense.clear()
            self.get_new_gen()
            x, y = self.get_start_point()
            cells = self.designer.generate_cells(x, y)
            self.game.set_cells(cells)
            count = 1

        if count % random.randint(10, 100) == 0:
            print("let's spice thing up a little")
            print("destroying world")
            print("Species survived %s cycle" % count)
            self.game.destroy_world()
            self.gene_bank.add_gene(self.designer.genome)
            self.sense.clear()
            self.get_new_gen()
            x, y = self.get_start_point()
            cells = self.designer.generate_cells(x, y)
            self.game.set_cells(cells)
            count = 1

        canvas = []

        # this where the cells are "painted" onto the canvas
        # The canvas is based on the grid pattern from the
        # gameoflife script
        for i in self.game.world:
            if not i:
                canvas.append(WHITE)
            else:
                canvas.append(RED)
        self.sense.set_pixels(canvas)
        self.game.run()
```

```
                count = count + 1
                time.sleep(0.1)
            except:
                print("Destroy world")
                print("%s generation tested" % len(self.gene_bank.bank))
                self.sense.clear()
                break

if __name__ == "__main__":
    # instantiate the class GeneLab
    lab = Genelab()
    # start the game
    lab.run()
```

The first helper script is designer.py. The code listing follows with the addition of my own comments:

```
import random

class CellDesigner(object):
    # initialization
    def __init__(self, max_point=7, max_gene_length=10, genome=[]):
        self.genome = genome
        self.max_point = max_point
        self.max_gene_length = max_gene_length

    # a genome is made up of 1 to 10 genes
    def generate_genome(self):
        length = random.randint(1, self.max_gene_length)
        print(length)
        for l in range(length):
            gene = self.generate_gene()
            self.genome.append(gene)

    # a gene is an (+/-x, +/-y) cooordinate pair; x, y range 0 to 7
    def generate_gene(self):
        x = random.randint(0, self.max_point)
        y = random.randint(0, self.max_point)
        x_dir = random.choice([1, -1])
        y_dir = random.choice([1, -1])
        return ((x * x_dir), (y * y_dir))

    def generate_cells(self, x, y):
        cells = []
        for item in self.genome:
            x_move, y_move = item
```

```python
            new_x = x + x_move
            if new_x > self.max_point:
                new_x = new_x - self.max_point
            if new_x < 0:
                new_x = self.max_point + new_x

            new_y = y + x_move
            if new_y > self.max_point:
                new_y = new_y - self.max_point
            if new_y < 0:
                new_y = self.max_point + new_y
            cells.append((new_x, new_y))
        return cells

    def cross_breed(self, seq_x, seq_y):
        if len(seq_x) > len(seq_y):
            main_seq = seq_x
            secondary_seq = seq_y
        else:
            main_seq = seq_y
            secondary_seq = seq_x

        for i in range(len(main_seq)):
            gene = random.choice([ main_seq, secondary_seq ])
            if i > len(gene):
                continue
            self.genome.append(gene[i])

    def mutate(self, sequence):
        # Just mutate one gene
        for i in sequence:
            mutate = random.choice([ True, False ])
            if mutate:
                gene = self.generate_gene()
                self.genome.append(gene)
            else:
                self.genome.append(i)

    def destroy(self):
        self.genome = []

class GeneBank(object):
    def __init__(self):
        self.bank = []

    def add_gene(self, sequence):
        self.bank.append(sequence)
```

```
def random_choice(self):
    if not self.bank:
        return None
    return random.choice(self.bank)
```

The second helper script is gameoflife.py. There is only a small portion of this script that is actually used as a helper for the main script. I have included it all for the sake of completeness and to provide you with the code, in case you want to run a single-generation Game of Life, which I will explain shortly. The complete code listing follows with my own comments added:

```
import time
world = [
    0, 0, 0, 0, 0, 0, 0, 0,
    0, 0, 0, 0, 0, 0, 0, 0,
    0, 0, 0, 0, 0, 0, 0, 0,
    0, 0, 0, 0, 0, 0, 0, 0,
    0, 0, 0, 0, 0, 0, 0, 0,
    0, 0, 0, 0, 0, 0, 0, 0,
    0, 0, 0, 0, 0, 0, 0, 0,
    0, 0, 0, 0, 0, 0, 0, 0,
]

max_point = 7 # We use a square world to make things easy

class GameOfLife(object):
    def __init__(self, world=world, max_point=max_point,
value=1):
        self.world = world
        self.max_point = max_point
        self.value = value

    def to_reproduce(self, x, y):
        if not self.is_alive(x, y):
            neighbor_alive = self.neighbor_alive_count(x, y)
            if neighbor_alive == 3:
                return True
        return False

    def to_kill(self, x, y):
        if self.is_alive(x, y):
            neighbor_alive = self.neighbor_alive_count(x, y)
            if neighbor_alive < 2 or neighbor_alive > 3:
                return True
        return False
```

```
def to_keep(self, x, y):
    if self.is_alive(x, y):
        neighbor_alive = self.neighbor_alive_count(x, y)
        if neighbor_alive >= 2 and neighbor_alive <= 3:
            return True
    return False

def is_alive(self, x, y):
    pos = self.get_pos(x, y)
    return self.world[pos]

def neighbor_alive_count(self, x, y):

    neighbors = self.get_neighbor(x, y)
    alives = 0
    for i, j in neighbors:
        if self.is_alive(i, j):
            alives = alives + 1
    # Because neighbor comes with self, just for easiness
    if self.is_alive(x, y):
        return alives - 1
    return alives

def get_neighbor(self, x, y):
    #neighbors = [
    #    (x + 1, y + 1), (x, y + 1), (x - 1, y + 1),
    #    (x + 1, y),     (x, y),     (x, y + 1),
    #    (x + 1, y - 1), (x, y - 1), (x - 1, y - 1),
    #]
    neighbors = [
        (x - 1, y - 1), (x - 1, y), (x - 1, y + 1),
        (x, y - 1),     (x, y),     (x, y + 1),
        (x + 1, y - 1), (x + 1, y), (x + 1, y + 1)
    ]
    return neighbors

def get_pos(self, x, y):
    if x < 0:
        x = max_point
    if x > max_point:
        x = 0
    if y < 0:
        y = max_point
    if y > max_point:
        y = 0

    return (x * (max_point+1)) + y
```

```python
# I am seriously thinking of having multiple species
def set_pos(self, x, y):
    pos = self.get_pos(x, y)
    self.world[pos] = self.value

def set_cells(self, cells):
    for x, y in cells:
        self.set_pos(x, y)

def unset_pos(self, x, y):
    pos = self.get_pos(x, y)
    self.world[pos] = 0

def run(self):
    something_happen = False
    operations = []
    for i in range(max_point + 1):
        for j in range(max_point + 1):
            if self.to_keep(i, j):
                something_happen = True
                continue
            if self.to_kill(i, j):
                operations.append((self.unset_pos, i, j))
                something_happen = True
                continue
            if self.to_reproduce(i, j):
                something_happen = True
                operations.append((self.set_pos, i, j))
                continue
    for func, i, j in operations:
        func(i, j)
    if not something_happen:
        print("weird nothing happen")

def print_world(self):
    count = 1
    for i in self.world:

        if count % 8 == 0:
            print("%s " %i)
        else:
            print("%s " %i) #, end = "")
        count = count + 1
    print(count)

def print_neighbor(self, x, y):
    neighbors = self.get_neighbor(x, y)
    count = 1
```

```python
        for i, j in neighbors:
            pos = self.get_pos(i, j)
            if count %3 == 0:
                print("%s " %self.world[pos])
            else:
                print("%s " %self.world[pos]) #, end = "")
            count = count + 1
        print(count)

    def everyone_alive(self):
        count = 0
        for i in self.world:
            if i:
                count = count + 1
        if count:
            return True
        return False

    def destroy_world(self):
        for i in range(len(self.world)):
            self.world[i] = 0

def main():
    game = GameOfLife()
    cells = [ (2, 4), (3, 5), (4, 3), (4, 4), (4, 5) ]
    game.set_cells(cells)
    print(cells)
    while True:
        try:
            game.print_world()

            game.run()
            count = 0
            time.sleep(5)
        except KeyboardInterrupt:
            print("Destroy world")
            break

def debug():
    game = GameOfLife()
    cells = [ (2, 4), (3, 5), (4, 3), (4, 4), (4, 5) ]
    game.set_cells(cells)
    test_cell = (3, 3)
    game.print_neighbor(*test_cell)
    print("Cell is alive: %s" % game.is_alive(*test_cell))
    print("Neighbor alive: %s" % game.neighbor_alive_
    count(*test_cell))
```

```
    print("Keep cell: %s" % game.to_keep(*test_cell))
    print("Make cell: %s" % game.to_reproduce(*test_cell))
    print("Kill cell: %s" % game.to_kill(*test_cell))
    game.print_world()
    game.run()
    game.print_world()

if __name__ == "__main__":
    main()
    #debug()
```

Test Run

First, ensure that the genelab.py, designer.py, and gameoflife.py scripts are in the pi home directory before running this command:

```
python genelab.py
```

The Raspberry takes a moment to load everything. You should begin to see the cells appear on the Sense HAT LED array, as well as status messages on the console screen. Figure 10-9 is a photograph of the LED array while my script was running.

Figure 10-9. *Sense HAT LED array with the Game of Life running*

Figure 10-10 shows the console display while the game was running.

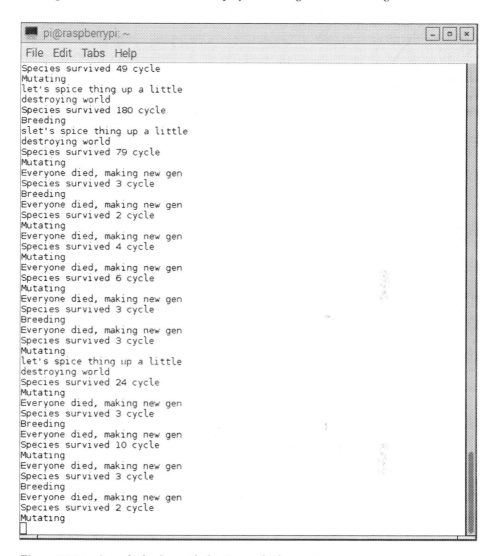

```
pi@raspberrypi ~

File  Edit  Tabs  Help
Species survived 49 cycle
Mutating
let's spice thing up a little
destroying world
Species survived 180 cycle
Breeding
slet's spice thing up a little
destroying world
Species survived 79 cycle
Mutating
Everyone died, making new gen
Species survived 3 cycle
Breeding
Everyone died, making new gen
Species survived 2 cycle
Mutating
Everyone died, making new gen
Species survived 4 cycle
Mutating
Everyone died, making new gen
Species survived 6 cycle
Mutating
Everyone died, making new gen
Species survived 3 cycle
Breeding
Everyone died, making new gen
Species survived 3 cycle
Mutating
let's spice thing up a little
destroying world
Species survived 24 cycle
Mutating
Everyone died, making new gen
Species survived 3 cycle
Breeding
Everyone died, making new gen
Species survived 10 cycle
Mutating
Everyone died, making new gen
Species survived 3 cycle
Breeding
Everyone died, making new gen
Species survived 2 cycle
Mutating
```

Figure 10-10. *Console display with the Game of Life running*

Single Generation of the Game of Life

It is also entirely possible to experiment with only a single generation of the Game of
Life. This script simply adheres to the rules for the cell neighbors that were previously
specified, with no cell or gene mutations allowed. The following script is named main.py.
It is available on the same GitHub website as the previous scripts.

```python
from sense_hat import SenseHat
from gameoflife import GameOfLife
import time

WHITE = [ 0, 0, 0 ]
RED = [ 255, 0, 0 ]

def main():

    game = GameOfLife()

    sense = SenseHat()
    # cells = [(2, 4), (3, 5), (4, 3), (4, 4), (4, 5)]
    cells = [(2, 4), (2, 5), (1,5 ), (1, 6), (3, 5)]
    game.set_cells(cells)

    while True:
        try:
            canvas = []
            for i in game.world:
                if not i:
                    canvas.append(WHITE)
                else:
                    canvas.append(RED)
            sense.set_pixels(canvas)
            game.run()
            if not game.everyone_alive():
                sense.clear()
                print("everyone died")
                break
            time.sleep(0.1)
        except:
            sense.clear()
            break

if __name__ == "__main__":
    main()
```

Enter the following command to run this script:

```
python main.py
```

The initial cell configuration is set by this statement:

```
cells = [(2, 4), (2, 5), (1, 5), (1, 6), (3, 5)]
```

You can try another configuration by uncommenting the prior cells array, and then comment out this one. I did that very action and then ran the script. I observed an unusual display, which I will not describe. I will leave it for you to discover.

I want to caution that what I am about to describe can become quite addictive. It is testing the consequences of new initial starting patterns. There are more than a few AI researchers who have dedicated their careers to the study of cellular automata, which includes researching the fascinating evolving patterns from the Game of Life.

Figure 10-11 illustrates some starting configurations that you may wish to try. The companion cell configuration array values are shown next to each of the patterns.

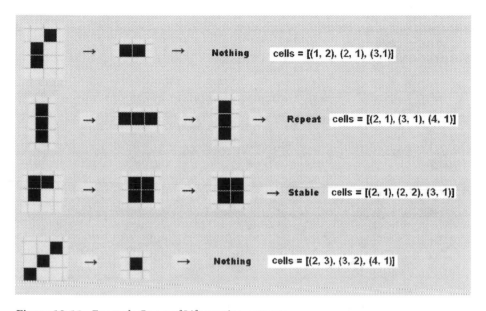

Figure 10-11. *Example Game of Life starting patterns*

Two of the patterns immediately disappear (die), one goes into a bi-stable state, and the fourth pattern enters a stable state. I tested each pattern and confirmed it acted as shown.

Figure 10-12 shows other initial patterns that you can experiment with to see how they evolve according to the rules set. The companion cell array values are shown next to each pattern.

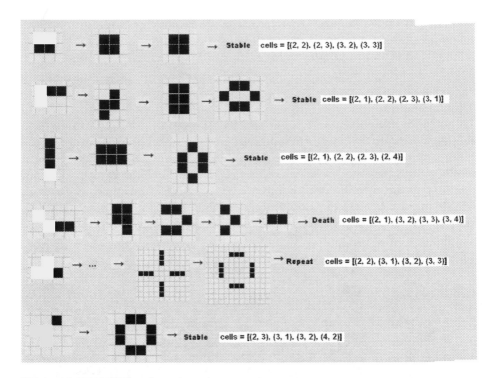

Figure 10-12. Additional starting patterns

There are a series of patterns that are dynamic, which means that they constantly move across the grid and repeat their patterns. Figure 10-13 shows the glider that moves around the grid and repeats its pattern every fourth generation.

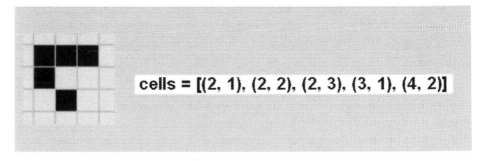

Figure 10-13. Glider pattern

A similar dynamic pattern is the *lightweight spaceship,* which is shown in Figure 10-14. It moves across the grid too.

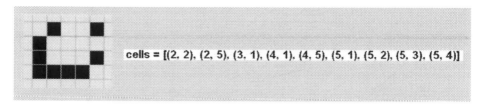

Figure 10-14. *Lightweight spaceship pattern*

Conway discovered several patterns that took many generations to finally evolve and become both predictable and periodic. Incidentally, he made these discoveries without the aid of a computer. He called these patterns *Methuselahs*, after a man who was described in the Hebrew Bible to have lived to the age of 969 years. The first of these long-lived patterns is named F-pentomino, which is shown in Figure 10-15. It becomes stable after 1101 generations.

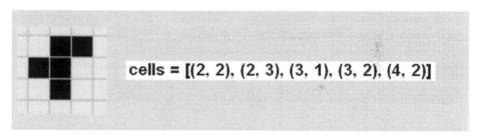

Figure 10-15. *F-pentomino pattern*

The Acorn pattern shown in Figure 10-16 is another example of a Methuselah that becomes stable and predictable after 5206 generations.

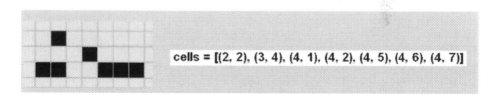

Figure 10-16. *Acorn pattern*

Readers who wish to experiment with more patterns can go to Alan Hensel's webpage at radicaleye.com/lifepage/picgloss/picgloss.html, where he has compiled a fairly large list of other common patterns.

This completes the initial foray into cellular automata using Conway's Game of Life as the tool. You should now be empowered to further experiment with this tool to gain more experience and confidence in this powerful AI topic. I also highly recommend Dr. Stephen Wolfram's book *A New Kind of Science* (Wolfram Media, 2002), in which he examines the entire field of cellular automata using the Mathematica application, which he created. Incidentally, the Mathematica application is now freely provided with the latest Raspian distributions available from `raspberrypi.org`.

Summary

This chapter was concerned with evolutionary computing. I began the chapter with a story relating how evolution and mutation were integral parts of EC.

The first demonstration showed how evolutionary programming could be used to find solutions to fairly simple problems using both evolution and mutation techniques. The solution was first calculated manually and then automatically by a Python script.

The second demonstration introduced the EC subtopic of genetic algorithms and genetic programming. I used a Python version of Conway's Game of Life as the means to explain and demonstrate these concepts. This section also introduced the concept of cellular automata, which is central to the game.

There were two game versions shown: one that used genetic evolution and mutation, and another that was more deterministic in that you could specify the starting patterns. The latter version was further used to examine a variety of cellular patterns that generated some unusual behaviors.

A Sense HAT accessory board was used with a Raspberry Pi 3 to display the Game of Life simulations.

CHAPTER 11

■ ■ ■

Behavior-Based Robotics

Behavior-based robotics (BBR) is an approach to control robots. Its origins are in the study of both animal and insect behaviors. This chapter presents an in-depth exploration of this approach.

Parts List

For the second demonstration, you need the parts that are listed in Table 11-1.

Table 11-1. *Parts Lists*

Description	Quantity	Remarks
Pi Cobbler	1	40-pin version, either T or DIP form factor acceptable
solderless breadboard	1	300 insertion points with power supply strips
solderless breadboard	1	300 insertion points
jumper wires	1 package	
ultrasonic sensors	2	type HC-SR04
4.9kΩ resistor	2	1/4 watt
10kΩ resistor	5	1/4 watt
MCP3008	1	8-channel ADC chip

There is a robot used in a demonstration discussed in this chapter that you can build by following the instructions in the appendix. The parts list includes items required beyond those needed for the basic robot.

The underlying formal structure for BBR is called *subsumption architecture*. In 1985, MIT professor Dr. Rodney Brooks wrote an internal technical memo titled "A Robust Layered Control Mechanism for Mobile Robots." At the time, Dr. Brooks worked in MIT's Artificial Intelligence Laboratory. His memo was subsequently published in 1986 as a paper in *the IEEE Journal of Robotics and Automation*. His paper changed the nature

© Donald J. Norris 2017
D. J. Norris, *Beginning Artificial Intelligence with the Raspberry Pi*,
DOI 10.1007/978-1-4842-2743-5_11

and direction of robotics research for many years. The gist of the paper described a robot control organization that he called subsumption architecture. The theory behind this architecture is based, in part, on the evolutionary development of the human brain.

Human Brain Structure

On a very broad scale, the human brain can be divided into three levels or parts. The lowest level is the most primitive part, which is responsible for basic life-supporting activities, such as respiration, blood pressure, core temperature, and so forth. The brain stem is the organic brain section that hosts these primitive functions. Figure 11-1 illustrates the brain stem and the limbic system.

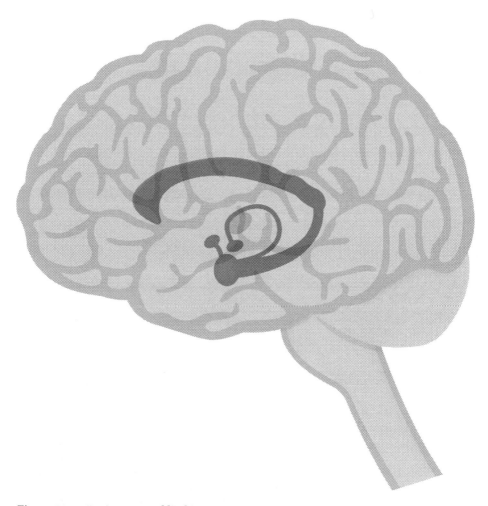

Figure 11-1. Brain stem and limbic system

The next highest level of brain function has been termed the *reptile brain* or *limbic system*. It is responsible for eating, sleeping, reproduction, flight or fight, and similar behaviors. The limbic system is made up of the hippocampus, amygdala, hypothalamus, and the pituitary gland. Finally, the highest cognitive level is the neocortex, which is responsible for learning, thinking, and similar high-level complex activities. The brain components composing the neocortex, or cerebral cortex, are the frontal, temporal, occipital, and parietal lobes. Figure 11-2 illustrates the four lobes that comprise the cerebral cortex.

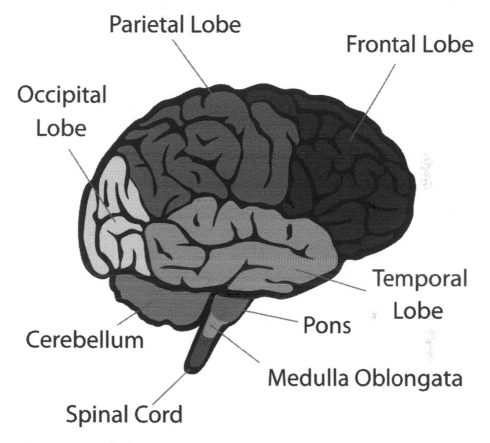

Figure 11-2. *Cerebral cortex*

Most often, these various brain levels function quite independently of each other but they can and often have conflicts. Perhaps you have a "high-strung" personality and find food a welcoming diversion to ease stress. The higher-level function knows that eating too much of the wrong types of food is no good for you, but the lower-level reptile brain still craves it. Which brain level overrides and changes your behavior is problematic. Sometimes the lower level wins and other times the higher level wins. However, if you have an addiction, it is always the case that the lower level wins and changes your

315

behavior, usually for the worst. Anyone can have many different brain-level behaviors ready to activate at a given time, but only one "wins" out and causes the current active behavior to be displayed. This interplay between brain behaviors was one source of Dr. Brooks' subsumption architecture.

Subsumption Architecture

A definition of subsumption will help at this point in the discussion. However, what really has to be defined is the word *subsume*, because subsumption is circularly defined as the act of subsuming.

> *subsume: incorporating something under a more general category; to include something in a larger group or a group in a higher position*

These definitions imply that complex behaviors can be decomposed into multiple simpler behaviors. There is another perspective that must be added to the definition. This addition is the word *reactive*, because in the real world, robots depend on sensors to react or change behaviors based on sensory inputs. These inputs are constantly reacting to changes in the robot's environment. Reactive behavior is also called *stimulus/response behavior*, which is appropriate for insects. Insects are a lower-level life form when compared to mammals, and they do not have a highly developed learning capability. What they do have is called *habituation*, which allows an insect to adapt to certain types of environmental changes. This can easily be seen by blowing air on a cockroach. The insect initially retreats from the blowing air. However, repeatedly blowing air on the cockroach causes it to ignore the air because it is perceived as non–life threatening. This type of low-level learning is useful for robots, especially autonomous robots.

One way to display the traditional approach for a reactive system is shown in Figure 11-3.

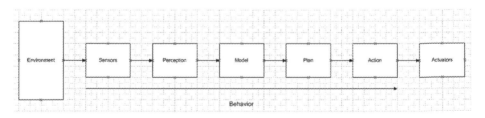

Figure 11-3. *Flowchart for a sensor-based system*

The collection of serial processes, from sensors to action, may be thought of as a behavior. This layout of serial processes or tasks is slow and relatively inflexible. Sensors acquire data without attempting to process it in any way. That job is left to the perception block, which must sort out all relevant sensory data before passing it on to the model block. The model block transforms this filtered data into a contextual sense or state. The plan block has rules that are followed based upon the state it receives from the model block. Finally, the action block implements the appropriate rules received from the plan block and sends the required control signals to the actuators, which are shown in the final block in the diagram. Having all of these blocks in a serial architecture makes for a slow response, which is not a good robotic attribute.

The serial blocks shown in the diagram represent a complex behavior that can be represented by a single layer. A layer in a behavioral sense may be considered a goal to be achieved by an agent or a robot.

Complex behaviors maybe decomposed into simpler behaviors. This is the key to subsumption architecture. Figure 11-4 shows a two-layer decomposition in place of the complex single-layer behavior stream shown in Figure 11-3.

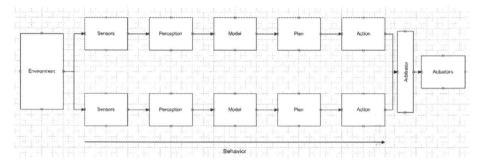

Figure 11-4. *Two-layer behavior serial stream*

Each layer or path is considered related to a specific task, such as following a wall or detecting an obstacle. This is the subsumption architecture proposed by Dr. Brooks. Notice that there is an additional arbitrator block that processes all of the action block signals before sending selected ones to the actuators. This arbitrator block is another important element in subsumption architecture.

Systems can be made much more responsive by essentially converting a single, complex behavior into multiple parallel paths. It is also easy to envision that many more layers can be added without disturbing any of the existing layers. The feature of extending code without modifying existing code closely mimics the software composition principle discussed in an earlier chapter. It is always a good thing to be able to extend existing code without too much "disturbance" to the existing code.

The subsumption architecture does not provide any guidance on how to decompose a complex behavior into simpler multiple tasks. In addition, the perception block is generally regarded as the hardest of all the blocks to define and implement. The problem is to create a meaningful data set from a limited number of environmental sensors. This data set then feeds the model block that effectively creates the robot's world or state. At this point, BBR differs significantly from the more traditional approach. I discuss the traditional approach first, followed by the BBR approach.

Traditional Approach

In the traditional approach, the model block stores a complete and accurate model of the real world that the robot operates within. This may be accomplished in a variety of ways, but there is usually some type of geometric coordinate system involved for mobile robots to establish the current state and predict the future state. Sensor data must be calibrated and accurate for the state to be precisely determined. Ideal state information is either stored or computed based upon the sensor data set. Deviations from the ideal state are errors that are passed onto to the plan block so that appropriate control measures can be taken to minimize these errors. Controllers or actuators must also be precise and accurate to ensure that the corrective motions are done in strict conformance with the commands created by the plan and action blocks.

The traditional approach often involves a lot of computer memory to store or compute the necessary state information. It is slower than the BBR approach, which in turn makes the robot less responsive.

Behavior-Based Robotics Approach

It is worth digressing a bit before discussing BBR. In the study of animal behavior, also known as *ethology*, it has been shown that infant seagulls respond to parent models. Figure 11-5 shows such a parent model with a feature circled in the figure, which will trigger the infant gull's instinct feeding behavior.

Figure 11-5. *Seagull ethology*

All that matters to the infant gulls is that the parent gull model has a sharp beak with a colored spot near the beak tip. The babies open their beaks awaiting food delivery. These infant gulls use a very limited real-world representation, but it has been shown to be perfectly adequate for the gull species to survive.

Similarly, real-world robots can use a limited real-world representation or model, so that it should be adequate to carry out the desired requirements without reliance on an overly detailed world model.

These limited representations are often referred to as "snapshots" of the local environment. Behaviors are then designed to react to these snapshots. Two of the important points are that the mobile robot does not need to maintain a geometric coordinate system, and it does not have to have a memory-laden real-world model. By utilizing reflex-like direct responses, mobile robots minimize the complexity of the model, plan, and action blocks. The behavior stream almost reverts to a simple behavior diagram, as shown in Figure 11-6.

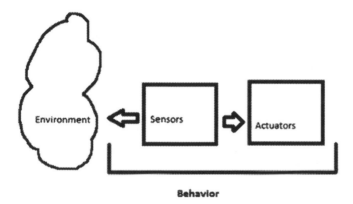

Figure 11-6. Simple behavioral stream

How can environmental snapshots be related to robot behaviors? Initially, a data set has to be created that consists of the sensor data generated when the environmental conditions exist, which should trigger the desired robotic reflexive behavior. These are termed *sensor signatures*. Now all that needs to be done is to link the signatures to a specific behavior using interpretive routines, normally done in the Prediction block. However, there could be an issue that given the relatively coarse-grained sensor data signatures, simultaneous stimulus/response pairings could happen. Assigning priorities to the simple behaviors alleviates this situation. In addition, default or long-term behaviors are normally assigned a lower priority than emergent or "tactical" behaviors. The tactical signature happens if the robot encounters an environment condition that requires immediate attention from the robot control system.

Instituting a behavior prioritization scheme has an unintended positive outcome. Robots usually operate with the same behavior, such as moving forward. All behaviors acting in sequence should strive to maintain this normalcy. Only when environmental conditions warrant should a behavior direct the robot to deviate from the normal. When deviations happen, the higher-priority behaviors take control and try to restore normalcy.

BBR also incorporates long-term progress indicators to help avoid a "looping" situation, as might be the case where the robot continually bounces between two barriers or is locked into a wall corner. These long-term progress indicators effectively generate a strategic trajectory in which the robot moves in a general direction or path. When progress is impeded, a different set of behaviors is selected to return to the normal state.

In a layered subsumption model, a low-level layer might have the goal to "avoid an obstacle." This layer could be "beneath" a higher level of "roam around." The higher level of "roam around" is said to subsume the lower-level behavior of "avoid an obstacle." All layers have access to sensors to detect environment changes, as well as the ability to control actuators. An overall constraint is that separate tasks have the ability to suppress any input and to inhibit output sent to actuators. In this way, the lowest levels can be very responsive to environment changes, much the way reflexes function in living organisms. Higher levels are more abstract and devoted to satisfying goals.

The following behaviors may be represented by a variety of graphical or mathematical models:

- Functional notation

- Stimulus/response diagram

- Finite state machine (FSM)

- Schema

I use the FSM model because it provides a good representation of behavior interactions without much mathematic abstraction. A basic FSM model is shown in Figure 11-7.

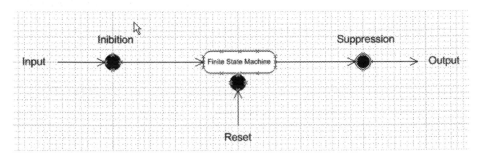

Figure 11-7. Basic FSM model

Figure 11-8 shows multiple behaviors with interrelationships, including sensory inhibitions and actuator suppressions. Notice the layered behavior sequences and behavior prioritization discussed earlier.

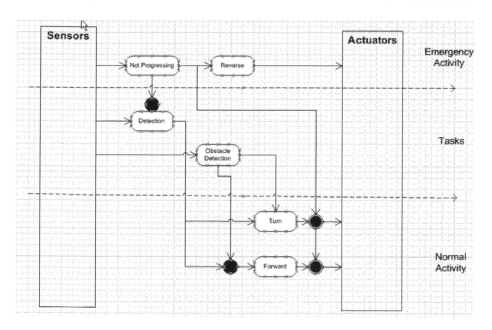

Figure 11-8. *Multilayered FSM model*

At this point in the discussion, I would normally proceed to show you a Python implementation for a subsumption architecture that runs on a Raspberry Pi. Next, however, I divert from the norm to discuss a very nice robot simulation project that can implement subsumption and a whole lot more.

Demo 11-1: The Breve Project

The breve project is the work of Jon Klein, who developed it as part of his undergraduate and graduate thesis work. It is available from Jon's website at www.spiderland.org for Windows, Linux, and Mac platforms. I am using it on a MacBook Pro and it seems to perform quite flawlessly. Just be aware that Jon states on his website that he is no longer actively updating the application but continues to make it available, at least in the Mac format.

Here are Jon's own words to describe what breve is all about: "breve is a free, open-source software package which makes it easy to build 3D simulations of multi-agent systems and artificial life. Using Python, or using a simple scripting language called steve, you can define the behaviors of agents in a 3D world and observe how they interact. breve includes physical simulation and collision detection so you can simulate realistic creatures. It also has an OpenGL display engine so you can visualize your simulated worlds."

There is extensive HTML-formatted documentation on the website that I urge you to review; particularly the introductory pages showing how to run one of the many available demo scripts. These scripts are both in the "steve" front-end language as well as Python. It is impossible for me to go through the many documentation pages, which would constitute an entire book to itself. I did run the following Python script, titled RangerImage.py, in breve. The listing is shown here to provide a glimpse of the power and flexibility that you have using breve.

```
import breve

class AggressorController( breve.BraitenbergControl ):
    def __init__( self ):
        breve.BraitenbergControl.__init__( self )
        self.depth = None
        self.frameCount = 0
        self.leftSensor = None
        self.leftWheel = None
        self.n = 0
        self.rightSensor = None
        self.rightWheel = None
        self.simSpeed = 0
        self.startTime = 0
        self.vehicle = None
        self.video = None
        AggressorController.init( self )

    def init( self ):
        self.n = 0
        while ( self.n < 10 ):
            breve.createInstances( breve.BraitenbergLight, 1 ).
            move( breve.vector( ( 20 * breve.breveInternal
            FunctionFinder.sin( self, ( ( self.n *
            6.280000 ) / 10 ) ) ), 1, ( 20 * breve.
            breveInternalFunctionFinder.cos( self, ( ( self.n *
            6.280000 ) / 10 ) ) ) ) )
            self.n = ( self.n + 1 )

        self.vehicle = breve.createInstances( breve.
        BraitenbergVehicle, 1 )
        self.watch( self.vehicle )
        self.vehicle.move( breve.vector( 0, 2, 18 ) )
        self.leftWheel = self.vehicle.addWheel( breve.vector
        ( -0.500000, 0, -1.500000 ) )
        self.rightWheel = self.vehicle.addWheel( breve.vector
        ( -0.500000, 0, 1.500000 ) )
        self.leftWheel.setNaturalVelocity( 0.000000 )
        self.rightWheel.setNaturalVelocity( 0.000000 )
        self.rightSensor = self.vehicle.addSensor( breve.
        vector( 2.000000, 0.400000, 1.500000 ) )
        self.leftSensor = self.vehicle.addSensor( breve.vector
        ( 2.000000, 0.400000, -1.500000 ) )
        self.leftSensor.link( self.rightWheel )
        self.rightSensor.link( self.leftWheel )
        self.leftSensor.setBias( 15.000000 )
        self.rightSensor.setBias( 15.000000 )
        self.video = breve.createInstances( breve.Image, 1 )
```

```
        self.video.setSize( 176, 144 )
        self.depth = breve.createInstances( breve.Image, 1 )
        self.depth.setSize( 176, 144 )
        self.startTime = self.getRealTime()

    def postIterate( self ):
        self.frameCount = ( self.frameCount + 1 )
        self.simSpeed = (self.getTime()/(self.getRealTime()-
        self.startTime))
        print '''Simulation speed = %s''' % (  self.simSpeed )
        self.video.readPixels( 0, 0 )
        self.depth.readDepth( 0, 0, 1, 50 )
        if ( self.frameCount < 10 ):
            self.video.write( '''imgs/video-%s.png''' %
            (self.frameCount))

        self.depth.write16BitGrayscale('''imgs/depth-%s.png''' %
        (self.frameCount))

breve.AggressorController = AggressorController

# Create an instance of our controller object to initialize the
simulation
AggressorController()
```

Figure 11-9 shows the actual robot running in the breve display, which was created by the preceding script.

Figure 11-9. *breve world*

You may have noticed in the script that there are references to BraitenbergControl, BraitenbergLight, and BraitenbergVehicle. These are based on a thought experiment conducted by Italian-Austrian cyberneticist Valentino Braitenberg, who wrote *Vehicles: Experiments in Synthetic Psychology* (The MIT Press, 1984), which I highly recommend for readers desiring to learn more about his innovative approach to robotics. In his experiment, he envisions vehicles directly controlled by sensors. The resulting behavior might appear complex, or even intelligent, but in reality, it is based on a combination of simpler behaviors. That should remind you of subsumption at work.

A Braitenberg vehicle may be thought of as an agent that autonomously moves around based on its own sensory inputs. In these thought experiments, the sensors are primitive and simply measure a stimulus, which is often just a point light source. The sensors are also directly connected to the motor actuators so that a sensor can immediately activate a motor upon stimulation. Again, this should remind you of the simple behavioral stream shown in Figure 11-4.

The resulting Braitenberg vehicle behavior depends on how the sensors and motors are connected. In Figure 11-10, there are two different configurations between the sensors and the motors. The vehicle to the left is wired so that it avoids or drives away from the light source. This contrasts with the vehicle on the right, which drives toward the light source.

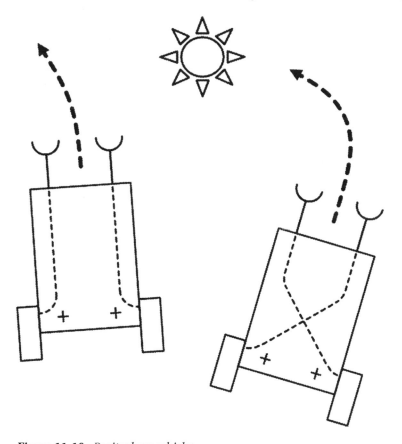

Figure 11-10. Braitenberg vehicles

It is not too much of a leap to say that the vehicle on the left "fears" the light, while the vehicle on the right "likes" the light. I have assigned human-like behaviors to a robot, which is precisely the result that Braitenberg was seeking.

Another Braitenberg vehicle has one light sensor with the following behaviors:

- More light produces faster movement.

- Less light produces slower movement.

- Darkness produces standstill.

This behavior can be interpreted as a robot that is afraid of the light and moves quickly to get away from it. Its goal is to find a dark spot to hide.

Of course, the complementary Braitenberg vehicle is one that features these behaviors:

- More darkness produces faster movement.

- Less darkness produces slower movement.

- Full light produces standstill.

In this case, the behavior can be interpreted as a robot that is seeking light and moves quickly to get to it. Its goal is to find the brightest spot to park.

Braitenberg vehicles exhibit complex and dynamic behavior in a complex environment with multiple stimulation sources. Depending on the configuration between the sensors and the actuators, a Braitenberg vehicle might move close to a source, but not touch it, run away very quickly, or make circles or figures-of-eight around a point. Figure 11-11 illustrates these complex behaviors.

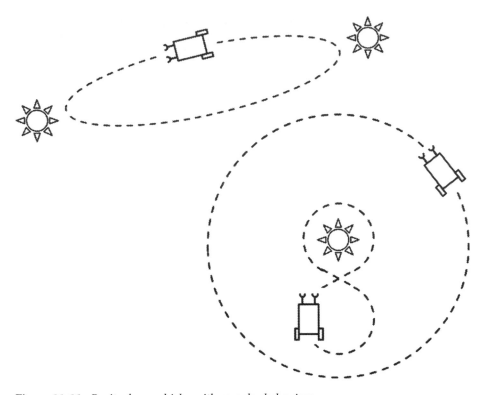

Figure 11-11. *Braitenberg vehicles with complex behaviors*

These behaviors may appear to be goal-directed, adaptive, and even intelligent in much the same way that minimal intelligence is attributed to a cockroach's behavior. But the truth is that the agent is functioning in a purely mechanical way, without any cognitive or reasoning processes at play.

There are a few items in the breve Python example that I want to further explain in preparation for a step-by-step example in which you create your own Braitenberg vehicle. The first item to note is that all breve simulations require a controller object, which specifies how the simulation is to be set up. The controller's name in this simulation is AggressorController. In the controller definition, there is at least one initialization method named `init`. In this specific case, because this is a Python script, there is another initialization method named `__init__`. The first initialization method is called when a breve object is instantiated. The second initialization method is automatically called when a Python object is instantiated. breve takes care of sorting out the relationships between breve and Python objects using a third object called a *bridge*. You don't ordinarily have to be concerned with these bridge objects. In fact, if you only use the steve scripting language (instead of Python), you never see a bridge object.

The `init` method creates 10 Braitenberg light objects, a few of which you can see in Figure 11-7. They are the spheres named `'n'` surrounding the Braitenberg robot, which is also created by the `init` method and is referred to as `vehicle`.

The __init__ method creates all the attributes needed for the simulation, and then it calls the init method that instantiates all the required simulation objects and assigns real values to the attributes. Once that is accomplished, all that is needed to click the play button to view the simulation.

The step-by-step demonstration starts here. The following listing creates a non-functioning Braitenberg vehicle and a light source:

```
import breve
class Controller(breve.BraitenbergControl):
    def __init__(self):
        breve.BraitenbergControl.__init__(self)
        self.vehicle = None
        self.leftSensor = None
        self.rightSensor = None
        self.leftWheel = None
        self.rightWheel = None
        self.simSpeed = 0
        self.light = None
        Controller.init(self)

    def init(self):
        self.light = breve.createInstances(breve.BraitenbergLight, 1)
        self.light.move(breve.vector(10, 1, 0))
        self.vehicle = breve.createInstances(breve.BraitenbergVehicle, 1)
        self.watch(self.vehicle)

    def iterate(self):
        breve.BraitenbergControl.iterate(self)

breve.Controller = Controller
Controller()
```

I named this script firstVehicle.py to indicate that it is the first of several generated in the process of developing a working simulation. Figure 11-12 shows the result after I loaded and "played" this script in the breve application.

Figure 11-12. *breve world for the firstVehicle script*

This script defines a Controller class that has the two initialization methods mentioned earlier. The init method instantiates a Braitenberg light object and a Braitenberg vehicle. The __init__ method creates a list of attributes, which is filled in by a follow-on script. This method also calls the init method.

There is also a new method called iterate that simply causes the simulation to run continuously.

The next step in developing the script is to add sensors and wheels to the vehicle to allow it to move through and explore the breve world. The following statements add the wheels and set an initial velocity that causes the vehicle to turn in circles. These statements go into the init method.

```
self.vehicle.move(breve.vector(0, 2, 18))
self.leftWheel = self.vehicle.addWheel(breve.
vector(-0.500000,0,-1.500000))
self.rightWheel = self.vehicle.addWheel( breve.
vector(-0.500000,0,1.500000))
self.leftWheel.setNaturalVelocity(0.500000)
self.rightWheel.setNaturalVelocity(1.000000)
```

The next set of statements adds the sensors. These are also added to the init method. The sensors are also cross-linked between the wheels (i.e., right sensor controls the left wheel and vice versa). The setBias method sets the amount of influence that a sensor has on its linked wheel. The default value is 1, which means that the sensor has a slightly positive influence on the wheel. A value of 15 means that the sensor has a strongly positive influence on the wheel. Bias can also be negative, meaning the influence is directly opposite to wheel activation.

```
self.rightSensor = self.vehicle.addSensor(breve.vector
(2.000000, 0.400000, 1.500000))
self.leftSensor = self.vehicle.addSensor( breve.vector
(2.000000, 0.400000, -1.500000 ) )
```

```
self.leftSensor.link(self.rightWheel)
self.rightSensor.link(self.leftWheel)
self.leftSensor.setBias(15.000000)
self.rightSensor.setBias(15.000000)
```

The preceding sets of statements were added to the init method. The whole script name was changed to secondVehicle.py. The sensors are designed to have a natural affinity toward any light source. However, if the sensors do not detect any light source, they will not activate their respective linked wheels. In this script configuration, the sensors do not immediately detect the light source and the vehicle simply stays still, which is the reason for my setting an initial natural velocity for each wheel. These settings guarantee that the robot will move. It may not move in the direction of the light source, but it moves. Figure 11-13 shows the updated breve world with the enhanced vehicle.

Figure 11-13. *Breve world for the secondVehicle script*

At this stage, the simulation is working, but it is a bit dull because the vehicle has no purpose other than to turn in circles in the breve world, and perhaps to catch a glimpse of the solitary light source. It is time to give the vehicle a better goal to realize the rationale behind a simulation. I make the goal really simple, as this is a "hello world" type demonstration and its purpose is to clarify, not obscure how a breve simulation works. The goal is to have the vehicle seek out a number of light sources and simply "run through" them.

These additional Braitenberg light sources are generated by the following loop that is added to the init method.

```
self.n = 0
    while (self.n < 10):
        breve.createInstances( breve.BraitenbergLight, 1).move(
        breve.vector((20 * breve.breveInternalFunctionFinder.
        sin(self, ((self.n * 6.280000) / 10))), 1,(20 * breve.
        breveInternalFunctionFinder. cos(self, ((self.n *
        6.280000 ) / 10)))))
        self.n = ( self.n + 1 )
```

I also commented out the single light source created in the initial script. In addition, I reset the natural velocities back to 0.0 because there are now a sufficient number of light sources that the vehicle sensors can likely detect. Figure 11-14 shows the updated breve world, with some of the additional light sources and the vehicle going through them. The new script was renamed thirdVehicle.py.

Figure 11-14. *breve world for the thirdVehicle script*

This last script completes my introductory lesson on how to create a robot simulation in the breve environment using Python. This lesson just scratches the surface on what breve has to offer—not just in robotic simulations but in a whole host of other AI applications. Look at Figure 11-15 and see if you recognize it.

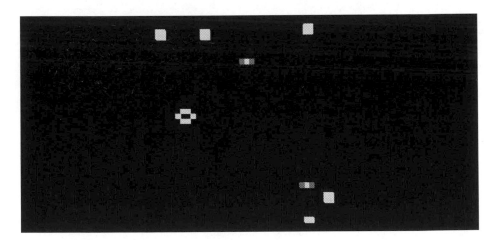

Figure 11-15. *breve snapshot*

It is a snapshot of Conway's Game of Life running in breve. This script is named PatchLife.py. It is available in the Demos menu selection in both Python and steve formats. In fact, most demos are available in both formats. There are many demos available for you to try, including the following:

- Braitenberg: vehicles, lights

- Chemistry: Gray Scott diffusion, hypercycle

- DLA: diffusion limited aggression (fractal growth)

- Genetics: Game of Life both 2D and 3D

- Music: play midi and wav files

- Neural networks: multilayer

- Physics: springs, joints, walkers

- Swarms: swarming robots and other lifeforms

- Terrain: robots, creatures exploring terrain features

It is now time to conclude the breve discussion and return to subsumption.

Demo 11-2: Building a Subsumption-Controlled Robot Car

This section's objective is to describe how to program a Raspberry Pi that directly controls a robot car. The robot car is the same platform used in Chapter 7, but now uses subsumption architecture to control the car's behaviors. Python is the implementation language for the subsumption classes and scripts.

After searching through GitHub, I was inspired by Alexander Svenden's EV3 post that used Python to implement a generic subsumption structure. I also relied on my experience with developing subsumptive Java classes with leJOS. You can read more about these Java classes at `www.lejos.org`. There are two primary classes required: one abstract class named `Behavior` and the other named `Controller`. The `Behavior` class encapsulates the car's behavior using the following methods:

- `takeControl()`: Returns a Boolean value indicating if the behavior should take control or not.

- `action()`: Implements the specific behavior done by the car.

- `suppress()`: Causes the action behavior to immediately stop, and then returns the car state to one in which the next behavior can take control.

```python
import RPi.GPIO as GPIO
import time
class Behavior(self):
    global pwmL, pwmR

    # use the BCM pin numbers
    GPIO.setmode(GPIO.BCM)

    # setup the motor control pins
    GPIO.setup(18, GPIO.OUT)
    GPIO.setup(19, GPIO.OUT)

    pwmL = GPIO.PWM(18,20) # pin 18 is left wheel pwm
    pwmR = GPIO.PWM(19,20) # pin 19 is right wheel pwm

    # must 'start' the motors with 0 rotation speeds
    pwmL.start(2.8)
    pwmR.start(2.8)
```

The `Controller` class contains the main subsumption logic that determines which behaviors are active based on priority and the need for activation. The following are some of the methods in this class:

- `__init__()`: Initializes the `Controller` object.

- `add()`: Adds a behavior to the list of available behaviors. The order in which they are added determines the behavior's priority.

- `remove()`: Removes a behavior from the list of available behaviors. Stops any running behavior if the next highest behavior overrides it.

- `update()`: Stops an old behavior and runs the new behavior.

- `step()`: Finds the next active behavior and runs it.

- `find_next_active_behavior()`: Finds the next behavior wishing to be active.

- `find_and_set_new_active_behavior()`: Finds the next behavior wishing to be active and makes it active.

- `start()`: Runs the selected action method.

- `stop()`: Stops the current action.

- `continously_find_new_active_behavior()`: Monitors in real-time for new behaviors desiring to be active.

- `__str__()`: Returns the name of the current behavior.

The `Controller` object also functions as a scheduler, where one behavior is active at a time. The active behavior is decided by the sensor data and its priority. Any old active behavior is suppressed when a behavior with a higher priority signals that it wants to run.

There are two ways to use the Controller class. The first way is to let the class take care of the scheduler itself by calling the start() method. The other way is to forcibly start the scheduler by calling the step() method.

```python
import threading
class Controller():

    def __init__(self):
        self.behaviors = []
        self.wait_object = threading.Event()
        self.active_behavior_index = None

        self.running = True
        #self.return_when_no_action = return_when_no_action

        #self.callback = lambda x: 0

    def add(self, behavior):
        self.behaviors.append(behavior)

    def remove(self, index):
        old_behavior = self.behaviors[index]
        del self.behaviors[index]
        if self.active_behavior_index == index:  # stop the old
        one if the new one overrides it
            old_behavior.suppress()
            self.active_behavior_index = None

    def update(self, behavior, index):
        old_behavior = self.behaviors[index]
        self.behaviors[index] = behavior
        if self.active_behavior_index == index:  # stop the old
        one if the new one overrides it
            old_behavior.suppress()

    def step(self):
        behavior = self.find_next_active_behavior()
        if behavior is not None:
            self.behaviors[behavior].action()
            return True
        return False

    def find_next_active_behavior(self):
        for priority, behavior in enumerate(self.behaviors):
            active = behavior.takeControl()
            if active == True:
                activeIndex = priority
        return activeIndex
```

```
    def find_and_set_new_active_behavior(self):
        new_behavior_priority = self.find_next_active_behavior()
        if self.active_behavior_index is None or self.active_
        behavior_index > new_behavior_priority:
            if self.active_behavior_index is not None:
                self.behaviors[self.active_behavior_index].suppress()
            self.active_behavior_index = new_behavior_priority

    def start(self):  # run the action methods
        self.running = True
        self.find_and_set_new_active_behavior()  # force it once
        thread = threading.Thread(name="Continuous behavior checker",
                                  target=self.continuously_find_
                                  new_active_behavior, args=())
        thread.daemon = True
        thread.start()

        while self.running:
            if self.active_behavior_index is not None:
                running_behavior = self.active_behavior_index
                self.behaviors[running_behavior].action()

                if running_behavior == self.active_behavior_index:
                    self.active_behavior_index = None
                    self.find_and_set_new_active_behavior()
            self.running = False

    def stop(self):
        self._running = False
        self.behaviors[self.active_behavior_index].suppress()

    def continuously_find_new_active_behavior(self):
        while self.running:
            self.find_and_set_new_active_behavior()

    def __str__(self):
        return str(self.behaviors)
```

The Controller class is very general by allowing a wide variety of behaviors to be implemented using the general-purpose methods. The takeControl() method allows a behavior to signal that it wishes to take control of the robot. The way it does this is discussed later. The action() method is the way a behavior starts to control the robot. The obstacle avoidance behavior kicks off its action() method if a sensor detects an obstacle impeding the robot's path. The suppress() method is used by a higher priority behavior to stop or suppress the action() method of a lower priority behavior. This happens when an obstacle avoidance behavior takes over from the normal forward motion behavior by suppressing the forward behavior's action() method and having its own action() method activated.

The Controller class requires a list or array of Behavior objects that comprise the robot's overall behavior. A Controller instance starts with the highest array index in the Behavior array and checks the takeControl() method's return value. If true, it calls that behavior's action() method. If it is false, the Controller checks the next Behavior object's takeControl() method return value. Prioritization happens by the assignment of index array values attached to each Behavior object. The Controller class continually rescans all the Behavior objects and suppresses a lower priority behavior if a higher priority behavior asserts the takeControl() method while the lower priority action() method is activated. Figure 11-16 shows this process with all the behaviors that are eventually added.

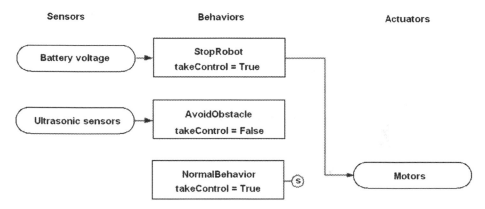

Figure 11-16. *Behavior state diagram*

It is now time to create a relatively simple behavior-based robot example.

Demo 11-3: Alfie Robot Car

The target robot is Alfie, which was used in previous chapters. The normal or low-priority behavior is to drive in a forward direction. A higher-priority behavior is obstacle avoidance, which uses ultrasonic sensors to detect obstacles in the robot's direct path. The obstacle avoidance behavior is to stop, back up, and turn 90 degrees to the right.

The following class is named NormalBehavior. It reinforces the layered behavior approach. This class has all the required Behavior method implementations.

```
class NormalBehavior(Behavior):
    def takeControl():
        return true
    def action():
        # drive forward
        pwmL.ChangeDutyCycle(3.6)
        pwmR.ChangeDutyCycle(2.2)
```

```
    def suppress():
        # all stop
        pwmL.ChangeDutyCycle(2.6)
        pwmR.ChangeDutyCycle(2.6)
```

The takeControl() method should always return the logical value true. Higher priority behaviors are always allowed control by the Controller class; it really doesn't matter if this lower priority requests control.

The action() method is very simple: power the motors in a forward direction using the full-power setting.

The suppress() method is also very simple: it stops both motors.

The obstacle avoidance behavior is a bit more complex, however. It still implements the same three methods specified in the Behavior interface. I named the class AvoidObstacle to indicate its basic behavior.

```
class AvoidObstacle(Behavior):
global distance1, distance2
    def takeControl():
        if distance1 <= 25.4 or distance2 <= 25.4:
            return True
        else:
            return False

    def action():
        # drive backward
        pwmL.ChangeDutyCycle(2.2)
        pwmR.ChangeDutyCycle(3.6)
        time.sleep(1.5)
        # turn right
        pwmL.ChangeDutyCycle(3.6)
        pwmR.ChangeDutyCycle(2.6)
        time.sleep(0.3)
        # stop
        pwmL.ChangeDutyCycle(2.6)
        pwmR.ChangeDutyCycle(2.6)

    def suppress():
        # all stop
        pwmL.ChangeDutyCycle(2.6)
        pwmR.ChangeDutyCycle(2.6)
```

There are a few items to point out regarding this class. The takeControl() method returns a logical true only if the distance between the ultrasonic sensor and the obstacle is 10 inches or less. This behavior is never active without asserting a true value.

The action() method causes the robot to back up for 1.5 seconds, as seen by the time.sleep(1.5) statement. The robot next rotates for 0.3 seconds based on stopping the right motor and allowing the left motor to continue to run. The robot then stops waiting for the next behavior to activate.

The suspense() method simply stops both motors because there is no other obvious behavioral intent regarding suspending obstacle avoidance.

The next step is to create a test class named testBBR that instantiates all of the classes defined earlier, and a Controller object. Note that I also added the StopRobot class to this listing, which I discuss next. I did this to avoid another long code listing. The following listing is named subsumption.py:

```python
import RPi.GPIO as GPIO
import time
import threading
import numpy as np

# next two libraries must be installed IAW appendix
instructions
import Adafruit_GPIO.SPI as SPI
import Adafruit_MCP3008

class Behavior():
    global pwmL, pwmR, distance1, distance2

    # use the BCM pin numbers
    GPIO.setmode(GPIO.BCM)

    # setup the motor control pins
    GPIO.setup(18, GPIO.OUT)
    GPIO.setup(19, GPIO.OUT)

    pwmL = GPIO.PWM(18,20) # pin 18 is left wheel pwm
    pwmR = GPIO.PWM(19,20) # pin 19 is right wheel pwm

    # must 'start' the motors with 0 rotation speeds
    pwmL.start(2.8)
    pwmR.start(2.8)

class Controller():

    def __init__(self):
        self.behaviors = []
        self.wait_object = threading.Event()
        self.active_behavior_index = None

        self.running = True
        #self.return_when_no_action = return_when_no_action

        #self.callback = lambda x: 0

    def add(self, behavior):
        self.behaviors.append(behavior)
```

```python
    def remove(self, index):
        old_behavior = self.behaviors[index]
        del self.behaviors[index]
        if self.active_behavior_index == index:  # stop the old
        one if the new one overrides it
            old_behavior.suppress()
            self.active_behavior_index = None

    def update(self, behavior, index):
        old_behavior = self.behaviors[index]
        self.behaviors[index] = behavior
        if self.active_behavior_index == index:  # stop the old
        one if the new one overrides it
            old_behavior.suppress()

    def step(self):
        behavior = self.find_next_active_behavior()
        if behavior is not None:
            self.behaviors[behavior].action()
            return True
        return False

    def find_next_active_behavior(self):
        for priority, behavior in enumerate(self.behaviors):
            active = behavior.takeControl()
            if active == True:
                activeIndex = priority
        return activeIndex

    def find_and_set_new_active_behavior(self):
        new_behavior_priority = self.find_next_active_behavior()
        if self.active_behavior_index is None or self.active_
        behavior_index > new_behavior_priority:
            if self.active_behavior_index is not None:
                self.behaviors[self.active_behavior_index].suppress()
            self.active_behavior_index = new_behavior_priority

    def start(self):  # run the action methods
        self.running = True
        self.find_and_set_new_active_behavior()  # force it once
        thread = threading.Thread(name="Continuous behavior checker",
                                  target=self.continuously_
                                  find_new_active_behavior,
                                  args=())
        thread.daemon = True
        thread.start()
```

```
        while self.running:
            if self.active_behavior_index is not None:
                running_behavior = self.active_behavior_index
                self.behaviors[running_behavior].action()

                if running_behavior == self.active_behavior_index:
                    self.active_behavior_index = None
                    self.find_and_set_new_active_behavior()
            self.running = False

    def stop(self):
        self._running = False
        self.behaviors[self.active_behavior_index].suppress()

    def continuously_find_new_active_behavior(self):
        while self.running:
            self.find_and_set_new_active_behavior()

    def __str__(self):
        return str(self.behaviors)

class NormalBehavior(Behavior):

    def takeControl(self):
        return True

    def action(self):
        # drive forward
        pwmL.ChangeDutyCycle(3.6)
        pwmR.ChangeDutyCycle(2.2)

    def suppress(self):
        # all stop
        pwmL.ChangeDutyCycle(2.6)
        pwmR.ChangeDutyCycle(2.6)

class AvoidObstacle(Behavior):

    def takeControl(self):
        #self.distance1 = distance1
        #self.distance2 = distance2
        if self.distance1 <= 25.4 or self.distance2 <= 25.4:
            return True
        else:
            return False
```

```python
    def action(self):
        # drive backward
        pwmL.ChangeDutyCycle(2.2)
        pwmR.ChangeDutyCycle(3.6)
        time.sleep(1.5)
        # turn right
        pwmL.ChangeDutyCycle(3.6)
        pwmR.ChangeDutyCycle(2.6)
        time.sleep(0.3)
        # stop
        pwmL.ChangeDutyCycle(2.6)
        pwmR.ChangeDutyCycle(2.6)

    def suppress(self):
        # all stop
        pwmL.ChangeDutyCycle(2.6)
        pwmR.ChangeDutyCycle(2.6)

    def setDistances(self, dest1, dest2):
        self.distance1 = dest1
        self.distance2 = dest2

class StopRobot(Behavior):

    critical_voltage = 6.0

    def takeControl(self):
        if self.voltage < critical_voltage:
            return True
        else:
            return False

    def action(self):
        # all stop
        pwmL.ChangeDutyCycle(2.6)
        pwmR.ChangeDutyCycle(2.6)

    def suppress(self):
        # all stop
        pwmL.ChangeDutyCycle(2.6)
        pwmR.ChangeDutyCycle(2.6)

    def setVoltage(self, volts):
        self.voltage = volts

# the test class
class testBBR():
```

```python
def __init__(self):

    # instantiate objects
    self.nb = NormalBehavior()
    self.oa = AvoidObstacle()
    self.control = Controller()

    # setup the behaviors array by priority; last-in = highest
    self.control.add(self.nb)
    self.control.add(self.oa)

    # initialize distances
    distance1 = 50
    distance2 = 50
    self.oa.setDistances(distance1, distance2)

    # activate the behaviors
    self.control.start()

    threshold = 25.4 #10 inches

    # use the BCM pin numbers
    GPIO.setmode(GPIO.BCM)

    # ultrasonic sensor pins
    self.TRIG1 = 23 # an output
    self.ECHO1 = 24 # an input
    self.TRIG2 = 25 # an output
    self.ECHO2 = 27 # an input

    # set the output pins
    GPIO.setup(self.TRIG1, GPIO.OUT)
    GPIO.setup(self.TRIG2, GPIO.OUT)

    # set the input pins
    GPIO.setup(self.ECHO1, GPIO.IN)
    GPIO.setup(self.ECHO2, GPIO.IN)

    # initialize sensors
    GPIO.output(self.TRIG1, GPIO.LOW)
    GPIO.output(self.TRIG2, GPIO.LOW)
    time.sleep(1)

    # Hardware SPI configuration:
    SPI_PORT   = 0
    SPI_DEVICE = 0
    self.mcp = Adafruit_MCP3008.MCP3008(spi=SPI.SpiDev(SPI_
    PORT, SPI_DEVICE))
```

```python
    def run(self):
        # forever loop
        while True:
            # sensor 1 reading
            GPIO.output(self.TRIG1, GPIO.HIGH)
            time.sleep(0.000010)
            GPIO.output(self.TRIG1, GPIO.LOW)

            # detects the time duration for the echo pulse
            while GPIO.input(self.ECHO1) == 0:
                pulse_start = time.time()

            while GPIO.input(self.ECHO1) == 1:
                pulse_end = time.time()

            pulse_duration = pulse_end - pulse_start

            # distance calculation
            distance1 = pulse_duration * 17150

            # round distance to two decimal points
            distance1 = round(distance1, 2)

            time.sleep(0.1) # ensure that sensor 1 is quiet

            # sensor 2 reading
            GPIO.output(self.TRIG2, GPIO.HIGH)
            time.sleep(0.000010)
            GPIO.output(self.TRIG2, GPIO.LOW)

            # detects the time duration for the echo pulse
            while GPIO.input(self.ECHO2) == 0:
                pulse_start = time.time()

            while GPIO.input(self.ECHO2) == 1:
                pulse_end = time.time()

            pulse_duration = pulse_end - pulse_start

            # distance calculation
            distance2 = pulse_duration * 17150

            # round distance to two decimal points
            distance2 = round(distance2, 2)

            time.sleep(0.1) # ensure that sensor 2 is quiet

            self.oa.setDistances(distance1, distance2)
```

```
        count0 = self.mcp.read_adc(0)
        # approximation given 1023 = 7.5V
        voltage = count0 / 100

        self.control.find_and_set_new_active_behavior()

# instantiate an instance of testBBR
bbr = testBBR()

# run it
bbr.run()
```

At this point, it is a good opportunity to show how easy it is to add another behavior.

Adding Another Behavior

The new class encapsulates a stop behavior based on the battery voltage level. You certainly wish to halt the robot if the battery voltage drops below a critical level. You also need to build and connect a battery monitoring circuit, as shown in the Figure 11-17 schematic.

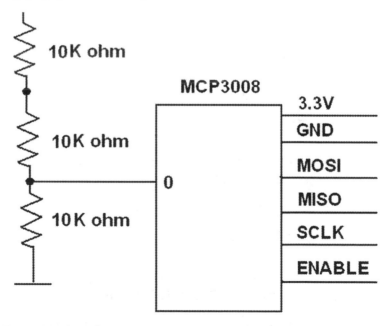

Figure 11-17. Battery monitor schematic

This circuit uses the MCP3008 ADC chip discussed in earlier chapters. You should review the installation and configuration for this chip because it uses SPI, which requires a specialized Python interface library.

The new `Behavior` subclass is named `StopRobot`. It implements all three `Behavior` subsumption methods, as well as one more that sets a real-time voltage level. The following is the class code:

```
class StopRobot(Behavior):

    critical_voltage = 6.0 # change to any value suitable for robot

    def takeControl(self):
        if self.voltage < critical_voltage:
            return True
        else:
            return False

    def action(self):
        # all stop
        pwmL.ChangeDutyCycle(2.6)
        pwmR.ChangeDutyCycle(2.6)

    def suppress(self):
        # all stop
        pwmL.ChangeDutyCycle(2.6)
        pwmR.ChangeDutyCycle(2.6)

    def setVoltage(self, volts):
        self.voltage = volts
```

The `testBBR` class also has to be slightly modified to accept the additional behavior. The following code shows the two statements that must be added to the `testBBR` class. Notice that the `StopRobot` behavior is the last one added, making it the highest priority—as it should be.

`self.sr = StopRobot()` (Add this to the bottom of the list of instantiated `Behavior` subclasses.)

`self.sr.setVoltage(voltage)` (Add this right after the voltage measurement.)

Test Run

The robot was run using an SSH session to make the robot car completely autonomous and free of any encumbering wires or cables. The script started with the following command:

```
python subsumption.py
```

The robot immediately drove forward in a straight line until in encountered an obstacle, which was a cardboard box. When the robot closed to about 10 inches from the box, it quickly paused, turned right, and proceeded to drive in a straight line. For this demonstration's purpose, it is sufficient to stop at this point; although the robot's behaviors may be continuously fine-tuned as additional requirements are placed on the robot.

Readers who wish to pursue more in-depth research into BBR should take a look at the following recommended website and online articles:

- `https://sccn.ucsd.edu/wiki/MoBILAB`

- `http://www.sci.brooklyn.cuny.edu/~sklar/ teaching/boston-college/s01/mc375/iecon98.pdf`

- `http://robotics.usc.edu/publications/media/ uploads/pubs/60.pdf`

- `http://www.ohio.edu/people/starzykj/network/ Class/ee690/EE690 Design of Embodied Intelligence/Reading Assignments/robot- emotion-Breazeal-Brooks-03.pdf`

Summary

Behavior-based robotics (BBR) was this chapter's theme. BBR is based on animal and insect behavior patterns, especially the ones related to how organisms react to sensory stimulation within their environment.

A brief section discussed how the human brain exhibits multilayer behavioral functions, which range from basic survival behaviors to complex reasoning behaviors. An introduction to the subsumption architecture followed; it is closely modeled after the human brain's multilayered behavioral model.

Further in-depth discussion went through both simple and complex behavioral models. I choose to use the finite state model (FSM) for this chapter's robot car demonstration.

I next demonstrated an open source, graphical robotic simulation system named breve. A simple Braitenberg vehicle simulation was created and run that further demonstrated how the stimulus/response behavior pattern functions.

The final demonstration used the Alfie robot car, which was controlled by a Python script created using the subsumption architecture model. The script contained three behaviors, each with its own priority level. I showed how subsumptive-based behavior could take over the robot, depending on the environmental conditions that the robot encountered.

APPENDIX A

■ ■ ■

Build Instructions for the Alfie Robot Car

An oblique front view of the robotic car is shown in Figure A-1. It was constructed from a kit available from the Parallax Corporation (www.parallax.com).

© Donald J. Norris 2017

D. J. Norris, *Beginning Artificial Intelligence with the Raspberry Pi*,
DOI 10.1007/978-1-4842-2743-5

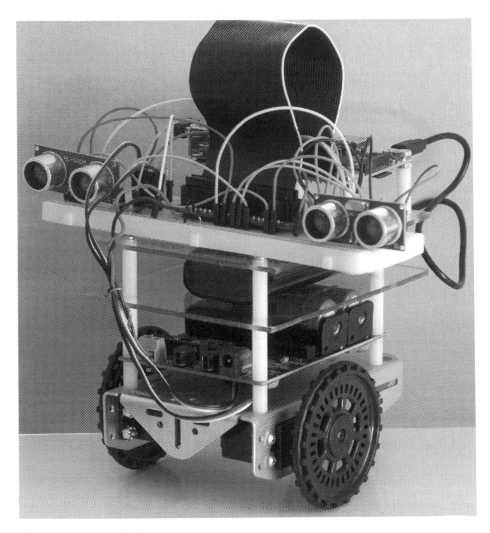

Figure A-1. *Finished robotic car*

A straight-on back view of the car is shown in Figure A-2.

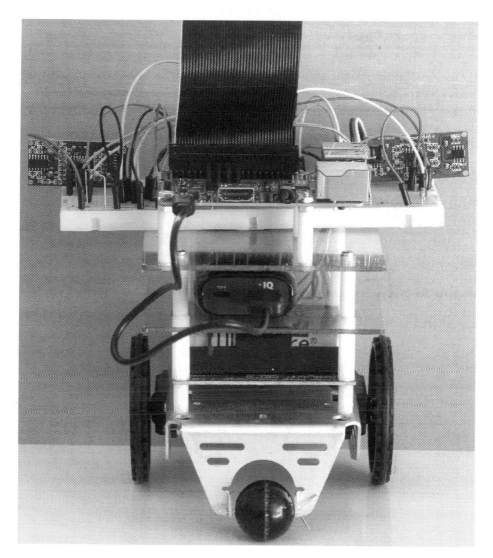

Figure A-2. *Straight-on back view of the finished robot car*

Parallax named this robot model the Boe-Bot, which is short for *board of education robot*. The company sells several versions of the Boe-Bot, which include different microcontrollers. I purchased the kit controlled by their propeller activity board. However, there is a basic model 28124 parts kit available without a microcontroller, which allows you to build only the robot car platform, and then you add your own Raspberry Pi.

The car is powered by two continuous rotation (CR) servos on the underside of the robot, as seen in Figure A-3.

Figure A-3. *Underside of the robotic car*

It is easy to quickly build the basic robotic car platform. You can go to the Parallax website to download the assembly instructions if you want a preview of what is involved in the platform assembly.

Robotic Car Power Supply

The two CR servos driving the robot car require more voltage and current than provided by a cell battery eliminator, which powers the Raspberry Pi. Fortunately, Parallax provides a nice alternative power supply for both CR servos. In addition, its form factor matches nicely with the robotic car's chassis. Figure A-4 shows the Li-ion battery power supply mounted on the robotic car's chassis.

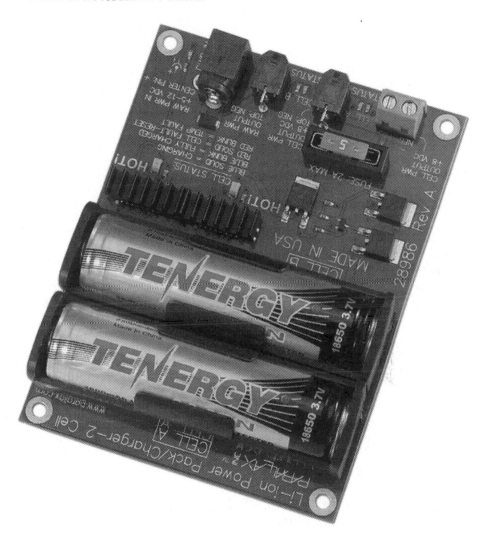

Figure A-4. *Li-ion battery power supply mounted on the robot car's chassis*

The Parallax part number for the power supply with two Li-ion batteries is 28989. It has a built-in charging system for the two 18650-size Li-ion cells. Each cell provides 3.7 VDC that will provide over 1 A when fully charged. Two cells in the series provide 7.4 VDC to the CR servos, which is plenty of power to allow them to be operated at maximum capacity if so desired.

CR Servo Drive Pulse Width Modulation (PWM)

The motors on the robot car are CR servos, which mean they must be driven using appropriate PWM signals. The PWM pulse duration ranges from 1.0 to 2.0 milliseconds (ms) for the CR servos used on this robot car. Sending a 1.5 ms pulse duration signal will cause the CR servos to remain motionless with no rotation. The `ChangeDutyCycle(arg)` Python command sets the servo's rotation speed. I experimentally determined the `arg` values as follows:

- 2.6: No rotation

- 3.6: Full speed in the counterclockwise direction

- 2.2: Full speed in the clockwise direction

You will see these values in the various Python scripts that control the robot car.

▓ **Note**   I used Raspberry Pi model 3, which has two independent PWM channels, suitable for directly controlling each CR servo. If you use a model 2 B or B+, there is only one PWM channel available on these boards. You need to use an external multiplexer board to enable the two channels for CR servo control. I refer you to Adafruit's Learn tutorial at `https://learn.adafruit.com/adafruit-16-channel-servo-driver-with-raspberry-pi/overview`, where the installation and setup of a 16 -channel multiplexed servo driver is discussed in an excellent fashion. In other projects, I set up this board according to the tutorial instructions without any difficulty.

Mount Plates

The robot car incorporates two mount plates designed to hold the cell battery eliminator's power supply and a Raspberry Pi. Figure A-5 is a side view of the robot car with all the plates installed with the battery eliminator, Raspberry Pi, and solderless breadboard.

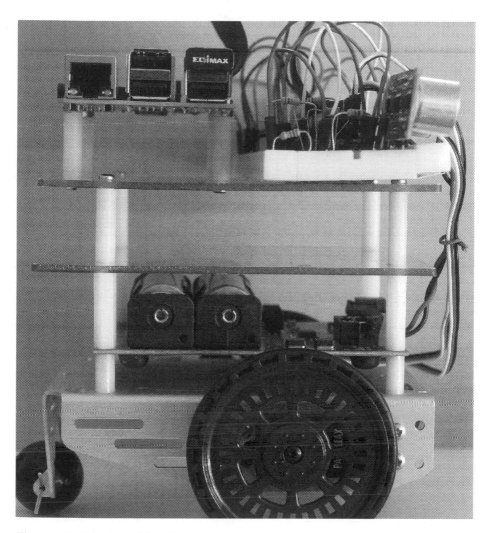

Figure A-5. *Side view of the robot car*

I used four non-threaded 1/2-inch nylon spacers with four 7/8-inch 4-40 machine screws to mount the Li-ion power supply to the car chassis. The 4-40 machine screws were threaded into 1-inch nylon spacers with internal 4-40 threads. The battery eliminator plate is secured between the top of the 1/2-inch nylon spacers and the bottom of the 1-inch threaded nylon spacers. Figure A-6 is a detailed drawing of the battery eliminator mount plate.

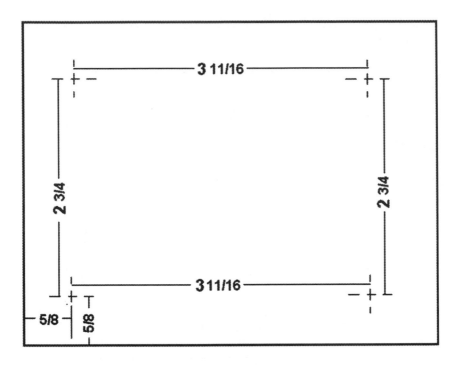

material: 1/8" Lexan sheet stock

all dimensions: inches

all holes: 1/8 inch diameter

Figure A-6. *Battery eliminator mount plate construction drawing*

The next mount plate holds the Raspberry Pi and a solderless breadboard. Figure A-7 shows a construction drawing for this mount plate.

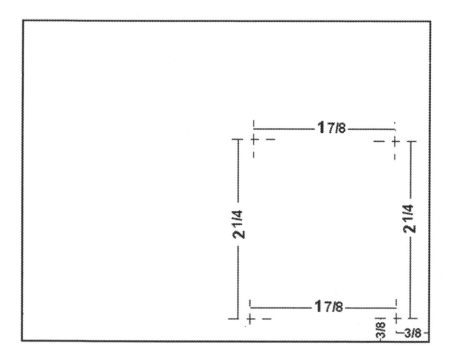

material: 1/8" Lexan sheet stock

all dimensions: inches

all holes: 1/8 inch diameter

Base stock: Repeat Figure A-6 construction
add additional holes for the Raspberry Pi

Figure A-7. *Raspberry Pi mount plate*

This plate is secured to the battery eliminator mount plate using the four 1-inch threaded nylon spacers with four 4-40 1/2-inch machine screws.

Finally, the Raspberry Pi is secured to the Raspberry Pi mount plate with 7/8-inch non-threaded nylon spacers coupled with 1-1/4-inch 4-40 machine screws and nuts.

I plugged in two Ping ultrasonic sensors into the breadboard along with a MCP3008 ADC chip. Figure A-8 is a close-up of the solderless breadboard with all the components plugged in.

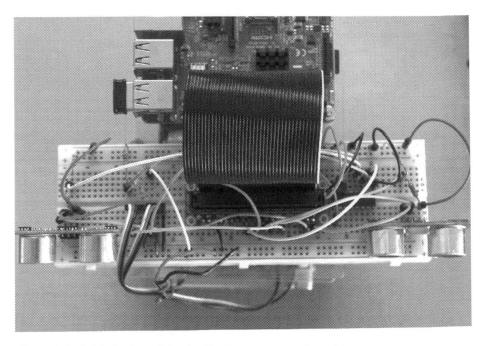

Figure A-8. *Solderless breadboard with all components plugged in*

The solderless breadboard is attached to the mount plate using double-sided tape, which allows easy removal if desired. I strongly recommend that you do not use the adhesive backing that comes with the solderless breadboard because it is practically impossible to remove the breadboard once it is attached to the plastic mount plate.

This completes the mechanical build instructions for the robotic car. Next, I present the electrical and wiring instructions that will energize the car and sensors.

Electrical and Wiring Instructions

The electrical connections for the car are fairly simply, as shown in the Figure A-9 schematic of both the propulsion drive electrical schematic and the ultrasonic sensor interconnections.

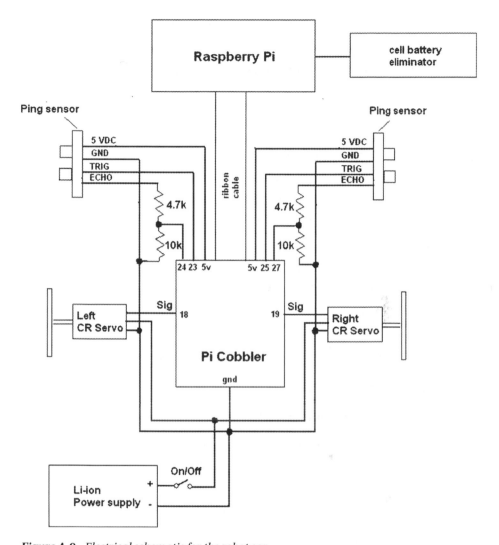

Figure A-9. *Electrical schematic for the robot car*

The main power source for the two CR servos is the Li-ion power supply, which provides 7.4 VDC and has an energy capacity of approximately 2600 mAh when fully charged. This capacity should provide the CR servos with more than 6 hours of runtime before they need a recharge.

The Raspberry Pi is powered by a separate cell battery eliminator module. The Raspberry Pi model 3 draws an average current of about 120 ma, which means that a 2100 mAh battery eliminator provides more than 15 hours of power to the Raspberry Pi before requiring a recharge.

Ping Sensor

I purchased several inexpensive HC-SR04 Ping sensors from Amazon.com. Figure A-10 shows close-up front and back views of this sensor.

Figure A-10. *HC-SR04 Ping sensor*

The Ping sensor contains an embedded microprocessor as part of the sensor hardware. This processor controls the ultrasonic transmitter and receiver transducers that physically measure distance by bouncing discrete ultrasonic sound wave pulses off objects, and timing how long the sound takes to transit from the sensor transmitter to the sensor receiver. The distance is easily calculated because the speed of sound is relatively constant at 1130 ft/sec. This is method of operation is quite similar to the way that bats navigate in caves and attics. Figure A-11 is a block diagram of the sensor and all the principal components.

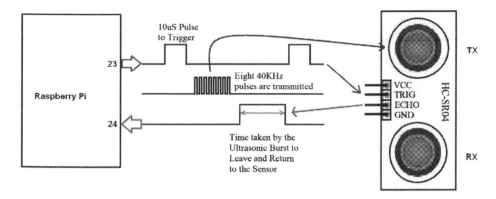

Figure A-11. *Ping sensor block diagram*

The distance is proportional to the length of the digital pulse, which is sensed by any processor that needs it—in this case, the Raspberry Pi. The digital pulse generated by the Ping has a 10-μsec time measurement resolution, which translates to approximately 1-inch distance measurement uncertainty in its total range of up to 100 inches. Of course, distance measurements also depend upon the size and texture of the reflecting object. A hard wall provides excellent reflection, whereas a curtain would be more problematic.

Note that the Ping sensor requires 5 VDC for its power supply, and as a consequence, the digital output pulse from the Ping sensor is also at a 5 VDC level. This level is incompatible with the Raspberry Pi maximum 3.3 VDC GPIO input level. This is the reason I used resistive dividers as shown in the Figure A-9 schematic.

The digital communication protocol between the Ping sensor and Raspberry Pi commences when the Raspberry Pi (host device) generates a 10-μsec trigger pulse that in turn causes the Ping sensor to emit a short burst of 40-kHz ultrasonic sound waves. This burst travels through the air, hits an object, and then bounces back to the Ping sensor. The Ping simultaneously starts its digital pulse when it receives the host's trigger pulse. This pulse terminates when an echo return is detected. Therefore, the width of the digital pulse is proportional to the distance to the target.

The electrical schematic in Figure A-9 shows the interconnections between the Raspberry Pi and the Ping sensors. Besides the V_{cc} and ground wires, there are two other wires connecting each Ping sensor to the Raspberry Pi: one wire carries the pulse initiation trigger from the Raspberry Pi to the Ping and the other wire sends the digital timing pulse from the Ping to the Raspberry Pi. The actual range measurement is calculated within the Raspberry Pi's Python script.

MCP3008 Analog-to-Digital Converter (ADC)

One of the significant shortfalls of the Raspberry Pi—at least as far as it concerns experimenters—is the lack of any analog-to-digital converters. Unlike most popular microcontroller boards, such as the Arduino Uno or the Beaglebone Black, the Raspberry Pi has never come equipped with this option. Therefore, it is necessary to use an external chip for this function. A very popular and inexpensive solution is the Microchip MCP3008, 8-channel, 10-bit, ADC chip. Figure A-12 shows the pinout for this chip.

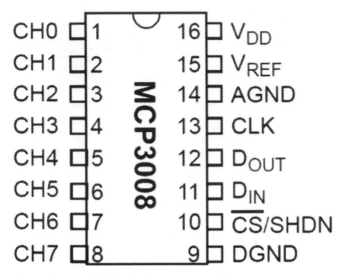

Figure A-12. *MCP3008 pinout*

The following pins must be used to convert analog voltages to equivalent digital numbers:

- V_{DD} (power)
- V_{REF} (analog voltage reference)
- DGND (digital ground)
- AGND (analog ground)
- DOUT (data out from MCP3008)
- CLK (clock pin)
- DIN (data in from Raspberry Pi)
- /CS (chip select)
- An analog input, channels 0 to 7

  Table A-1 lists the interconnections used for several robot car circuits in this book's projects.

Table A-1. *MCP3008/Pi Cobbler Interconnections*

MCP Pin	MCP Description	Pi Cobbler Pin	Pi Cobbler Description
9	DGND	6	GND
10	$\overline{CS}$ /SHDN	24	CE0
11	DIN	19	MOSI
12	DOUT	21	MISO
13	CLK	23	SCLK
14	AGND	6	GND
15	V_{REF}	1	3.3V
16	V_{DD}	1	3.3V
1	Analog Channel 0	N/A	

Software Installation

I used Adafruit's MCP3008 library to interface the MCP3008 to the Raspberry Pi. You must first ensure that the SPI interface is enabled in the Jessie distribution. Use the raspi-config application to enable SPI, if it hasn't already been enabled. You should enter the following commands once the SPI interface is enabled:

```
sudo apt-get update
sudo apt-get install build-essential python-dev python-smbus
python-pip
sudo pip install adafruit-mcp3008
```

There is an `examples` folder in the `Adafruit_Python_MCP3008` directory once the Adafruit library is installed. Go to the `examples` directory and run this command:

```
python simpletest.py
```

You should see a display similar to what is shown in Figure A-13.

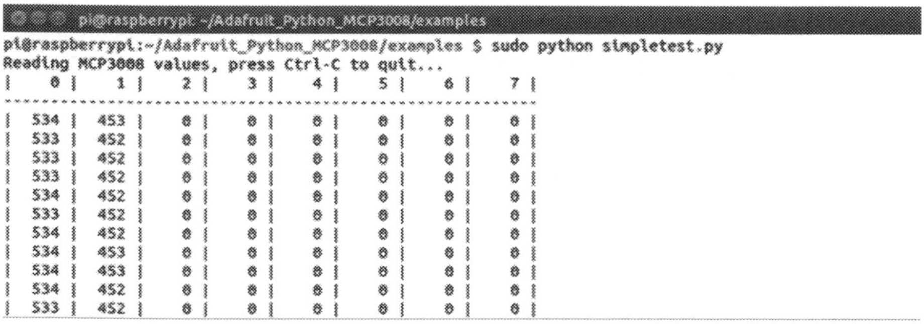

Figure A-13. *simpletest.py display*

Final Thoughts

I believe that I sufficiently provided you with detailed information on how to build and set up a robot car for use in this book's demonstrations, as well as for your own experiments. You can obviously modify and adjust the build instructions to suit your own situation. This is part of the fun and excitement of being a maker.

Index

© Donald J. Norris 2017
D. J. Norris, *Beginning Artificial Intelligence with the Raspberry Pi*,
DOI 10.1007/978-1-4842-2743-5

Get the eBook for only $5!

Why limit yourself?

With most of our titles available in both PDF and ePUB format, you can access your content wherever and however you wish—on your PC, phone, tablet, or reader.

Since you've purchased this print book, we are happy to offer you the eBook for just $5.

To learn more, go to http://www.apress.com/companion or contact support@apress.com.

Apress®

31901060982529

Printed in the United States
By Bookmasters